Morals under the Gun

MORALS UNDER THE GUN

The
Cardinal Virtues,
Military Ethics, and
American Society

JAMES H. TONER

THE UNIVERSITY PRESS OF KENTUCKY

Scholarly publisher for the Commonwealth,
serving Bellarmine College, Berea College, Centre
College of Kentucky, Eastern Kentucky University,
The Filson Club Historical Society, Georgetown College,
Kentucky Historical Society, Kentucky State University,
Morehead State University, Murray State University,
Northern Kentucky University, Transylvania University,
University of Kentucky, University of Louisville,
and Western Kentucky University.
All rights reserved.

Editorial and Sales Offices: The University Press of Kentucky
663 South Limestone Street, Lexington, Kentucky 40508-4008

04 03 02 01 00   5 4 3 2 1

Library of Congress Cataloging-in-Publication Data

Toner, James Hugh, 1946-
    Morals under the gun : the cardinal virtues, military ethics, and
American society / James H. Toner.
        p.   cm.
    Includes bibliographical references and index.
    ISBN 0-8131-2159-0 (cloth : alk. paper)
    1. Military ethics—United States. 2. Cardinal virtues. 3. United
States—Armed Forces. 4. United States—Moral conditions. I. Title.
U22.T6497   2000
174'.9355—dc21   99-089730

To the Memories of my Grandparents:

James Henry Toner (1884–1914)
Ethel Mathews Toner Aldrich (1891–1943)
Joseph John Leahy (1871–1954)
Ellen Cotter Leahy (1877–1950)
for the life you gave
for the example you set
for the heritage you created
CCC#958
2 Macc. 12:43–46
Job 19:25

The worst temptation for mankind, in the epochs of dark night and universal perturbation, is to give up Moral Reason. Reason must never abdicate. The task of ethics is humble but it is also magnanimous in carrying the mutable application of immutable moral principles even in the midst of the agonies of an unhappy world, as far as there is in it a gleam of humanity.

—Jacques Maritain (1882–1973)

Contents

Preface

I like prefaces. I read them. Sometimes I do not read any further.
—*Malcolm Lowry*

If you think about what you ought to do for other people, your character will take care of itself.

—*Woodrow Wilson*

I want my readers to read this preface—and more. So, in an effort to attract and keep your interest, I will tell you at once what *Morals under the Gun* is all about. My argument is, at its heart, very simple: moral life in America is "out of order" to a considerable extent.[1] Consequently, there is moral confusion in the armed forces, whose people, after all, are drawn from society. But the armed forces do have a standard (the traditional military ethic), the virtues of which can provide an ethical reference point for soldiers so that they can chart a course for doing the right thing. The core values—the main virtues—of the armed services are wisdom, justice, courage, and temperance, which are found both in sacred Scripture[2] and in the writing of the ancient Greeks. If the armed forces (and other institutions) adhere to these cardinal virtues, they can help all of us to resolve the moral confusion we have been experiencing for some time. President Wilson was correct: if we do gracious things for others, we will be all right. Martin Luther King Jr. said the same thing: "Life's most persistent and urgent question is: What are you doing for others?" The correct answer to that question is what the profession of arms is—or should be—all about. Is it not interesting that the right answer to that question, as C.S. Lewis once told us, is what religion is also all about?[3]

So this is a book about connections. Theological ethics and philosophy have much to teach us—the concept that justice is superior to law is only one example of that. We civilians have much to teach the armed forces—the concept of civilian control of the armed forces is only one example of that. The armed forces have much to teach us, their civilian superiors—the concept of sacrifice is only one example of that. Civilians and soldiers alike must never again forget the macroethical lessons of the just war and the microethical lessons of being good, kind, and decent human beings. That takes us back to Wilson, to King, and to religion: concern for others. That is one reason this book ends with a chapter on character.

A Peculiar Assortment

A glance at the bibliography, a list of the articles and books to which I owe the inspiration for this work, will confuse any interested reader. It is an odd assortment, this bibliography. There are "military books" such as *The Downsized Warrior,* by McCormick, and *Dereliction of Duty,* by McMaster. There are international geopolitical books such as *The Grand Chessboard,* by Brzezinski, and *The Clash of Civilizations,* by Huntington. This is sensible because, after all, I do teach at a war college run by the U.S. Air Force. But there are also books by such Christian writers as Servais Pinckaers and Norman Geisler, evangelist Josh McDowell, and apologists Peter Kreeft and C.S. Lewis. There are some of the great works of philosophy by Plato and Aristotle. There are a number of books about classical education, such as *Who Killed Homer?* and *Cultivating Humanity;* about writing and fiction, such as Flannery O'Connor's *The Habit of Being* and David Denby's *Great Books;* and about contemporary American life, such as *For Shame* and *One Nation after All.* A cursory glance at the bibliography signifies what I try to do here—connect ethics and moral theology with the profession of arms.

I have explained already that this book is about the U.S. armed forces. But it is not that simple. I am now in my tenth year of teaching ethics at the Air War College at Maxwell Air Force Base in Montgomery, Alabama. Before coming to the War College, I taught at a military college for thirteen years. Before that, for a year I taught international politics to Naval ROTC midshipmen at Notre Dame. Before that I was an army infantry officer whose only real achievement in four years of active duty was earning my parachute badge. I joined the army on 14 May 1968, my birthday; although I was honorably discharged six years later, I have been around the U.S. military now for more than thirty years.

I am not a soldier, sailor, airman, marine, or Coast Guardsman, but I have written for, lectured to, and otherwise been involved with educational programs with all five services. In talking principally about contemporary ethics with members of the five services, I have discovered that soldiers (I use the term generically) find most philosophy too convoluted and abstract to have a serious impact on their world. I do not mean this in a negative or pejorative way. Consider the average army captain, whose pace of operations today is often extremely busy. As a professor, I hope he finds time to read. When he does, he is likely to read books related to his military specialty and, perhaps, a book or two about an area of the world to which he may be assigned. Can you reasonably blame him for not plowing through *The Nicomachean Ethics* by Aristotle? Should he read Kant? Saint Thomas Aquinas? John Stuart Mill? Sartre? The fact is that most soldiers know smatterings of philosophy and theology, but—understandably—they have rarely thought about philosophy systematically. Moreover, many, if not most, military chaplains, as busy as they are with pastoral concerns, find little time for review of theological ethics, which they may not even have studied years before in seminary. There are, in short, too many soldiers ignorant of philosophy.

BRIDGING GAPS

I have also been appalled over the years to discover that only a handful of our country's colleges seem to have even the foggiest notions of what "military ethics" is all about. Very recently, I had an E-mail exchange with the administration of a large university in Nebraska, initially asking a question about a chair in military ethics. The question was referred to an army captain in ROTC who patiently explained to me, via E-mail, how army ROTC is conducted on the campus. That the idea of a chair in military ethics was lost on the captain, I could understand. That the university administration seemed, at least at first, not even to understand the idea was, however, more typical than one would customarily think. Many colleges teach philosophy courses along the idea of "just war." But when problems such as Tailhook, the Flinn case, the Lavelle affair, and the like occur, philosophy instructors who may not know the difference between an M16 and an F-16 are understandably puzzled by the military ethos. There are, in short, too many philosophers ignorant of military affairs.

As a teacher, I seek to bridge the gap whenever and wherever I can. Among the courses I teach at the Air War College are "Command and Conscience" and "Core Values." In writing and in lecturing at both civilian and military institutions, I try to explain ethics as best I can to military professionals and military professionalism as best I can to civilian academics and students. Some years ago, at a state university in New England, I discovered that the students to whom I lectured (mostly juniors and seniors in history and political science) knew little, if anything, about the realist school of international politics, which was, certainly on that campus, entirely out of faculty favor. My students at the war college, although largely untutored in philosophy, understand, I think, that one can teach ethics without being ordained (and that I really do not regard *everything* as a paramount moral concern). What is of grave concern to me, though, is that "liberal" academics and "conservative" soldiers—the stereotype is pretty accurate—seem increasingly not to be talking with one another, not only because they do not share similar interests but also because they do not share a similar language.

To some extent, this problem is rooted in the foolish notion that ROTC should be banned from many university campuses. Thirty years ago, ROTC cadets and their military officer-instructors were reflexively regarded on some campuses as mindless automatons, representatives of an ultraconservative power establishment. Today, there is often a surprising and disturbing bitterness on the part of military officers toward academics and journalists, representatives, they often think, of an ultraliberal power establishment. Meanwhile, all around us are caustic, if critical, debates about inflammatory issues, the roots of which go back at least a quarter-century (and some to the dawn of time). Few of these issues are "military," and fewer still involve soldiers, who are (or who are supposed to be) nonpolitical. The university used to accommodate a "universe" of opinion but seek truth. Now, too often, I fear, the university houses approved ideologies but dismisses truth as delusion or superstition.[4] Civilians, although properly suspicious of the people with the artillery, must relearn that soldiers, whether in military service for three or for thirty years, will again be civilians themselves. And soldiers, although properly troubled by civilian apathy or even antagonism toward the military, must never forget whom and what they serve.

I believe that philosophy and theological ethics are relevant to military science, and I have tried to make that case in the pages that follow. In trying to make connections between philosophy and military science, I have attempted to make sometimes arcane and abstruse philosophical concepts available to military readers who rarely have the time for in-depth philosophical explorations. At the same time, I have tried to make the spirited and sometimes perplexing world of military ethics plainer to interested civilians.

THE TITLE OF THE BOOK

Military ethics, of course, refers to morals under the (literal) gun. In civilian society morals are under the (figurative) gun. Unless the cardinal virtues of wisdom, justice, courage, and temperance are a vital part of military operations and expectations, there will be no "military ethics" worthy of the name, but only moral corrosion. I argue that the same is true of our increasingly morally bewildered society: unless we can restore the classical notions of wisdom in education, justice and truthfulness in our politics, moral courage in all that we do, and temperance in what we put into our bodies and what we do with our bodies, we may learn our part in an ancient lamentation that our children will recall sadly: "How lonely lies Jerusalem, once so full of people! Once honored by the world, she is now like a widow; the noblest of cities has fallen into slavery. . . . The enemy was watching for us. . . . Swifter than eagles swooping from the sky, they chased us down. They tracked us down in the hills; they took us by surprise in the desert. . . . Our ancestors sinned, but now they are gone, and we are suffering for their sins" (Lam. 1:1, 4:18a–19, 5:7).

A remarkable movie appeared in 1998 that helps me to corroborate a point I often try to make when I lecture on ethics. That is that ethics is best understood in the single five-letter word *owing*. Ethics is about having a sense of responsibility both to what will come about because of who we are and what we do and to those who have gone before and who have given us our moral starting point.[5] *Saving Private Ryan* tells the fictional tale of a young soldier whose brothers are killed in combat in 1944 and whom the U.S. Army wants to save from death, lest all the Ryan brothers perish (as did the Sullivan brothers in real life). A squad of soldiers under the command of Captain Miller is dispatched on a mission to find and save Ryan. They accomplish their mission, dying in the process. With his last breath, Miller tells Ryan to earn the gift of life he has been given. At the movie's end, Private Ryan, now an old man, has returned to an American military cemetery in France to visit the grave of Captain Miller. Kneeling and in tears, he turns to his

wife and family, asking whether he has fulfilled the "mission" his captain gave him. Has he led a good, decent life? Has he paid the debt? Has
he earned the gift?

A Personal Thought about "Owing"

I hope that will explain the dedication of this book, which is to people I
deeply regret I never really knew. I vaguely remember my maternal grandfather, who died when I was eight years old, and my maternal grand-
mother, who died when I was four. They spent their lives working in a
mill on a pond in Monson, a small town in western Massachusetts. They
never owned a house or a car and only very rarely made a trip to the "big
city" of Springfield. They never attended high school. But they had their
faith and their hard work and their simple pleasures—a porch to sit on, a
radio to listen to, and a town baseball game on a hot summer day. And
three daughters to live for. And a new country, America! to cherish, after
their trips here from Ireland. My paternal grandfather, a thirty-year-old
stricken with respiratory disease, died more than thirty years before I
was born, as he worked for union causes and was finally attending college in the bright world of early 1914. With a 1902 diploma in hand
from a prep school but too poor for college at a time when Irish Catholics were expected only to work in mills or quarries (or perhaps as maids
or policemen), he died in July that year, as the lamps were going out all
over Europe. His widow was left penniless, a twenty-three-year-old with
a four-year-old son to raise. When I am in Monson, I always visit the
cemetery where my grandparents and parents are. Like Private Ryan, I
wonder if I have earned the gift. Like Private Ryan, I know some debts
are never paid.

My father and mother stayed in Monson, graduating from the high
school there in 1928 and 1931, respectively. My wife, Rebecca, and I
stayed there as well, graduating in 1966 and 1964, respectively. But
then the world—college and graduate school and the service and jobs—
took us away, probably, except for the occasional visit, never to return.
Can you take your roots with you? Absolutely. Though some debts are
never paid, some things are never forgotten.

And some things provide a source of unending joy. My sons, now
grown, wonder why I trot out family albums whenever I can, trying to
link their future to my (and their) past. It is emotionally hard for me to
explain it to them; maybe this book can do that job for me vicariously.

To my wife, Rebecca (Prov. 31:29); to my sons and daughters, Chris and Ruth, Patrick and Shannon; and to Jamey—thank you (Prov. 3:5–6). Enough said.

I gladly acknowledge and greatly appreciate the advice, encouragement, and high professionalism of Lois Crum, whose recommendations to me have helped to make this a far better book than it would have been without her careful editing.

The Air War College, where I teach and write, has been very generous—and very stimulating. Every year about 40 officers from allied countries around the world and about 210 U.S. officers and a few selected civilians make their way to Maxwell Air Force Base for ten months of education at the War College, where they study international politics, campaign planning, military history, and other subjects, including ethics. These are accomplished, highly intelligent, energetic men and women. Teaching them is a rare privilege. I am truly honored to have been in their company this past decade. Without the sabbatical I was generously given by the War College, I could not have finished this book.

Particular thanks are due Peter Bowen of the Sangreal Group in California and Brig. Gen. Malham Wakin, USAF (Ret.), both of whom made, directly or indirectly, a number of very helpful suggestions about this book. The opinions I express here are mine, and I do not represent them as having the approval of the Department of Defense, the U.S. Air Force, Air University, or the Air War College.[6]

The Necessary Immorality of the Military Profession

Science has always defeated religious dogma point by point when differences between the two were meticulously assessed.

—*Edward O. Wilson*

[It is useful for a leader] to appear merciful, faithful, humane, religious, upright, and to be so, but with a mind so framed that should you require not to be so, you may be able and know how to change to the opposite.

—*Machiavelli,* The Prince

One of the great difficulties involved in reading, writing, and teaching about military ethics is the tendency of people in the field, and I do not exclude myself, to be rather self-congratulatory about the moral climate we associate with the profession of arms. Blithely we contend that honor and truth-telling are functional military imperatives. Glibly we maintain that cheating and stealing contravene the norms of the professional military ethic. Rather smugly we declare our common allegiance to, and membership in, a self-proclaimed citadel of modern chivalry, whose corrupt knights—one thinks of Lieutenant Calley at My Lai—are supposedly the great aberrations. So we, the anointed, quickly condemn the very few exceptions to our confraternity of high purpose and noble aim, feel better about ourselves for the condemnation, and go about our business with all the calm self-assurance of the saved.

THE NEED FOR REALISM

Reality intrudes, of course. Clearly, Calley was an exception. To argue to the contrary would be to besmirch the names and reputations of thousands of gallant soldiers who found themselves in Calley's circumstances but not in Calley's shoes. The arguments in this book are not intended to advocate war crimes or to exonerate war criminals. After all is said and written, however, the American military exists to kill the national enemies of the United States or, at a minimum, to prepare to kill them. That is not the sole purpose of the military; neither is it even the primary purpose of the military, which can deter, just as it can wage, war. But, for example, following the attack on Pearl Harbor in 1941, after all else had failed, the army and the navy were called upon to do what soldiers and sailors have done, or tried to do, throughout the ages: find, fix, fight, and finish their national enemies.[1] That is an unpleasantness, but it is also a truth. The ultimate reality of military service is that soldiers, sailors, airmen, and marines are paid to destroy the enemies of their country.

A man by the name of Palamarchuk, a car thief, claims that during World War II, he was trained as an underwater demolitions expert, being paid "$54 a month to kill people." Consequently, stealing cars hardly disturbed him ethically.[2] The American military has been recognized by writers and jurists alike as a separate society, yet one still part of its larger civilian element. The law, the custom, the ritual, and the training of the profession of arms owe much to the recognition that the military requires a certain latitude forbidden to civilian agencies. If the military is to discharge all of its possibly fearsome tasks, Private Jones, U.S. Army, must be held to an accounting different from the expectations we might have for Mr. Smith, civilian employee of any business. Private Jones can be ordered to risk his life and to kill; Mr. Smith, of course, is free to walk away from such liabilities. After teaching Jones—and Palamarchuk—how to kill, is it entirely rational to teach them not to lie, not to cheat, not to steal?

MAJOR ERRORS AND MINOR TRANSGRESSIONS

Here stands in uniform before the Congress of the United States a lieutenant colonel in the U.S. Marine Corps. See the colonel deceive, dissemble, delude, lie. Observe the self-satisfied smugness with which far too many of us peremptorily condemn what we brand as the machinations of a power-mad marine. But hear the colonel explain, with feeling and with manly self-confidence, that his is a higher ethic. Feel the colonel's outrage that the politics of a vacillating Congress could, in his judgment, displace the legitimate security concerns of greater patriots and of more enlightened professionals. Soldiers kill and soldiers die. As Murray Kempton put it, more than thirty years ago, "The good soldier will [also] lie under orders as bravely as he will die under them."[3] And so it is with Oliver North: "I'm not in the habit of questioning my superiors."[4] He recognized both opportunity and challenge and responded with innovation and alacrity; for doing his duty, he was subsequently ravaged.

We in the field of military ethics all too quickly condemn our errant knight, finding when and where we can reasons to mitigate North's ethical "lapse" because he had been such a good marine until the unfortunate episode described. And it is easy to understand North's confusion, confronted as he was with the timidity and, some might say, the treachery about him. He may have misled the Congress, but his was a nobler cause and a grander calling. We stand in judgment of North because we apply to him as a man the hoary notions of a Gothic standard he learned as a naive midshipman; when his country called him as an adult, he was ready to do whatever he had to do, but many of the innocents in his profession were not.

Oliver North had been done a monumental disservice by the pious platitudes of the Naval Academy's Code of Honor. For there are most certainly times to lie. To cheat. To steal. To kill. Even the Bible tells us that "there is an appointed time for everything, and a time for every affair under the heavens" (Eccles. 3:1). Only the ethically stunted can hold, for example, that the Pole harboring a Jew in his basement in 1939, asked by an SS officer if he knows the whereabouts of any Jews, should tell the shining truth and thereby betray the greater good. It is silly to object that when the crewmen of the captured ship *Pueblo* in effect cheated their captors by flashing their middle fingers in photos, calling the gesture the "Hawaiian good luck sign," they were morally wrong. Should anyone have objected to purloining Communist secrets through espionage as CIA agents did for years? One may well dispute whether Lieutenant Colonel North was actually serving his country by lying; one has trouble doubting, however, that Lieutenant Colonel North thought he was being truly patriotic. He had been ill served by an absolutist code that taught him things as a midshipman that the adult world belied.

The professional military can and does kill. Are we to believe that it cannot lie or cheat or steal? Are we to believe that it cannot tolerate those who do? But how many professional military members are lying, right now, as they fill out Officer Effectiveness Reports (OERs) on subordinates? How many justify what amounts to lying on the very real foundation stone of group loyalty? How many career soldiers truly want to work for the boss who tells the strict truth that Major Blue is a good officer—rather than that Major Blue is an outstanding officer, deserving of immediate promotion? Is the colonel who is filling out that report a debauched and evil man, undeserving of trust? Or is he a good and compassionate commander, as anxious to advance his soldiers' careers as is another colonel, in another division, far away, filling out an OER on Major Green? And is Captain Orange an immoral or corrupt man because he uses the DSN (military telephone system) for occasional personal calls, or photocopies private materials on government machines, or takes an occasional pen or pencil for personal use?

We have listened for years to the impassioned rhetoric of those who say that minor slightings of the truth will lead inexorably to treason—or to some other equally catastrophic moral failing. It is as if they have been unable to distinguish between grave moral failure and, for example, the rather inconsequential youthful indiscretions to which we are all heir as we grow up. Once again, even the Bible is clear that there are both grave sins and sins that are less consequential.[5]

For instance, how many cadets, candidates, trainees, or midshipmen have been ignominiously and peremptorily dismissed from service academies or other officer preparation courses because of "lying," which, in many cases, may amount to no more than forgetfulness or the desire to be loyal to a friend? Take the case of Cadet Khaki who knows that his roommate, Cadet Brown, has not shined his shoes to prepare for an inspection. When Brown is asked if he has shined his shoes, he lies, contending that he has indeed shined his shoes. In fact, the response is a function of habit, for the harried cadet almost always shines his shoes; this once, however, he did not; asked about it, he accidentally gave an incorrect, "untruthful" response. Now Khaki is on the horns of a terrible dilemma. He knows that Brown has misled the inspecting officer. Does he turn Brown in for "lying" and risk the expulsion of his friend from the school, or can he overlook what is, after all, a trifling error and remain loyal to his friend? The writer E.M. Forster once contended, "If I had to choose between betraying my country and betraying my friend, I hope I should have the guts to betray my country."[6]

Can there be no hierarchy of values, no sophistication whatsoever, in the values preached and taught? Do we really want a military organization that encourages preparation for maiming and mutilating the enemy to be unable to find it in its heart publicly to tolerate the soldier who takes home a yellow legal pad for personal use? Surely reason itself leads us to see how threadbare and fallacious is the old argument that he who steals a government pen will soon be misappropriating a fortune in government funds. In September 1993 a major cheating scandal at the Naval Academy was uncovered. The U.S. Naval Academy does not have an honor code but an "honor concept," and it does not oblige midshipmen to turn in peers who cheat. A *Newsweek* article suggests that "the discretion allowed by the code may have provided students with a rationale for looking the other way."[7] It may also have provided students the opportunity for developing a mature moral judgment. Although instances of felony or grand larceny or espionage should, of course, be reported, which army major or navy lieutenant commander, for example, has ever turned in a peer for stealing a government pen or a wrench or two or for government communications equipment used for purely personal matters? There can be such a thing as excessive scrupulousness. As one Naval Academy graduate put it after the cheating scandal at USNA indicted 125 midshipmen, leading to the possibility of massive expulsions, "Should we brand kids for life for a single mistake? Even in the criminal world we don't do that."[8] There are, after all, times to look the other way. Certain instances of "cheating" may, in fact, more nearly be instances of keen initiative.[9]

There is a difference, then, between a major offense and a minor transgression. The tyranny of ethical absolutism, however, preaches no distinctions. For moral martinets there is hardly a difference between a crime and a mistake, between a felony and a misdemeanor, between the seven deadly sins[10] and the social "lies" we tell every day. (For example, your wife asks you, before you go to a party, "Honey, do I look O.K.?" You respond, "No, you look tired, your makeup is terrible, and your choice of colors is abominable." That is the truth; it would also most likely be the end of your marriage. All of us know that the preferred response—"Sweetheart, you look fine!"—although perhaps not perfectly true, is by far the more sensible.)

THE COURAGE TO "LIE"

Modern military ethics instruction is too often a feeble Potemkin Village, exhorting us never to lie or cheat or steal when the very essence of combat obliges soldiers to do exactly those things—or much worse. POWs in Vietnam and Korea routinely lied to their captors or cheated them whenever feasible. In destroying enemy installations and equipment, soldiers are in effect stealing from their enemy's national treasury. Such activities not only are not discouraged; they are often handsomely rewarded. Self-righteously shrouding the essence of such behavior is the veil of moral purity, which so frequently confounds and confuses the very soldiers it is intended to enlighten.[11] I was once informed by an instructor at the U.S. Army Ranger School at Fort Benning, Georgia, that whenever inspectors of any type are around, ranger students are told that they have a moral obligation to collect prisoners of war after sweeping a battlefield. When the inspectors depart, however, the students are counseled that fallen enemies on the battlefield should be dispatched with pistol or bayonet (the practice of "double-tapping"), lest they shoot passing rangers in the back. (Besides, there is no real way for commandos to take care of such POWs.) Of course that real-world combat advice is perfectly correct (and, tragically, a time-tested, valid recommendation) but our hypocritical mask of purity obliges instructors to have one set of "public" instructions and another set of "private" instructions.

Pronunciamentos of ethical purity among soldiers do little to resolve the real-world tensions for professionals who are possibly obliged to kill—and to lie, cheat, and steal—on occasion for their government. Great lip service is paid to codes and paradigms that, in actual circumstances, are silly, sophomoric, or senseless. The result is moral confusion. Instead of a guide to ethical conduct that informs soldiers that, regrettably, as there will be times and circumstances that may warrant killing other human beings whom your country labels as "enemy," so there will be times and circumstances when lying or cheating or stealing is also required for the greater good. As you may be asked to risk your life for your country, so also in its service may you be asked to risk your privileged sense of personal purity.

There is a Latin phrase—*Ultra posses nemo obligatur* (no one is obligated to do more than he can)—which seems to capture the essence of my argument. Soldiers are not morally bound to be saints; that is, in today's ethical climate, no one expects soldiers to be perfectionists. There is, and ought to be, some discretionary morality, some latitude afforded to soldiers in the matter of lying, cheating, and stealing. It would be easy to mistake my position. Not for a moment do I hold that rampant lying ought to be permissible; but there are times and circumstances when truth-telling is not the prudent policy. As Col. Anthony Hartle has said, "Is it unethical for a military officer to mislead the enemy? We can confidently say no. The requirements of the practice of truth-telling extend only to fellow participants in the practice."[12]

The *New York Times* reported in August 1993 that officials in the Strategic Defense Initiative program had "rigged a crucial 1984 test and faked other data in a program of deception that misled Congress as well as the intended target, the Soviet Union, four [unnamed] Reagan Administration officials said."[13] Total honesty can, apparently, thwart or frustrate government officials in the discharge of their official duties. Machiavelli pointed out more than four hundred years ago that "men are so simple, and so subject to present necessities, that he who seeks to deceive will always find someone who will allow himself to be deceived."[14] Reason of state can oblige soldier-statesmen to lie, and they are ill fitted to do so when they have learned a mechanical, banausic ethical creed that permits no room for moral discretion.

Consider carefully the prudent advice tendered by Machiavelli: "A wise lord cannot, nor ought he to, keep faith when such observance may be turned against him, and when the reasons that caused him to pledge it exist no longer. If men were entirely good this precept would not hold, but because they are bad, and will not keep faith with you, you too are not to observe it with them. Nor will there ever be wanting to a prince legitimate reasons to excuse this nonobservance."[15]

THOSE WHO DO NOT DESERVE THE TRUTH

In 1998, during a lecture at the Naval War College, I showed an excerpt from a video tape of a remarkable exchange that took place during a military ethics conference held in Philadelphia about ten years before.[16] During that conference, Peter Jennings of ABC was asked the following. If he had been an American reporter allowed to be among the enemy (no doubt to give their story to the American public) and he happened to see an American patrol approaching an enemy ambush, would he attempt to warn his countrymen? Jennings initially avers that he would try to do so. Mike Wallace of CBS is shocked at Jennings's reply to the question. "You're a reporter!" Wallace objects, contending that the reporter's first job is to get the story. A lively debate ensues. After a fashion, Jennings relents, saying that he had "chickened out," wishing that he had made Wallace's choice of getting the story—and allowing the American infantrymen to be killed from ambush. At the war college, the tension was palpable among the officers, many of whom were seeing this excerpt for the first time. In the tape, a marine colonel, outraged by the moral poltroonery of Jennings and Wallace, responds by saying that, in this hypothetical scenario, the next day these journalists are themselves wounded and lying in a no-man's zone, begging for help. Should U.S. marines now risk their lives to help the wounded Jennings and Wallace? After all, by their own choice, they are not Americans but only journalists. "You can't have it both ways," the colonel says. Wallace has the logical powers to understand at least that. But the colonel points out that he *will* send marines out to save the pair, and that it is likely that some marines will die, saving a pair of—and he fairly spits out the word—"journalists." Many of the naval officers, entirely understandably, cheered.

What is owed by soldiers to journalists more interested in getting a story than in saving American lives? Some time ago a very high-ranking U.S. officer, speaking at the Air War College under the promise of nonattribution, told the audience about his appearance on *60 Minutes*. His taped interview was edited in such a way that he seemed to give flip, thoughtless answers to sometimes delicate questions. The show caused a great deal of concern about him and his service. The officer's sensible advice to his subordinates was never to appear on that program. "The *right to the communication* of the truth is not unconditional," one important religious text counsels us. We are required "in concrete situations to judge whether or not it is appropriate to reveal the truth to someone who asks for it. . . . No one is bound to reveal the truth to someone who does not have the right to know it."[17] If we know that the enemy, or journalists, or politicians will misuse the truth, we are not morally obliged to reveal it.

During American operations in Somalia, efforts to capture Somalian warlord Mohammed Farah Aidid proved fruitless. One source suggested that U.S. military headquarters in Somalia had issued a report, as the magazine put it, "about yet another bungled attempt" to capture Aidid, which, in fact, was "an invention to cover up an operation by the supersecret Delta Force." The Deltas really were retaliating against a previous mortar attack but "cover[ed] their tracks . . . [by] invent[ing] a plausible fiction."[18] Such "plausible fictions" may not be in the same league as the possible murder in 1969 of a suspected North Vietnamese double agent and its alleged cover-up,[19] but the basic premise holds: lies and duplicities are sometimes required by, and in the probable best interest of, the well-being of the state, as well as of the military unit involved.

The pietistic platitudes of customary military ethics are thus not innocuous; those who hear them may become puzzled and perplexed about the nature of the real world. The oddity is that most, if not all, scholars in military ethics will quickly admit that we have not yet seen the end of war and that there does exist such a compelling notion as reason of state. In serving the republic, soldiers are expected to put the well-being of country ahead of self. Zealous devotion to ethical purity (as in "I never lie!") can be seen, therefore, as a kind of ethical egoism and crass self-indulgence. As there are times to lie to the enemy and perhaps even to certain congressional or other governmental agents (as, apparently, in the matter of SDI testing), and as there are clearly times to stretch the truth on OERs, so is there need of a modified ethical creed that states that soldiers will lie under orders as bravely as they will die under them. The soldier who, in extreme conditions, will not risk life or limb for country and comrades-in-arms may well be a physical coward, preferring his own safety above all else; the soldier who, in extreme conditions, will not compromise truth for country and comrades-in-arms may well be a moral coward, preferring his own integrity above all else.

It may be tragic that both human beings and the statecraft they practice are imperfect and imperfectible, but it is an indisputable fact. In the face of this reality, the maintenance of strict codes of honor and conduct oblige those subject to them to carry medieval standards of conduct to absurd contemporary lengths. Moral rigidity in developing standards of officer conduct creates an inflexibility wholly inconsistent not only with the needs of the combat arms but also with the civil responsibilities necessarily discharged, upon occasion, by soldier-statesmen.

Of course, no one will dispute the idea that soldiers ought to tell the truth when permitted to do so by appropriate circumstances. Soldiers should similarly refrain from killing when permitted to do so by circumstances. But in the heat of combat on the battlefield, there will be times when killing is not only morally permissible but also ethically mandatory. And in the heat of combat in the bureaucratic battles there too will be times when lying is not only morally permissible but also ethically mandatory. Outdated and ancient codes and creeds that create ethical paralysis impede clear thinking and obstruct swift and decisive action. As Machiavelli put it, the prince, or the leader, must "have a mind ready to turn itself accordingly as the winds and variations of fortune force it . . . not to diverge from the good if he can avoid doing so, but, if compelled, then to know how to set about it."[20]

Absolutist prohibitions against lying, cheating, and stealing result, at best, in hypocrisy and in the numbness properly associated with the moral somnolence now frequently parading as moral instruction in the military. The flat, catechetical tones of much of contemporary military moral instruction represent a tyranny of the mind, refusing to foster genuine intellectual growth among the young and denying moral latitude and discretion to the mature. There are no pat, simple answers to the kinds of questions soldiers must answer, in the combat either of bureaucratic or of battlefield warfare. To insist upon the rigor mortis of an uncompromising, rule-based set of expectations is the moral equivalent of sending soldiers off to battle with pikes and body armor. If, when justified by circumstance, soldiers can violate one of the greatest of all commandments—Thou shalt not kill—then they can certainly lie, cheat, or steal when appropriate circumstances arise.

The Call of Business

Up to a point, it is even permissible for soldiers to advance their own careers by modified duplicity; executives, after all, do it all the time. To argue the reverse is to expect divine conduct of the human, and that is a manifestly unfair expectation and a forlorn hope. We need to bet with, not against, human nature. Currently we demand of soldiers that they elevate country ahead of self. But there are few saints among us. We need to develop a modern approach to soldierly conduct, which emphasizes rational self-interest instead of relying upon the crusty and clearly obsolete invocations of patriotic devoutness and self-sacrifice. That is not to denigrate these notions, but modern psychology testifies in a plangent voice that people customarily act in their own self-interest. A step in the right direction, to be sure, is the military's devotion to Total Quality Management (TQM), stemming from a recognition that old ways of doing business are out of place in today's military.[21] Indeed, William Perry, a former secretary of defense, "want[ed] to run defense like a business," according to one magazine.[22] It is déjà vu for many senior officers, some of whom remember reforms of this nature that were introduced a generation ago, under Secretary of Defense Robert S. McNamara. Thirty years ago, hidebound careerists rejected, to the extent they feasibly could, the kinds of innovations and modern business practices now receiving the choruses of approval too long overdue.

A few years ago the *Wall Street Journal* used this as a subheadline: "Ethics are [*sic*] nice, but they can be a handicap, some executives declare." The article explained that about a quarter of 671 managers surveyed by a research firm contended that being ethical can damage a successful career; that group believed that more than half the executives they knew would bend the rules to get ahead. One fifty-year-old executive said, "I know of unethical acts at all levels of management. I have to do it in order to survive."[23] A publication by Jay L. Walker entitled *The Complete Book of Wall Street Ethics* has 158 blank pages.[24] As business management practices become increasingly important in the contemporary profession of arms, one can find such books as *Duty, Honor, Company: West Point Fundamentals for Business Success.*[25] A recent poll revealed that 75 percent of its respondents believed that there was less honesty in government at that time than there had been a decade before.[26] (And this poll took place before the revelations about the Clinton administration.) To attempt to inculcate into young soldiers today codes of honor and conduct that are clearly atavistic and obviously anachronistic is professionally irresponsible and ethically ill advised.

Today's soldiers are businessmen and businesswomen in green, blue, or tan suits. The codes by which they lived on the streets before entering the military and the expectations of the businesses to which they will return after their service are demonstrably at odds with an archaic ethic that paralyzes the mind and hence the ethical faculties. Soldiers are presumably imbued with an absolutist ethic in modern times when elementary answers do not square with complicated questions. A number of today's soldiers must deal with matters of acquisition, procurement, and logistics. When they negotiate with their occasionally less scrupulous civilian counterparts, they are at a decided disadvantage. It is as if cheating were legalized for, and expected of, civilian managers but forbidden to military officers with similar duties.

An old bit of doggerel I learned in Officer Candidate School may help to explain this: "Here lie the bones of Lieutenant Jones, the pride of the institution. He died one night in his first fire fight, by applying the school solution." For too long now, the profession of arms has been trussed by an ethic suitable for medieval knights but painfully out of step with the times in which we now live. "When I was a child," the apostle Paul says in one of his epistles, "I used to talk like a child, think like a child, reason like a child. When I became a man, I put childish ways aside" (1 Cor. 13:11). It is past time to teach all soldiers that they, not some ancient code, must bear the burden of deciding the right and of choosing the true; it is past time to teach all soldiers that the ethics of simple answers and the morals of school solutions frequently result in absence of thought and poverty of action; it is past time to teach all soldiers that insistence upon never lying, never cheating, never stealing, and never killing results, not in a powerful armed service, but in the virtual destruction of the modern American military.

If, in sorrow, we recognize that lives and politics are imperfectible, we nonetheless have the responsibility of teaching the difficult truth that the exigencies of military life result, unavoidably, in the occasional commission of "immoralities" and that machinations are not always evil, much as Machiavelli once tried to teach us. It is time, as TQM counsels us, to empower our soldiers and trust their discretion in the combat both of battlefield and of bureaucracy. Knowing as we do that it is sometimes permissible, even desirable, to kill for our country, we have begun to recognize at long last that it also sometimes permissible, even desirable, to lie for our country. The empowered soldier has put away the simple slogans and the silly shibboleths he or she learned when young. Now that mature soldier decides whether, when, and to whom to tell the "truth." He or she has put away the things of a child such as illogical absolutes, outdated honor codes, and shallow religious dogma. At last, much as St. Paul suggests we put away "childish things," we have allowed the soldier to grow up.

2

A New Beginning

Men and women are always called to direct their steps toward a
truth which transcends them. Sundered from that truth,
individuals are at the mercy of caprice, and their state as person
ends up being judged by pragmatic criteria based essentially upon
experimental data, in the mistaken belief that technology must
dominate all.

—*Pope John Paul II*

If we do not confront the soft relativism that is now disguised as
virtue, we will find ourselves morally and intellectually disarmed.

—*William J. Bennett*

I must apologize: almost everything in chapter 1 is deceitful or distorted;
it is a hoax. I have misled my readers. In fact, I hope that parts of chapter
1 irritated or even angered readers. I took a dialectical liberty in the first
chapter of presenting a set of fraudulent ideas so that I could offer reasoned alternatives throughout the rest of the book. If you were discom-
fited or exasperated, I apologize, first, for misleading you; I do not
knowingly do it in the rest of the book. Second, I thank you for bothering to turn to this page, trusting that I might "get better." Third, the rest
of the book is just that: an attempt, the best I have in me, to help us all
"get better."

The authors of the epigraphs to the first chapter, E.O. Wilson and
Machiavelli, are individuals who I think are terribly wrong.[1] The epi-
graphs to this chapter, by contrast, are right on target, in my judgment.
The rest of the book explains why. I am what can be described as an

absolutist: I believe that there are moral norms and imperatives that transcend race, culture, and country.[2] With Job, I believe that "my Redeemer liveth" (Job 19:25), and, with the third president of our republic, I think "Prudence . . . dictate[s] that Governments long established should not be changed for light and transient Causes . . . and [that we should rather] suffer, while Evils are sufferable, than to right [our]selves by abolishing the Forms to which [we] are accustomed" (Declaration of Independence). Finally, as a former (one-tour, noncombat) army officer and a ten-year employee of the U.S. Air Force, I write as one convinced that the profession of arms often has been a truly noble calling, even though it—like all other professions—has too often suffered from despicable deviations from the code of chivalry that endows it with honor. Let me set the record straight about chapter 1. There is a great deal of fallacious logic there, accompanied by some highfalutin' language suggesting what amounts to absurd comparisons and analogies, misuse of authorities and respected texts (such as the Bible—but we know, with Shakespeare, that "the devil can cite Scripture for his purpose"), some nonsense about the "greater good" (which is corrected in chapter 4 about moral reasoning and chapter 6 about justice), and some morally meaningless notions about corrupt business, "plausible fiction," and the like. The codes and canons learned by young officers are, indeed, the ethical essence of the profession. There is not—there must not be—one set of ethical criteria for cadets and an entirely different set for older officers.[3]

Can we lie to the Nazi who asks us if we are harboring a Jew? Unlike Kant, I think we can. Some of our responsibilities may well wind us up in the terrain of what I call "dueling duties" (also explained in chapter 6). We must learn to reason well. But we are hardly relieved from the duty of truth-telling merely because we would, with real remorse, lie to the Nazi. For an act to be moral, one must consider the end, the means, and the circumstances involved. It is true, as I suggest in chapter 1, that there are people (e.g., Nazis) who do not deserve the truth. The same, of course, *cannot* be said of journalists and politicians, especially those in Congress. Although it may be necessary on occasion for officers to testify in executive session (behind closed doors), and although one may not be obliged to tell everything one knows to everyone one meets, one must tell the truth—if not always all the truth. (But neither is deliberately leaving a mistaken impression acceptable.)[4]

I offer two quick observations before we (truly) begin: a professor at Amherst College tells a joke about an attorney who is promised complete success in both love and business, for which the price to be exacted is simply giving up his soul. He asks only, "What's the catch?"[5] Blaise Pascal once said, "Our whole duty is to think as we ought."[6] "The catch" is (1) that we have an immortal soul and (2) that its "sale" should be nonnegotiable. Every man, in short, does *not* have his price. Pascal tells us in his apothegm that we must think *well* and in the context of a *standard*. We know that four times eight is thirty-two; that is a mathematical law. We may wish that the answer were thirty or thirty-three; but the law exists independent of our wish or our taste. Are there such moral laws— truths—that also may exist independent of our taste? I think there are, and I think we can find them in the cardinal virtues of wisdom, justice, courage, and temperance. Once we know we have a soul, we know we have a standard we can use to measure our thoughts and our actions. In the context of this book, we then have criteria against which to judge the profession of arms. That is, in brief, what this book is all about. Really.

A NOTE ABOUT MORALITY AND RELIGION

Morality flows from religious principle. That conviction is always implicit or explicit throughout this book (see chapter 5 for the development of the argument). The task of religious people is always to be righteous without becoming self-righteous. For civil servants and officers, the task is to be true to one's spiritual convictions (and thus the moral creeds that derive from them) without proselytizing. Treating subordinates as a captive audience for religious indoctrination is wrong. Using government time, money, or resources for purposes of religious propagation is wrong. Extending favoritism to fellow church members in professional matters is wrong. Quoting Bible verses or other religious references on government E-mail or other means of communication is wrong. But it is not wrong—it is, in fact, morally quite "on target"—for government officials and military officers to speak and to behave publicly as they believe privately. There is such a thing as freedom *from* religion; no one should be coerced by importunate religious people intent upon spreading the word. There is also freedom *for* religion; no one should be made to feel shame or remorse for being faithful to his or her religious beliefs.[7] Although George Marsden has written, "Everyone is expected to accept the standard doctrine that religion has no intellectual relevance,"[8] he astutely argues the opposite: that there is compelling reason to appreciate the scholarship deriving from the Judeo-Christian tradition.

In this book, where we study the cardinal virtues and inquire into their relevance to the profession of arms, we can particularly prize Marsden's observation that "Christians [and, I would add, religious people in general] must remember that, much as they may value liberal institutions, they are participating in them on an ad hoc basis, *limited by higher allegiances.*" He tells us that "we should think of ourselves as 'resident aliens' . . . [who] should obey the laws of the land of our sojourn to the extent that they do not conflict with our higher allegiances."[9] In any book that concerns military power—which is *the logic of force*—I think one must also carefully consider necessary restrictions on the employment of that power—which is *the force of logic,* deriving in good measure from ethical judgment frequently rooted in religious conviction.[10] To help integrate the logic of force and the force of logic is a goal of this book.

In our democratic republic, I believe that we can agree, if only academically, about the religious roots of the cardinal virtues. Although we may arrive from demonstrably different avenues of approach, we can similarly agree about the hortatory merit and the practical usefulness of the four cardinal virtues. And we can agree, I think, that the cardinal virtues can be taught—without degrading or defiling them—in a successful, secular manner. After all, one need not be Jewish[11] or Christian[12] to espouse what we call the Golden Rule. The late Carl Sagan, no theist, called it the "most admired standard of behavior in the West."[13] Does that make Sagan a Christian apologist or evangelical? Does separation of church and state require us to stop teaching this precept? Of course not. Merely because we can often trace the sources of a morality precept to religion does not mean that all of us, religious and nonreligious, cannot benefit from its counsel and its application in our daily lives, both personal and professional. If one believes that, for example, the Bible, natural law, and other religious principles have an "Ultimate Author," I rather suspect that He will not object to the use of His principles even by those who think of sacred Scripture and the law of the heart as mere cultural artifacts, nevertheless useful, at least occasionally, for teaching. The most hidebound atheist will undoubtedly teach his or her children not to steal (without mention of Exod. 20:15). Do we thus indict the atheist for "preaching" in the secular city? We can—we should—use the fruits of religion for general moral nutrition.

THE BUSINESS OF THE MILITARY IS NOT "BUSINESS"

The first chapter of this book presents, rather starkly, a position I will label the "accommodationist" approach to military ethics. Accommodationists hold that the military ethic must be drawn increasingly closer to the norms and mores of the civilian sector. "Ethical accommoda-tionists" would argue that military ethics must be based on, or at least be much more similar to, the ethics one finds in the civilian community. Thus, if (or, to put it perhaps better, *to the extent that*) there is a pattern of ethical permissiveness and moral self-absorption, never mind occasional commercial corruption, in the civilian or business community, accommodationists make the case that the military ethic should be increasingly "sophisticated," "progressive," and "enlightened"; that is, it should follow suit.

Arguments suggesting that military professionals are business people are silly—and dangerous. The quackery of TQM should have no—let me say that again—*no* place in the U.S. military. The supposed debate over whether soldiers are leaders or managers is nonsense. There is no substitute for virtuous, valorous, vigorous leadership. It is an indictment of some upper-level military leaders that they even considered introducing the charlatanry of TQM into the profession of arms. Cooler—I dare to say "much brighter"—heads have prevailed, and TQM and other such puffery are going away, leaving military leaders with such teaching tools as "principles of leadership" and "traits of leaders," which deserve respectful attention, whereas TQM and similar business humbugs deserve a place in the cemetery of giddy ideas.

More than forty years ago, Samuel Huntington was pointing out that "liberalism's injunction to the military has in effect been: conform or die." Liberalism, he said, customarily attempts either to transmute or to extirpate military values.[14] In chapter 1 I tried to raise, with whatever sweet sophistry I could muster, the basic argument—perhaps made less fastidiously elsewhere by accommodationists—that the military profession is wholly out of step with the "times." Because others may lie or cheat or steal, I argued, the military may do the same. In order to purchase a grain of respectability for my enterprise, I held back from blanket endorsement of such transparently unethical behavior. As the saying goes, the road to hell is paved with good intentions. And I suspect that most of us, in straying from the paths of righteousness, do so by degrees. That is, we err most grievously at the margins. We lie or cheat or steal for the wolf of self-promotion or of self-gratification, which we routinely clothe in the sheep's raiment of patriotism, service loyalty, or family responsibility. The gravest vice is camouflaged as the greatest virtue.

There is hardly any doubt that virtue and character, traditionally understood, are under assault (see chapter 3).[15] In the *Chronicle of Higher Education* of 10 November 1993, for example, one reads of the new program in "Queer Studies" at a New England college (Wellesley).[16] At another New England institution, MIT, a recent survey indicates that more than eight out of ten undergraduates admit to cheating at least once in their college careers. More than two-thirds confessed to committing some form of plagiarism, and 11 percent cheated on at least one exam. The director of MIT's undergraduate program, who coauthored the study, observed: "Of course, it's worrisome, but *we're not looking at this in a moralistic way,* to say people who do this are [bad] and they're beyond helping."[17] My dictionary defines *moralistic* as "teaching the difference between right and wrong." The MIT undergraduate director would not presume to look at cheating and plagiarism "in a moralistic way," for such an old-fashioned attitude might also oblige that person to look at the "educational" programs being established at Wellesley, only a few miles away.

The departure from traditional canons of morality is much in evidence based on these "educational" developments at two presumably respected Massachusetts colleges (for an exploration of "Teaching and Truth," see "Obiter Dicta," following chapter 6). The size of the chasm between traditional virtues and the brave new world of modern education can be seen in this comment by Peter Kreeft: "If you confess at a fashionable cocktail party that you personally love to play with porcupines, or plan to sell CIA secrets to the communists, or that you are considering becoming a Palestinian terrorist, you will find a buzzing, fascinated crowd around you, eager to listen. But if you confess that Jesus is God, that he died to save us from sin, or that there really are a Heaven and a Hell, you will soon be talking to empty air, with a distinct chill in it."[18] And as George Roche points out, in modern times "we have come . . . to a totally animalistic view of life. We are but beasts sprung from the natural process; there is no God; there is no authority other than our own; there is no right or wrong; there is no imperative except the survival of the species, achieved by the strong preying on the weak. Indulge your every animal appetite, o modern man [person]! This is the drumbeat of our 'progressive' culture, its throb everywhere loosing the jungle instincts in us."[19]

What is the connection between the deterioration of traditional values on American campuses and the military ethic? It is simply this: the military ethic, based as it is upon the notion of heroism and self-sacrifice and reasoned patriotism, cannot hope to survive, let alone flourish, in an atmosphere in which ancestral virtue is regarded as poisonous. The essential character of the military ethic is based upon the conviction that there is something worth living for and perhaps dying for that is more important than one's own skin (see chapter 9). In a climate of nihilism, materialism, and ethical relativism, the military ethic is little more than an absurd anachronism. If we believe that the human mind is incapable of knowing objective truth—that all we can ever have is personal opinion—then there is no reasonable way to adjudicate between conflicting opinions other than the use of violence. As Robert Hutchins tells us, "force becomes the only way of settling differences of opinion. And, of course, if success is the test of rightness, right is on the side of the heavier battalions."[20] By denying standards, ethical relativism therefore invites conflict; ironically, should conflict spill over into combat, ethical relativism deprives military forces of any reason to risk life, for no sane person wishes to fight and die for ideas and institutions that are no better than those of anyone else.

American officers, we know, have not majored in "Queer Studies." American officers, we profoundly hope, have indeed been educated in "a moralistic way" on campuses where the faculty understands the difference between matters of taste and matters of truth. American officers, we believe, are and must be concerned with more than commercial interests, the preservation of American business ventures, or the viability of their own careers. At this point, the reader will recognize that I am, in addition to being an absolutist, a theist, and a conservative, also a romantic. But the best officers I have known have a touch of the romantic, the idealistic, the sentimental in them.[21]

It is likely that there will always be tension between the expectations of civil society and the requirements of the profession of arms. But if the larger civilian community ever effectively "extirpates" or "transmutes" the ancient and, I think, noble traditional values of the profession of arms, it will have lost a principal propaedeutic source of what it means to be a lady or a gentleman.

The best counter to the specious and somewhat minatory notions propounded in chapter 1 is a paragraph from a remarkable talk given at the Air Force Academy about thirty years ago. In that talk, Gen. Sir John Hackett offered the following explanation of how the military can serve the state:

> A man can be selfish, cowardly, disloyal, false, fleeting, perjured, and morally corrupt in a wide variety of other ways and still be outstandingly good in pursuits in which other imperatives bear than those upon the fighting man. He can be a superb creative artist, for example, or a scientist in the very top flight, and still be a very bad man. What the bad man cannot be is a good sailor, or soldier, or airman. Military institutions thus form a repository of moral resource that should always be a source of strength within the state.[22]

The business of the military, therefore, is war, the preparation for it, and the execution of it—a task to be conducted by ladies and gentlemen.

LADIES AND GENTLEMEN

In a recent book, I contended that the military code and spirit might serve as "a well from which our ethically beleaguered country may draw moral refreshment," and I quoted from the Hackett speech cited above. Joel Rosenthal, of the Carnegie Council on Ethics and International Affairs, subsequently stated that "to a certain extent" he agreed with Sir John Hackett but that he was unprepared to go quite as far as I had.[23] In point of fact, Rosenthal is right: the military ethic cannot serve as an "ethical well" for us if its waters are suspect, let alone poisoned. American military leaders must never take upon themselves the task of "enlightening" the body politic about proper moral conduct—that is neither their right nor their duty. But one can hardly spend time around military posts and bases without hearing it said that the standards of the military are and must be higher than those of civilian society. Military standards are, in fact, often higher. For example, too few civilian colleges have honor codes, but honor codes are at the heart of the education provided by the federal service academies. Moreover, any army private would have been unceremoniously and entirely justifiably booted out of the service had he or she been caught committing the sexual offenses of Bill Clinton.

I believe that the military ethic customarily adhered to by our service members is indeed a worthy moral code—one that must be preserved by the profession of arms if it is to serve our society with competence and character. To the extent that the military demonstrates honorable and exemplary moral behavior, however, it does so as a function of its responsibilities as an armed force *and not as a self-appointed ethical tutor to the nation.* The distinction is subtle, I concede, but critical. Officers who with more than a little sense of self-righteousness trumpet the military services as professors and paradigms of ethical excellence worthy of emulation by civilian moral sluggards deserve not praise but censure. But if officers insist upon maintaining the highest personal and professional standards, not only for themselves but also in and for their services, they are entirely commendable.

An analogy may help. We expect the clergy of, say, the Methodist Church to set the highest example of upright living. Their standards are very likely higher than the standards of those to whom they minister. But we do not expect Methodist clergy to go about celebrating their own high standards, proclaiming that they will thereby be moral saviors of the republic. The example they give, however critical to their ministry, is not a political effort and, in one sense at least, may be understood as a by-product of their ministry. By the same token, the profession of arms must maintain high moral standards but must never look upon itself as having a responsibility—let alone a major duty—of serving as the nation's main moral maestro. For example, former air force chief of staff Ronald R. Fogleman said in 1996, "Because of what we [in the military] do, our standards must be higher than those that prevail in society at large." But the context of that remark clearly indicated that there was nothing about it that was patronizing toward civil authority, let alone seditious.[24]

It may very well be that the idea of being a gentleman is "a waning ideal."[25] In 1950, according to Col. Lloyd Matthews, the Department of Defense pamphlet entitled *The Armed Forces Officer* had this to say about officers: "The military officer is considered a gentleman, not because Congress wills it, nor because it has been the custom of people in all times to afford him that courtesy, but specifically because nothing less than a gentleman is truly suited for his particular set of responsibilities."[26] As an army second lieutenant, I first received that pamphlet from my battalion commander in 1969. A 1975 revision refers to "gentle persons" (3) and "gentle qualities" (4), but the connection, albeit in tortuous language, is made between officership and the ideal of the gentleman (and the lady). The 1988 edition of that pamphlet, however, is changed, not only in style but also in substance. Observes Matthews, "Gone is the explicit insistence of the 1950 and the 1975 editions that officers be gentlemen. In its place we find a prize example of wafflespeak: 'The concept of military officers is based on the notion of "gentlemen."'" Here, in place of 'officers' and 'gentlemen' themselves, we hear of 'concepts' and 'notions.' Moreover, the relation between officers and gentlemen is left purposefully vague."²⁷ "It is a matter of some interest," says Colonel Matthews, "to inquire why the authors of the 1988 manual find themselves . . . so queasy over the prospect of unambiguously declaring that officers be gentlemen."²⁸ But isn't all of this a mere exegetical quibble?

Colonel Matthews says that the word *gentlemen* is "an emblem for those human beings who . . . are striving to achieve true excellence"; that word, therefore, is "simply too valuable to be expunged from the language by the zealots of radical egalitarianism."²⁹ Another army officer, Col. Anthony Hartle, has pointed out that if a military force has highly developed virtues (such as physical and moral courage, loyalty, discipline, and competence), "it will indeed be superior to one equal in ability but lacking such virtues." His argument, in short, is that good people make better warriors.³⁰ If we segue Hartle's contention into Matthews's, we understand why Matthews is passionate about what appears to be only a matter of language:

> Officers hold a professional monopoly on the instruments
> of military force, and they alone embody the martial spirit
> and technical expertise essential for the successful employ-
> ment of such instruments. Society can afford to entrust
> such awesome responsibility and capability only to its most
> civilized and enlightened members. So long, therefore, as
> "gentlemen" remains the most expressive term in our
> language for denoting such favorably endowed members of
> society, it is indispensable that armed forces officers [be] . . .
> among their number. That portion of the current edition of
> *The Armed Forces Officer* dealing with the officer as
> gentleman should be revised to make the foregoing man-
> date unequivocal.³¹

Much of what appears in this book can be subsumed into the simple but crucial idea that leaders must be ladies or gentlemen. As I look back over more than a half-century of my own life, I think of the people I have known, in various walks of life, for whom I have had great respect. Invariably, the word *lady* or *gentleman* leaps to mind when I think of such people.

There is one other bit of language worth considering here, as trivial as it first appears to be. I have known women who object to the term *lady.* Their argument is usually that a *lady* "belongs" to a gentlemen, and they do not like that one little bit. I agree. But I do not intend the word *lady* here in any such way. Nor am I referring to any physical qualities such as physical loveliness or sartorial elegance. All gentlemen are men. All ladies are women. But not all men are gentlemen, and not all women are ladies. I believe that almost all of us who are, say, forty and above would agree upon what we mean by *lady* and *gentleman.* (Try that verbal game in a group sometime.)

I have asked numerous senior officers whether they have ever counseled a subordinate for not being a gentleman or a lady. I am surprised— and more than a little pleased—that many say they have done exactly that. But these colonels and naval captains seem to share my belief that younger service members do not have the same unspoken understanding of these terms that they do. (In a class or at a meeting, you might compare their reactions to these words with the reactions of more senior people.)

The U.S. military Uniform Code of Military Justice (UCMJ) is a set of laws, established in 1950 and revised in 1968, that governs the conduct of service members, in addition to establishing a system of courts and judges to try service members accused of violating those regulations and laws. The UCMJ instructs armed forces cadets and officers that there is such a thing as "conduct unbecoming an officer and gentleman" (a term including both males and females).[32] In the "General Article" one reads that conduct "of a nature to bring discredit upon the armed forces" will be punished at the discretion of the appropriate court-martial.[33] In addition to that, there is the U.S. Code, Title 10, an intriguing adjuration of all U.S. officers:

> All commanding officers and others in authority in the
> naval service are required to show in themselves a good
> example of virtue, honor, patriotism, and subordination; to
> be vigilant in inspecting the conduct of all persons who are
> placed under their command; to guard against and suppress

all dissolute and immoral practices, and to correct, according to the laws and regulations of the Navy, all persons who are guilty of them; and to take all necessary and proper measures, under the laws, regulations, and customs of the naval service, to promote and safeguard the morale, the physical well-being, and the general welfare of the officers and enlisted persons under their command or charge.

(Although I have cited the section pertaining to U.S. Naval and Marine Corps officers [section 5947], the "requirement of exemplary conduct" is the same for officers in the U.S. Army [section 3583] and the U.S. Air Force [section 8583].) One cannot help observing that this is a "moralistic" demand, (justifiably and sensibly) placed upon military officers by the legal code of the United States—but one that is impossible and impracticable unless those officers are ladies and gentlemen.

THE CARDINAL VIRTUES

If we accept the ideal of lady and gentleman, the problem of how to cultivate that ideal still remains. Can we suppose that gentlemen possess in common certain attributes or traits that, if developed in a young man, will ensure "virtue"? The American diplomat and scientist Benjamin Franklin "conceived the bold and arduous project of arriving at moral perfection." He wished "to live without committing any fault at any time; [he] would conquer all that either natural inclination, custom, or company might lead [him] into." For this purpose he developed a list of virtues, which he intended to practice daily, keeping strict written accounts of his progress in each category:

1. Temperance: Eat not to dulness. Drink not to elevation.
2. Silence: Speak not but what may benefit others or yourself. Avoid trifling conversations.
3. Order: Let all things have their places. Let each part of your business have its time.
4. Resolution: Resolve to perform what you ought. Perform without fail what you resolve.
5. Frugality: Make no expence but to do good to others or yourself; i.e., waste nothing.

6. Industry: Lose no time. Be always employed in something useful. Cut off all unnecessary actions.
7. Sincerity: Use no hurtful deceit. Think innocently and justly; and, if you speak, speak accordingly.
8. Justice: Wrong none by doing injuries or omitting the benefits that are your duty.
9. Moderation: Avoid extremes. Forbear resenting injuries so much as you think they deserve.
10. Cleanliness: Tolerate no uncleanness in body, clothes, or habitation.
11. Tranquillity: Be not disturbed at trifles or at accidents common or unavoidable.
12. Chastity: Rarely use venery but for health or offspring—never to dulness, weakness, or the injury of your own or another's peace or reputation.
13. Humility: Imitate Jesus and Socrates.[34]

Between the list of the eighteenth-century American statesman-scholar Franklin and the following list of the twentieth-century states-man-scholar Sir Harold Nicolson there is a striking parallel. Nicolson described the ideal diplomat:

> These, then, are the qualities of my ideal diplomatist. Truth, accuracy, calm, patience, good temper, modesty, and loyalty. They are also the qualities of an ideal diplomacy.
> "But," the reader may object, "you have forgotten intelligence, knowledge, discernment, prudence, hospitality, charm, industry, courage and even tact." I have not forgotten them. I have taken them for granted.[35]

Moreover, William Bennett's 1993 bestseller, *The Book of Virtues: A Treasury of Great Moral Stories,* gives his favorite virtues: self-discipline, compassion, responsibility, friendship, work, courage, perseverance, honesty, loyalty, and faith.

The reason that lists of virtues have, or appear to have, so much in common is that the better ones, at least, share a common theological and philosophical heritage, deriving from the natural law. Natural law can be defined as a universal understanding of right and wrong toward which people can reason regardless of gender, class, culture, or country.[36] Natural law is deeply rooted in seven virtues, four of which are at the heart of this book. Faith, hope, and charity or love[37] are known as the theological, supernatural, or infused virtues. The four cardinal (or natural) virtues are found in the fourth book of Plato's *Republic* (chapter 6) as well as in the first book of his *Laws* (1.631). Reference is also made to the cardinal virtues in the deuterocanonical Old Testament book the Wisdom of Solomon (8:7). Saint Thomas Aquinas also argued in his classic work *Summa Theologica* that there are four classical virtues, all based upon right reason (and thus the natural law):

1. the good of reason present in the judgment is prudence;
2. the order of reason with regard to actions affecting others and present in the will as its subject is justice;
3. the order of reason with regard to the passions when these draw us to something irrational is temperance and is in the concupiscible appetite;
4. the order of reason with regard to the passions when these draw us away from a reasonable course of action is fortitude and is in the irascible appetite.[38]

In a book about the profession of arms, why is there mention of "concupiscible appetite" and "irascible appetite," which are terms from Scholastic philosophy? The answer is that they are fundamental to military concerns. Concupiscence is sensual desire; the word *irascibility* stems from *ira* (anger). If our passions and urges lead us toward something sensual that our reason tells us is wrong, we resist that temptation through the power of temperance. If our passions and urges lead us toward something that has to do with anger, wrath, or violence that our reason tells us is wrong, we resist that temptation through the power of fortitude or courage. Concupiscible desires and irascible desires are "merely psychological raw material for good or evil."[39] Desires for food, drink, sleep, sex, money, and the like are not evil in themselves. The point is that unless we are capable of regulating our appetites and passions—according to the standards of reason—we will be possessed by those urges; we will be in the control of vice and will have become not virtuous but vicious.

Ambition, for example, can be concupiscible (a matter of material desire) and irascible (a matter of aggressive yearning). If ambition leads to professionalism, it is to be commended; if it leads to careerism, it is to be condemned. Self-defense, similarly, is virtuous if politically and ethically reasonable; it is vicious if conducted disproportionately or maliciously. There is an old joke about a man of limited intellectual gifts who, upon being informed that a thermos will keep cold drinks cold and hot drinks hot, replied, "How does it know?" How do we know how to separate good and bad ambition or good and bad national defense? See chapter 4 for my attempt to explain how to separate the moral from the immoral.

Chapters 5–8 consider the cardinal virtues and the military profession. I explore prudence or wisdom using the B-52 crash at Fairchild Air Force Base as a case study. The argument there is that military officers at Fairchild lacked wise judgment in taking a mistaken course of action that resulted in the death of fellow service members. The cardinal virtue of justice or truthfulness is considered in the context of Gen. John Lavelle's choice of a course of action during the Vietnam War that necessarily resulted in his relief from command. In looking at the cardinal virtue of courage, I suggest that an army warrant officer, Hugh Thompson, displayed great courage during his actions at My Lai. And the recent circumstances surrounding the end of the apparently promising military career of a young air force lieutenant serve as a case study for examining the virtue of temperance.

If we, like Franklin, can follow a list[40] of virtues—even the four cardinal virtues—can we thereby develop the ideal officer and gentleman? In short, does a list of virtues lead to virtue itself? Can we, as writer Elizabeth Austin asks, get from Bennett's list to *Schindler's List*? The fundamental idea, she sensibly suggests, is to understand that "virtue is essentially about who you are, not what you do. . . . Because we have mislaid our understanding of virtue, we can't make the distinction between a genuine jerk and a basically good person who has made a couple of deeply regretted mistakes."[41] The idea is for the officer and gentleman to integrate the virtues, to develop character (see chapter 9) rather than a checklist or catalog of virtues. The character thus developed will be tested by the fire of difficult circumstances and conflict that one faces in the course of a career—or a life.

Nevertheless, there is no question, as James F. Keenan has told us, that the four virtues of prudence, justice, courage, and temperance are critical and fundamental. In fact, they are known as *cardinal* because they derive from the Latin word *cardo* (hinge). "Everything depends on those virtues. They are what it takes to make a complete human being,"

Keenan explains. According to Austin, "Justice [lies] at the heart of those virtues; self-discipline [temperance] and courage [help] the virtuous man to practice justice, while prudence [advises] him when to enter the fray and when to retreat in good order."[42]

In the end, this book is about good people trying to be good officers. By extension, it is about good people trying to be . . . good people.[43] A long time ago, in the seventh grade, I had a teacher named Miss Jones, who tried to teach us very rebellious kids basic math. The poor woman had no discipline in her class, and to this day I still have problems with ratios, fractions, and the like. But, while dodging spitballs, Miss Jones used to tell us, "Habit is a cable, and we weave a thread of it every day." In chapter 7 I use the important word *habitus* to refer not to automatic and unthinking response (particularly a physical habit) but instead to "stable [moral] dispositions that develop the power of our faculties and render us capable of performing actions of high quality."[44] Benjamin Franklin's list may or may not be valuable for the virtues it lists. But it is invaluable in trying to teach us that we must consciously and conscientiously practice what we preach. Aristotle knew that. And so did Miss Jones.

3

Morals under the Gun

Conscience cannot come to us from the rulings of society;
otherwise it would never reprove us when society approves us,
nor console us when society condemns.

—*Fulton J. Sheen*

It is often easier to fight for principles than to live up to them.

—*Adlai Stevenson*

Is a painting by El Greco beautiful? Is a symphony by Haydn beautiful? Is the scene of two lovers walking hand in hand down a moonlit road beautiful? Is an acrobatic catch in deep centerfield by Willie Mays off the bat of Vic Wertz in the 1954 World Series beautiful? Is a stinking garbage truck, spilling over with rubbish and filth, while making its rounds in the hot sun on a July afternoon in the streets of New York City beautiful? Is a picture of the My Lai massacre in Vietnam beautiful?

MATTERS OF TASTE AND MATTERS OF TRUTH

It is likely that we might agree on the beauty of El Greco, Haydn, and the walkers; we might think "the catch" (as it is known to baseball fans) was, in a way, beautiful. We are unlikely to think the garbage truck beautiful—unless its driver and crew see beauty in the scene because it is the source of their employment and they view it, properly, as an important city service. But could anyone but the twisted person see a photo of a massacre as "beautiful"? (Actually, during the Vietnam War, one U.S. Army officer sent out a Christmas card inscribed "Peace on Earth," with a photo of dead enemy bodies, though not at My Lai.)

Who is to say which music is the "best"? Who will tell us which art is the most "meaningful"? Beauty, truth, and goodness—all these things are matters of taste, opinion, personal preference, are they not? Therefore, virtue itself is a matter of individual choice, is it not? What is principle to me is mere prejudice to you. What is lovely to me is ugly to you. What is alluring to me is appalling to you. There are no standards, we are told, to sort out not just the tasteful from the tasteless, but even honor from shame, virtue from vice, right from wrong. We do, of course, have hectoring and importunate television preachers who espouse a loveless, intellectually barren, and peculiarly personalized form of "Gospel," invariably a grotesque caricature of what they are supposed to be about.[1] So is all that matters, then, what we decide, independent of any standard, any moral "touchstone"? That appears to be the regrettable case. "The student entering college today," observed Prof. Christina Hoff Sommers, "shows the effects of an educational system that has kept its distance from the traditional virtues."

> Unencumbered by the "old bag of virtues," the student
> arrives toting a ragbag of another stripe whose contents
> may be roughly itemized as follows: psychological egoism
> (the belief that the primary motive for action is selfishness),
> moral relativism (the doctrine that what is praiseworthy or
> contemptible is a matter of cultural conditioning), and
> radical tolerance (the doctrine that to be culturally and
> socially aware is to understand and excuse the putative
> wrongdoer). Another item in the bag is the conviction that
> the seat of moral responsibility is found in society and its
> institutions, not in individuals.[2]

"Happy is the man," Saint Augustine said, "who, in the course of a complete life, has everything he desires, provided he desire nothing amiss."[3] Can there be something "amiss"? Who is to say what is "wrong"? Suppose we are talking about a child who wishes to eat nothing but candy bars. Do we have a dietary standard to which we can resort in order to preserve his health? Suppose a student insists that the United States entered World War I in 1912 instead of 1917. Do we have a standard—an almanac or a history textbook or an encyclopedia—that we can employ to disabuse him of his mistaken idea? We do, certainly. If the child will not accept our dietary advice, we chalk it up to his immaturity. If the student will not accept the information from a reputable encyclopedia, we attribute it to his stubbornness. If we admit that there can be something "amiss" in the realm of eating and in the area of historical dating, is there, then, nothing "amiss" in the realm of morals?

The first chapter of this book was basically a hoax. It was based upon the assumption that most readers would disagree strongly with the idea that, as we grow and assume ever larger responsibilities, we must be willing much more frequently to lie or cheat or steal. Honor, I implied there, is all right for cadets; but senior officers must routinely compromise. Why would a reader grow impatient with that argument? Is it because most of us (I hope) believe deeply that honesty is not the property only of children? Without saying it, then, I was assuming that the readers would have a standard of honesty that would properly be offended by my arguments in chapter 1 (see my apology for them in chapter 2).

What do you do if your child is dying for want of medication that you cannot afford? Can you steal it? Suppose you are a prisoner of war, and one of your friends, because he is afraid he cannot stand up to torture and will tell the enemy about an impending operation, begs you to kill him in his sleep? Can you kill him? These and similar cases, I suppose, are interesting; but they have little to do with real-world ethics. With very few exceptions (see "Obiter Dicta" for more detail), lying, and cheating, and stealing, and killing are simply wrong, immoral, unjust, evil. Any society will die and decay that does not somehow prevent widespread lying, cheating, stealing, and killing. Even a gang of criminals must have some sense of honor (omertà) among its members.

In short, there are some things we know: "What has happened before will happen again. What has been done before will be done again. There is nothing new in the whole world" (Eccl. 1:9). There are some virtues we must have, we must teach, we must cultivate. Peter Kreeft tells the story of teaching ethics to a rather antihistorical and radical group of freshmen at Boston College in the 1960s. Anxious to be rid of the "old and outdated ideas" and fashion a new, enlightened society, they developed a cluster of virtues critical to their new world. When their project was finished, Professor Kreeft asked them to compare their ideas to Plato's in the *Republic*. "The students were truly amazed to find that . . . [the ideas] they had just discovered were precisely the main points of this bewhiskered old classic."[4] So Kreeft then had them explore Aristotle, Augustine, Aquinas, and so on, giving them the chance to find new old ideas (or is it old new ideas?). To compress this into two simple statements: just because we do not know everything does not mean that we do not know some things. And ultimately we can know that there is an Ultimate.

Professor Sommers spoke at the Air Force Academy a few years ago about these kinds of ideas. Her point was that we must relearn what we already know:

> The past few decades has [sic] seen an assault on the sustaining institutions of our society and these now need our *conscious* protections and care if they are to be pre-served. Our American society is in many ways admirable and enviable; in any case it is our society; in preserving it we preserve ourselves. We need to devote ourselves to strengthening the institutions and social arrangements that nurture us. If we again become alive to the value of our traditions and our institutions, if we become determined to preserve and protect them, we will be doing what needs to be done to redeem and to safeguard our future; our own lives and those of our children will be more secure, more dignified, more humane. We must again learn what we already know. And we must act on what we know.[5]

"DEFINING DEVIANCY DOWN"

A few years ago, Daniel Patrick Moynihan coined the phrase "defining deviancy down"[6] to describe how we increasingly legitimate behavior previously regarded as criminal or antisocial. Attitudes, language, and conduct that my friends and I, as public school students in western Massachusetts in the mid-1960s, would have regarded as completely outrageous are increasingly normal, even socially expected, today. Indeed, much that passes for routine conduct today would have been seen by ordinary students then as shameful. I agree with James Twitchell that "shame is the generator of much moral sense and the ignition for much moral action." The problem is that "no area of American culture has gone untouched by the desire to remove shame." He contends that "shame is the basis of individual responsibility and the beginnings of social conscience. It is where decency comes from."[7] Not for nothing did Nicolaus

Mills choose the title *The Triumph of Meanness,* subtitling his book *America's War against Its Better Self.*[8]

To suggest to many people today that their behavior (or language or clothing) are shameful seems a reproach both curious and quaint.[9] Is *anything* shameful today? We have politicians and ministers who are satyrs; priests who are pedophiles; movies filled with gore and sexual dissipation; insatiable appetites of all kinds; ubiquitous profanity; TV programs designed for cretins and voyeurs; unwed mothers proud of their "assertiveness"; boys who can perform the physical act of impregnating girlfriends without any sense of the manly, moral responsibility of raising their children; semiliterate and apathetic teachers; colleges and universities with hardly an inkling of what and how to teach the "students" attracted to their campuses, although there will be promises of almost everything—except academic rigor; a nation obsessed with sports but having legions of fat, out-of-shape teenagers incapable of running even two miles; a rampant consumerism that manifests itself in shop-till-you-drop TV and endless miles of malls, while the poor and homeless go begging; bumper stickers of a cartoon character urinating on various things, or wisely advising us that dung occurs, or urging us to question authority; "art" featuring sacred objects immersed in urine; T-shirts with language on them I did not hear even in airborne school; Michael Jackson; Jerry Springer; O.J. Simpson; Richard Nixon; Bill Clinton; Monica Lewinsky; Mike Tyson; drive-in churches and drive-in wakes; drive-by shootings; sadists and murderers who torment and kill homosexuals; teenagers who murder their newborn children and return to dances; students who murder classmates; children who murder parents; mothers who hire killers to eliminate their children's competitors; mothers and fathers willing to sell their children for drugs; tenured radicals inculcating ideology and tenured moral incompetents unable to distinguish good from evil; Dr. Kevorkian, who kills his patients, regardless of the oath he once took to preserve life;[10] medical professionals who commit abortion regardless of the oaths they took and then those who in fits of cowardice and misplaced morality bomb abortion "clinics"; partial-birth abortion or infanticide;[11] the Ku Klux Klan and others, black and white, who traffic in racial hate; drug peddlers who traffic in human misery and suffering; and then those of us—myself included—who have too often and too long been too lukewarm to say much about it all, lest we be thought bluenoses, scolds, or puritans. Today, after all, we think self-righteous and bigoted anyone who is not "mellowed out" about anything someone else does as amusement, as self-fulfillment, or as "social statement."

In the false name of freedom (which is actually license), anything goes as long as it is "fun," or "comedic." In the false name of tolerance[12] (which is actually moral apathy) we are told to give respect to actions and attitudes that are, in many cases, loathsome, unethical, or—how "quaint" can one get?—sinful.[13] As William Bennett has pointed out, tolerance

> can be a genuinely harmful force when it becomes a
> euphemism for moral exhaustion and a rigid or indifferent
> neutrality in response to every great moral issue—when in
> G. K. Chesterton's phrase, it becomes the virtue of people
> who do not believe in anything. . . . A rigid and inflexible
> embrace of moral truths is not the virus that has invaded
> America's body politic, nor are we suffering an oversupply
> of consistent moral judgments. To the contrary, we live in
> an era when it has become unfashionable to make judg-
> ments on a whole range of very consequential behaviors
> and attitudes. To take just one example: 70 percent of
> people between the ages of eighteen and thirty-four say that
> people who generate a baby out of wedlock should not be
> subject to moral reproach of any sort. . . . judgment
> [Bennett concludes] is not bigotry; and tolerance may be
> just another term for indifference.[14]

A recent comment by Francis Fukuyama is important here: "Although William J. Bennett and other conservatives are often attacked for harping on the theme of moral decline, they are essentially correct: the perceived breakdown of social order is not a matter of nostalgia, poor memory, or ignorance about the hypocrisies of earlier ages. The decline is readily measurable in statistics on crime, fatherless children, broken trust, reduced opportunities for and outcomes from education, and the like."[15] The impact of what Fukuyama calls "The Great Disruption" of our moral order is increasingly evident even to those who wish to avert their eyes. As Senator Moynihan points out, "over the past generation . . . , the amount of deviant behavior in American society has increased beyond the levels the community can 'afford to recognize' and . . . accordingly, we have been re-defining deviancy so as to exempt much conduct previously stigmatized, and also quietly raising the 'normal' level in categories where behavior is now abnormal by any earlier standard."[16]

Discussion, Debate, Dispute, Dissent, and Democracy

One of the problems with the "culture war" in which all of us, left, right, and middle, find ourselves involved is the question of whether, in defending our views and asserting our beliefs, we indeed cross a line of courtesy, decency, and respect for others into the territory of shrill self-righteousness and even criminality. The idea expressed in Isaiah—"Come now, and let us reason together" (1:18 AV)—is at the heart of the democratic process. The "debates" that one sees on *Jerry Springer* do little to achieve the kind of consensus and harmony at which democracy aims, however forlornly. At the same time, we know, both religiously and politically, that such consensus will forever elude us. Meanwhile, regardless of our political views and religious convictions, we must do the best we can to talk with one another: to discuss, debate, dispute, dissent according to the means and methods ethically open to us. One need only examine the record of the civil rights movement and the preaching of Martin Luther King Jr. to see how dispute, when it is taken to the level of dissent in action, may be conducted in ways that are in accord both with the dissenters' social conscience and with respect for law (although the actions of dissent may well be in violation of law, in which case, dissenters are prepared to accept the penalty of the law).

For example, one does not support the prolife movement by killing abortion doctors. Neither does one shout down or intimidate speakers at "universities," no matter how pernicious one may perceive their message as being. Should a speaker appear on an American campus and spew racist hatred, one wishes to believe that the evil of his views could and should be exposed more readily through reasoned debate than by physically assaulting the speaker. There is a fundamental assumption here, of course: in a democracy, respect for reason and civil decorum, though they can never guarantee "right answers," can at least guarantee "right means." "In a democratic society, all opinions must be heard, because some of them may be true. And those that are false must be vigorously, but respectfully, contested."[17]

There is widespread agreement, even in the midst of "culture wars," about the means of debate and dissent. But there is little agreement to-

day about the ends, standards, or ultimate principles of democracy: a
trenchant explanation of this is that of Pope John Paul II:

> Democracy cannot be idolized to the point of making it a
> substitute for morality or a panacea for immorality. Funda-
> mentally, democracy is a "system" and as such is a means
> and not an end. Its "moral" value is not automatic, but
> depends on conformity to the moral law to which it, like
> every other form of human behavior, must be subject: in
> other words, its morality depends on the morality of the
> ends which it pursues and of the means which it employs.
> . . . Even in participatory systems of government, the
> regulation of interests often occurs to the advantage of the
> most powerful, since they are the ones most capable of
> maneuvering not only the levers of power but also of
> shaping the formation of consensus. In such a situation,
> democracy ultimately becomes an empty word.
>
> It is therefore urgently necessary, for the future of
> society and the development of a sound democracy, to
> rediscover those essential and innate human and moral
> values which flow from the very truth of the human being
> and express and safeguard the dignity of the person: values
> which no individual, no majority and no state can ever
> create, modify, or destroy, but must only acknowledge,
> respect and promote.[18]

Morals under the Law

But the Pope's position is widely challenged. Philosopher Richard Rorty,
for example, contends that "there is nothing deep inside of us, no common human nature, no built-in human solidarity, to use [as] moral reference point. There is nothing to people except what has been socialized
into them—their ability to use language, and thereby to exchange beliefs and desires with other people."[19] Rorty (described by James Q.
Wilson as "perhaps the most important philosophical writer in present-
day America") "denies that there is anything like a 'core self' or an
inherently human quality, and so there is no way for us to say that some
actions are inherently inhuman, even when confronted with the horrors

of Auschwitz." But would Rorty be reduced to saying that death camps are *"O.K. for that country or culture"*? Rorty, says Wilson, "of course condemns [them], but only because history and circumstance have supplied him with certain 'beliefs.'"[20]

The well-known international relations theorist Hans J. Morgenthau wrote a little-known essay in 1959 from which a lengthy quotation is appropriate here:

> Is not morality . . . a relative thing, the ever-changing result of environment and circumstances? If this were so . . . , how do you explain that we can not only understand the moral relevance of the Ten Commandments, originating in a social environment and circumstances quite different from ours, but also make them [remember, he was writing more than forty years ago] the foundation for our moral life? How do you explain that the moral ideas of Plato and Pascal, of Buddha and Thomas Aquinas are similarly acceptable to our intellectual understanding and moral sense? If the disparate historic systems of morality were not erected upon a common foundation of moral understanding and valuation, impervious to the changing conditions of time and place, we could neither understand any other moral system but our own, nor could any other moral system but our own have any moral relevance for us.

"What is it," he asked, that all men have in common as moral beings? All men . . . in contrast to the animals, are born with a moral sense. . . [and are] capable of making moral judgments."[21]

Recently, James Q. Wilson, in challenging Rorty (and implicitly following Morgenthau's lead), supported one of the theses of this book, that ethics is about *owing;* it is about responsibly fulfilling our gift of life. We do have certain social and political obligations. But that simple sentence defies the rather libertarian and "fatally flawed assumption of many Enlightenment [modern] thinkers, namely that autonomous individuals can freely choose, or will, their moral life." Wilson concludes, "Believing that individuals are everything, rights are trumps, and morality is relative to time and place, such thinkers have been led to design laws, practices, and institutions that leave nothing between the state and the individual save choices, contracts, and entitlements. Fourth-grade children being told how to use condoms is only one of the more perverse of the results."[22]

By the same token Sissela Bok has concluded that there are three categories of values so critical to the survival of communities that they must be worked out even in the smallest group. She says that all human groups stress some sort of positive duties regarding mutual support, loyalty, and reciprocity. A second group of basic values consists of negative duties to refrain from harmful action. A third cluster of values amounts to a kind of due process, in an attempt to ensure a procedural fundamental fairness. No known society has ever tolerated "false witness," for example. This results in a "minimal interpretation of morality," something Bok also finds in the writings of Michael Walzer, who has distinguished between minimalist and maximalist moralities. He characterizes the former type as thin, universal, and abstract, in contrast to the latter, which he sees as thick, rooted in the particular, and full-blooded. "Perhaps the end product of this effort," she quotes him as saying, "will be a set of standards to which all societies can be held—negative injunctions, most likely, rules against murder, deceit, torture, oppression, and tyranny." The title of her book, not surprisingly, is *Common Values.*[23]

Bok does not cite Reo Christenson, who wrote more than twenty years before she did about a "mature sense of justice";[24] nor does she cite C.S. Lewis, who was writing about forty years before she did about a common moral law;[25] nor does she cite Samuel Pufendorf, the world's first professor of international law, who was writing three hundred years before she did about natural law, reason, and limited government; nor does she cite the book of Romans in the Bible, written more than nineteen hundred years before Bok's *Common Values:* "The demands of the law are written in [our] hearts" (2:15). Sometimes the oldest truths, as we have seen, are the newest discoveries. And we are amazed to find that "in the end, only a morality which acknowledges certain norms as valid always and for everyone, with no exception, can guarantee the ethical foundation of social coexistence, both on the national and international levels."[26]

OUTRAGE AND INIQUITY: AN OUTLINE

Charles Krauthammer wrote recently in a *Time* essay that today "when religion is a preference and piety a form of eccentricity suggesting fanaticism," we must revise Chesterton. Tolerance is not just the virtue *of* people who do not believe in anything; it extends only *to* people who do not believe in anything. "Believe in something, and beware."[27] It will be easy for readers to discern my Christian convictions in these pages. Because of those convictions I believe, with Pope John Paul II, that man's "history of sin begins when he no longer acknowledges the Lord as his Creator and himself wishes to be the one who determines, with complete independence, what is good and what is evil." As Professor Budziszewski says, "We do not want God to be God; each of us wants to be his own little god."[28]

That should be contrasted—sharply—to the naturalistic thesis propounded recently, although hardly originally, by Edward O. Wilson: "*Ought* is the product of a materialistic process."[29] It has never been said more economically before. Wilson says, first, there is no God ("The idea of a biological God, one who directs organic evolution and intervenes in human affairs . . . is increasingly contravened by biology and the brain sciences"[54]); second, he says there is hardly a difference between superstition and faith ("As cults [inevitably?] evolve into religions, the image of the Supreme Being is reinforced by myth and liturgy"[67]); and third, people are "just extremely complicated machines."[30] Let me give Prof. E.O. Wilson a paragraph to explain his thesis: "For many, the urge to believe in transcendental existence and immortality is overpowering. Transcendentalism, especially when reinforced by religious faith, is psychically full and rich; it feels somehow *right*. By comparison, empiricism seems sterile and inadequate. In the quest for ultimate meaning the transcendental route is much easier to follow.[31] That is why, even as empiricism is winning the mind, transcendentalism continues to win the heart. Science has always defeated religious dogma point by point when differences between the two were meticulously assessed. But to no avail."[32]

But Wilson is too easily discouraged. Alan Wolfe of Boston University tells us that Americans are supine in the face of "transcendentalism": "Reluctant to impose their value on others, they are committed to tolerance to such an extent that they have either given up finding timeless morality or would be unwilling to bring its principles down to earth if, by chance, they came across it." Wolfe is very clear that "middle-class Americans have never let God command them in ways seriously in conflict with modern beliefs."[33] Richard John Neuhaus argued more than a decade ago that in America much of public debate had turned hostile to religious conviction. Robert J. Nash, by contrast, suggests, not without good reason, that "the problem of the mainline churches is not that they are too doctrinal or authoritarian but that they have become far too secular." Stephen Carter is closer to Nash than to Neuhaus in observing that religion today is often treated as a kind of "hobby."[34]

The success of materialism/subjectivism/empiricism/logical positivism/existentialism (all of which deny either the essence of, or the possibility of knowing a living, loving God),[35] is widely testified to, very recently by Robert J. Nash, who takes severely to task some philosophers of virtue.[36] Each of these writers, says Nash, "preaches," "orates," "admonishes," "pontificates," "ridicules," "hyperbolizes," "lectures," "cajoles," "accuses," or—perhaps worst of all—"exhorts." One wonders what Nash must think of the Bible. But nothing is lost because, says Nash (who, by the way, teaches teachers): "Most of my students are postmodern in temperament, eschewing any belief in a universal metaphysical or moral archetype. These students question otherworldly views of reality, preferring to remain persistently grounded in the here-and-now. For them, reality is socially constructed ['*ought* is the product of a materialistic process']. Truth is always of the 'small-*t*' variety and continually revisable. And morality is contextually shaped and up for grabs."[37] But what of virtues? Is there nothing beyond culture? Nothing beyond time? Nothing beyond taste and preference and opinion and appetite? When they come to take the Jews to Auschwitz, what do we say? "It's a matter of choice or power or prevailing interests?" "I'm not Jewish, so I don't care"? "That's a decision made in that time by those people, so who am I to judge?" Confronted with such vincible ignorance, what does the good professor say? He says that he is "highly sensitive" about the problems concerning "the relevance of virtues in the late twentieth century." He quotes with approval, for example, from J.L.A. Garcia, who is concerned that virtues are "anachronistic," "reactionary," "unintelligible," "irrelevant," "arbitrary," "impractical" (although he means "impracticable"), "egoistic," "fatalistic," and "deterministic."[38]

In the section titled "Defining Deviancy Down," I list what I see as evils in society, among them abortion and euthanasia, consumerism[39] and opulence, sports mania, educational poverty, rising crime rates, and so on. E.O. Wilson would want empirical data to support these claims, Nash would find me guilty of "hyperbolizing" unless I offer corroboration, and Garcia would likely consider "reactionary" any prescriptions I might suggest. But we have sowed; and here, briefly, is what we have reaped.

Every day in America:

- 1,000 unwed teenage girls become mothers;
- 1,100 teenage girls get abortions;
- 4,200 teenagers contract sexually transmitted diseases;
- 500 adolescents begin using drugs;
- 1,000 adolescents begin drinking alcohol;
- 135,000 kids bring guns or weapons to school;
- 3,600 teens are assaulted; 80 are raped;
- 2,200 teens drop out of high school;
- 6 teens commit suicide.[40]

In 1996 alone there were over 1,221,500 abortions (roughly the combined populations of Cleveland, Atlanta, and Buffalo). Since 1973 there have been an acknowledged 35 million abortions (and many millions more when abortions produced by abortifacients are also considered).[41] Prof. David Carlin, who teaches in Rhode Island, has been clear on this: "In America today there is no issue more important, no worse crime, than the unwarranted homicide of more than a million unborn babies per year."[42] Euthanasia, since it was first legally permitted in Oregon, has gained ground. Our understanding—both of when life starts and when it stops—is changing dramatically and rapidly. If we are simply complicated "machines," of course, it makes little difference. Moreover, as Charles Krauthammer has pointed out, we can now produce headless mice and headless tadpoles. So what? Princeton biologist Lee Silver has explained that it is almost certainly possible to produce human bodies without a forebrain: "These human bodies without any semblance of consciousness would not be considered persons, and thus it would be perfectly legal to keep them 'alive' as a future source of organs." "Headlessness," says Krauthammer, "will be cloning's crowning achievement." "If we flinch [from banning cloning] in the face of this high-tech barbarity, we'll deserve the hell it heralds."[43]

The U.S. Catholic bishops said in a recent statement:

We are now witnessing the gradual restructuring of American culture according to the ideals of utility, productivity and cost-effectiveness. It is a culture where moral questions are submerged by a river of goods and services and where

the misuse of marketing and public relations subverts
public life.

The losers in this ethical sea change will be those who
are elderly, poor, disabled, and politically marginalized.
None of these pass the utility test; and yet, they at least
have a presence. They at least have the possibility of
organizing to be heard. *Those who are unborn, infirm and
terminally ill have no such advantage.* They have no
"utility," and worse, they have no voice. As we tinker with
the beginning, the end and even the intimate cell structure
of life, we tinker with our own identity as a free nation
dedicated to the dignity of the human person. When
American political life becomes an experiment on people
rather than for and by them, it will no longer be worth
conducting.[44]

Meanwhile the American prison population has topped 1.8 million, but, as Eric Schlosser has written, this has given rise to a "prison-
industrial complex" of businesses that sell everything from security
cameras to padded cells available in a "vast color selection."[45] Business
and crime have always been close; perhaps they will get closer now that
we know it is "intolerant" to preach against the love of money and often
"judgmental" to moralize about the evil of crime or its putative causes.
As Adam Walinsky has written:

For more than twenty years the children of the ghetto have
witnessed violent death as an almost routine occurrence.
They have seen it on their streets, in their schools, in their
families, and on TV. They have lived with constant fear.
Many have come to believe that they will not see twenty-
five. These are often children whose older brothers, friends,
and uncles have taught them that only the strong and
ruthless survive. Prison does not frighten them—it is a rite
of passage that a majority of their peers may have experienced. Too many have learned to kill without remorse, for a
drug territory or for an insult, because of a look or a bump
on the sidewalk, or just to do it: why not?

These young people have been raised in the glare of
ceaseless media violence and incitement to every depravity

of act and spirit. Movies may feature scores of killings in
two hours' time, vying to show methods ever more horrific;
many are quickly imitated on the street. Television com-
mercials teach that a young man requires a new pair of
$120 sneakers each week. Major corporations make and
sell records exhorting their listeners to brutalize Koreans,
rob store owners, rape women, kill the police. Ashamed
and guilt-ridden, elite opinion often encourages even
hoodlums to carry a sense of entitlement and grievance
against society and its institutions.[46]

Movie critic Michael Medved has charged that Hollywood has a
"sickness in the soul," a "bias for the bizarre," and that it dismisses and
denigrates religion, promotes promiscuity, maligns marriage, encourages illegitimacy, glorifies ugliness, celebrates foul language and violence, and bashes America. "Hollywood's dark distortions about who
we are and where we are going," he writes, "amount to more than an-
noyance or insult: they represent a serious threat to the well-being of our
children and our country."[47] He quotes Senator Byrd (D-W.Va.): "If we
in this nation continue to sow the images of murder, violence, drug abuse,
sadism, arrogance, irreverence, blasphemy, perversion, pornography and
aberration before the eyes of millions of children . . . day after day, we
should not be surprised if the foundations of our society rot away as if
from leprosy."[48]

As former Speaker of the House Newt Gingrich has said, "It is
impossible to maintain civilization with twelve-year-olds having babies,
fifteen-year-olds killing each other, seventeen-year-olds dying of AIDS,
and eighteen-year-olds receiving diplomas they cannot read."[49]

There are more than one million babies born out of wedlock in the
United States every year. The rate of illegitimate births in this country
stood at 5 percent in 1960. The estimate now is that it runs at about 40
percent. Among black women, the figure is about 65 percent—as much
as 80 percent in some cities.[50] About nine out of ten children who suffer
abuse and come from unstable families eventually become delinquent.
Humanitarian and athlete Arthur Ashe, deploring the moral decline among
blacks, plaintively asks:

What went wrong within black America? We might as well
ask what went wrong with America as a whole. What

happened to blacks is, to be sure, only a heightened degree
of the national weakening of morality and standards. . . .
The cruel irony of African American history is that although we are not nearly equal to whites in terms of
opportunities and freedoms, we have declined as a group
exactly at the time we achieved the highest degree of
freedom we have ever had, and secured the largest number
of rights we have ever had.[51]

These things are not difficult to fathom when we realize that sexual
activity (and sexual diseases) among the young have increased by 300
percent in the last twenty years; the average American now watches
fourteen thousand references to sex in the course of a year.[52] Meanwhile, nearly twice as many teenagers reported gangs in their schools in
1995 as did so in 1989.[53]

The "Cure"

What is the relevance of this disturbing catalog of moral horror to the
profession of arms? In a list of American problems and divisions,
Zbigniew Brzezinski, President Carter's national security adviser and
Columbia University political scientist, lists, among other difficulties, a
greedy wealthy class, deepening racial and poverty troubles, widespread
crime and decay, the spread of a massive drug culture, the inbreeding of
social hopelessness, the profusion of sexual license, the massive propagation of moral corruption by the visual media, the decline in civic consciousness, the emergence of a potentially divisive multiculturalism,[54]
and an increasingly pervasive sense of spiritual emptiness.[55] All of these
problems are national security concerns. The profession of arms draws
its people from, serves the cause of, and will return its veterans to civilian society. The military establishment is not immune to the spiritual
diseases infecting the larger social order. And neither has the military
been a paragon of purity; it has suffered from the same moral illness that
contaminates the body politic.

As these words are written, about one thousand World War II veterans are dying every day. As is true of practically any group anywhere,
these veterans have their saints and their sinners, good men and bad.
Tom Brokaw and Stephen Ambrose are very probably correct, however,
in calling this incredible group of people "the greatest generation." It is

too easy to compare the men who invaded Normandy in 1944 with the boys and girls who were at Woodstock in 1969.[56] What comparison can be made between Eisenhower and Clinton? How are we to replace this generation of men and women who made it through the Depression, fought World War II, returned to college (using the G.I. bill, one of the wisest pieces of legislation ever passed by Congress), built their homes, raised their families, and lived—for the most part—quiet, industrious, and decent lives? There is no replacement for them, and we are poorer every day in America as our fathers, uncles, and grandfathers die.

A well-known hymn, "Faith of Our Fathers," by Frederick W. Faber, urges us to be "true to thee till death." In a book of quotations, the editor makes this comment after a quotation from Faber's hymn: "If we retained the convictions of our fathers in geography, physics, medicine—and, indeed, in almost any department of human knowledge—we would be in a ludicrous and lamentable plight and utterly unable to function in the modern world."[57] Of course, that is correct. No one suggests that we should teach the science of 1944 in 2000. We have learned too much. But the editor is wrong about the faith of our fathers in matters of religion and ethics. G.K. Chesterton called the error of rejecting what we should learn from our ancestors to embrace instead the folly of our children the "eternal revolution."[58] In the main, our fathers taught us well; in our pride and self-centeredness, we have turned our backs on them and what they wished to give us as our heritage. A recent novel, for example, concludes this way: "The meaning of life has not much to do with good and evil, right and wrong, duty, honor, country, or any of that. It has to do with cutting the right deal."[59] We have forgotten—we have disdained—too much. We have abandoned our moral compass, which James Q. Wilson describes this way: "Mankind's moral sense is not a strong beacon light, radiating outward to illuminate in sharp outline all that it touches. It is, rather, a small candle flame, casting vague and multiple shadows, flickering and sputtering in the strong winds of power and passion, greed and ideology. But brought close to the heart and cupped in one's hands, it dispels the darkness and warms the soul."[60]

In the wake of the school shootings in spring 1999 in Littleton, Colorado, and Conyers, Georgia, writer David Gergen pointed out that "every generation, no matter how good, has had its share of loners, misfits and plain old wackos. When many of us were growing up, these social outcasts vented their frustrations with fists or knives. Now they can break into gun arsenals their folks keep at home; their heads are filled with violent pictures they have seen on television and in movies; their hard drives are filled with pornography that floods across the Internet." But Gergen states with equal force that domestic Armageddon and civil conflagration are neither imminent nor necessary. Most of our kids are decent, responsible, and compassionate.[61] Those who are growing up owe a tremendous debt of gratitude to those who went before. But those of us who are today's teachers similarly have a tremendous obligation: to serve as moral exemplars for those who in the decades ahead will take our places in society. Truly there is a kind of "moral contract" among the leaders of yesterday, the leaders of today, and those who will succeed us tomorrow. If there is much about us that cries out for reform, there is also much about us for which to be grateful; if there is reason for anxiety, there is also reason for hope.

Is it possible that the resurrection of the cardinal virtues of prudence or wisdom, justice or truthfulness, courage, and temperance can revivify American society? Can these virtues again be the chief part, not just of our education, but also of our daily business? I think so. But there I am assuming that we can learn from those who have gone before, that there are virtues worthy of emulation, that we can resurrect the ancient standards—called in our Declaration of Independence "the Laws of Nature and of Nature's God"—and apply them wisely to the problems of the day, and that there is a Supreme Being whose commands are made known to us if we will but have the eyes to see and the ears to hear.

4

Moral Reasoning and the Cardinal Virtues

Conscience has rights because it has duties.
—*John Henry Cardinal Newman*

"I'm sorry, Father [said the doctor], I feel that the laws of society are what makes something a crime or not. I'm aware that you don't agree. And there can be bad laws, ill-conceived, true. But in this case [euthanasia], I think we have a good law. If I thought I had such a thing as a soul, and that there might be an angry God in Heaven, I might agree with you."

Abbot Zerchi smiled thinly. "You don't *have* a soul, Doctor. You *are* a soul. You *have* a body, temporarily."
—*Walter M. Miller Jr.,* A Canticle for Leibowitz

General of the Armies John J. Pershing is supposed to have said once that a soldier needs to learn only how to shoot and salute. In rather the same way, those attending church are supposed to know how to "pray, pay, and obey." Nothing is said, in either of those witticisms, about selective obedience or disobedience on grounds of "conscience."[1] In fact, for the past few decades conscience has received something of a bad press. "Surely," the positivist might say in a wide-eyed and condescending way, "you don't believe in *that*"—as if conscience were in the same league as the tooth fairy and the Easter bunny. After all, is "conscience" not merely what society (or our parents, teachers, coaches, ministers, and even drill sergeants) might tell us?

A Moral Dilemma

We are impaled on the horns of a very difficult dilemma. On the one hand, soldiers are supposed to obey orders; on the other hand, they are supposed to disobey illegal orders. Soldiers are expected to have the decency and the moral power to distinguish, even in combat, orders that are "good" from those that are "bad." I submit that this task is burdensome enough, say, for a forty-two-year-old senior officer with a master's degree and twenty years of military experience. The same task for an eighteen-year-old private or airman is practically impossible. To the extent that there is relief from this dilemma we must depend upon, well, conscience—upon those "self-evident" truths to which Jefferson referred in 1776.

In basic training or boot camp, when should we teach "conscience"? After basic rifle marksmanship? Perhaps before nuclear/biological/chemical (NBC) training? After grenade throwing? Before hand-to-hand training? By whom should "conscience" be taught? By the chaplain? No, that would smack of enforced religiosity. By the drill sergeant? No, he is trained to inculcate only martial science. By the commander? No, the philosophical arts were not part of her education. By a corps of well-meaning civilians? No, they would have little credibility, particularly with newly minted privates and airmen.

If we admit that illegal—not just stupid—orders have occasionally been given and that we want our soldiers to recognize and refuse such orders, we must depend upon conscience, for our military manuals do exactly that. Because conscience is intimately related to natural law and thus to subjects seemingly arcane and ethereal, it is rarely, if ever, taught in basic military training. We thus leave our soldiers—officers and enlisted, experienced or inexperienced, more or less educated—in the intractable position of having the responsibility of disobeying illegal orders when they have never been instructed how to recognize such orders. It is as if we expected our riflemen to be expert marksmen without so much as a class—let alone practical work on the range—about the details of maintaining, loading, aiming, and firing weapons. We expect our soldiers to obey and, if necessary, to disobey; we train in the one but resolutely ignore the other. We expect of the religious person that he, too, will "pray, pay, and obey"—but only up to a point.[2] My concern in this chapter, then, is with conscience and natural law and their application to the crucial task of the soldier, sailor, airman, or marine, which is to obey orders insofar as informed conscience permits.

OBEDIENCE TO LAWFUL ORDERS

The professional military services are neither debating societies nor philosophical associations. They exist, primarily, to go to war. There can be no doubt that orders must be presumed to be legal. An army whose members quarreled about or questioned the legality of every order issued would soon fall into chaos and anarchy. Over my ten years of teaching ethics to senior officers, I have repeatedly asked this question: "How many illegal orders have you received in your career?" Occasionally someone will suggest that he has been told to do something manifestly wrong. But that is rare. The modern military is not the collection of sybarites it is occasionally painted as being.

We must be clear at the outset that, in the absence of better information, subordinates must obey superiors. In the absence of inflamed conscience in the matter of potentially illegal orders, subordinates must follow orders. Orders cannot be challenged, let alone ignored, for cavalier reasons. The *Manual for Courts-Martial,* for example, is very clear: any military person who "willfully disobeys a lawful command of his superior commissioned officer . . . shall be punished, if the offense is committed in time of war, by death or such other punishment as a court-martial may direct." The *MCM* states, even, that "the dictates of a person's conscience, religion, or personal philosophy cannot justify or excuse the disobedience of an otherwise lawful order" (art. 90).

In article 92, moreover, the *MCM* instructs us that any military person who, "having knowledge of any other lawful order issued by a member of the armed forces, which it is his duty to obey, fails to obey the order . . . shall be punished as a court-martial may direct." *Lawful* orders must be obeyed; but can article 92 be read as saying that soldiers have the duty of disobeying *unlawful* orders? Or is that merely a form of eisegesis (reading into a text what one wants to find there)?

Thus far, consideration has been given only to the issue of soldiers' disobeying unlawful orders. Suppose the soldier obeys the unlawful order. Does he incur legal and moral responsibility for *not* disobeying such orders? The *MCM* puts it this way: "It is a defense to any offense that the accused was acting pursuant to orders unless the accused knew the orders to be unlawful or a person of ordinary sense and understanding would have known the orders to be unlawful" (rule 916 [2:109]). In other words, soldiers must obey orders unless "a reasonably prudent person" (4:24) would know better than to follow such transparently unlawful orders.

But what is "ordinary sense and understanding"? And who, more precisely, is the "reasonably prudent person"? If we dispense with the tome known as the *Manual for Courts-Martial* and deal with the presumably clearer field manuals covering such subjects as obedience to and disobedience of certain orders, are we likely to resolve the problem at hand? Consider the air force manual *International Law—The Conduct of Armed Conflict and Air Operations*. We are instructed there that if an act "was committed pursuant to military orders," such is a defense "only if the accused did not know or could not reasonably have been expected to know that the act ordered was unlawful." "Members of the armed forces are bound to obey only lawful orders" (AFP 110–31 [15–6]). That same manual then attempts a clarification: "An order requiring the performance of a military duty may be inferred to be legal. An act performed manifestly beyond the scope of authority, or pursuant to an order that a man of ordinary sense and understanding would know to be illegal, or in a wanton manner in the discharge of a lawful duty, is not excusable."

The basic army manual on this topic, *The Law of Land Warfare,* which dates to 1956, is of little help. Its serpentine language is as follows:

> The fact that the law of war has been violated pursuant to
> an order of a superior authority, whether military or civil,
> does not deprive the act in question of its character of a war
> crime, nor does it constitute a defense in the trial of an
> accused individual, unless he did not know and could not
> reasonably have been expected to know that the act ordered
> was unlawful. In all cases where the order is held not to
> constitute a defense to an allegation of war crime, the fact
> that the individual was acting pursuant to orders may be
> considered in mitigation of punishment. (FM 27–10, #509)

That paragraph is followed by a masterpiece of obfuscation:

> In considering the question whether a superior order
> constitutes a valid defense, the court shall take into consid-
> eration the fact that obedience to lawful orders is the duty
> of every member of the armed forces; that the latter cannot
> be expected, in conditions of war discipline, to weigh

scrupulously the legal merits of the orders received; that certain rules of warfare may be controversial; or that an act otherwise amounting to a war crime may be done in obedience to orders conceived as a measure of reprisal. At the same time it must be borne in mind that members of the armed forces are bound to obey only lawful orders.

Former army lieutenant colonel Paul Christopher says, after quoting that confusing passage, "In other words, the relevant military manual advises soldiers to obey only lawful orders while at the same time acknowledging that they will often be unable to tell lawful orders from unlawful ones!"[3] We seem to have arrived at these conclusions: First, lawful orders must be obeyed, but in a proportionate manner. Second, unlawful orders must be disobeyed.[4] Third, people of ordinary sense and understanding—reasonable and prudent people—can, will, and must distinguish the one from the other. If soldiers of ordinary sense and understanding disobey a direct order in time of war and are subsequently court-martialed, they may be put to death—so they had better be right in their refusal to obey, even though bullets, grenades, and other missiles may be flying their way during the course of their moral meditations.[5]

DEVELOPING CONSCIENCE

If we need people of "ordinary sense and understanding," how are we to develop these people in the military forces? People of "ordinary sense and understanding" are, in fact, people of conscience and character. "Persons of strong character," writes Colonel Hartle, "are the ultimate resource for any military organization, and they are by definition persons of integrity—individuals whose actions are consistent with their beliefs."[6]

We could expend a great deal of time and effort debating the precise definition of such terms as *conscience, character,* and *integrity.* Let us take for granted that, like competence, conscience and character and integrity must be developed. Con-science, after all, means "with knowledge"; conscience must be formed. That implies that there are sources or "formers" whose function it is to develop "persons of strong character," people of "ordinary sense and understanding," "reasonable and prudent" people. Recently, the armed forces and numerous industries have embraced with some fervor the concept of "core values." I will not list here the "core values" of all the services; nor is it my intent to impugn in any manner what is an obviously honorable intention of bringing before service members' eyes the fundamental values of their profession. But one must raise the question whether there is a bridge between core values and disobedience of unlawful orders. Can a recitation of "core values," however well intended, lead to the kind of moral reasoning one must have in order to refuse unlawful orders?

One point must be made about core values; the air force core values—integrity, service before self, and excellence in all we do—can stand as an example. A scholar has noted that "a person can be forthrightly honest, forget about self, and achieve excellent results—all for the sake of an evil purpose." A number of Nazis, he says, shared in those values. He goes on, however, to point out that the USAF core values, understood in the framework of agent, act, and outcome, "are a comprehensive plan for framing ethical issues."[7] The argument, then, is that although core values may be necessary, they are certainly not sufficient. They cannot take the place of moral reasoning—nor are they intended to do so.[8] But there is a danger that memorizing a list of values may, in some quarters, be regarded as a permissible substitute for the kind of difficult analysis that attends moral reasoning. One wishes that a better, clearer, older list of virtues had been embraced by the services.

Athens and Jerusalem—shorthand for the ancient Greeks and Scholastic Christians—had "core values." In Plato's *Laws,* one reads that wisdom (or prudence) is paramount; then comes temperance (or moderation); from the union of these two with courage springs justice (or truthfulness); and courage is fourth.[9] In the book of Wisdom, one finds the list repeated (8:7).[10] The cardinal virtues are, at heart, means for developing that faculty of conscience which is the essence of a "reasonable and prudent" person; no one can lay claim to having "ordinary sense and understanding" without a well-formed conscience, which is the amalgamation of proper "core values."

If a soldier—let alone a commander—is deficient in any one of the four classic, cardinal virtues, one may reasonably predict ruin for his or her command and career. The cardinal virtues, as we have seen, are so called because they derive from the Latin word *cardo,* which means "hinge." All the other virtues hinge on or are related to these four. *Virtue,* first, is a habitual and firm disposition to do good.

> *Prudence* (or wisdom) encourages our power of reason to find our
> true good and to choose the proper means for attaining it.

Justice (or truthfulness) is the firm commitment to give God and
neighbor their due.
Courage (or fortitude) ensures firmness in difficulties and
constant pursuit of goodness.
Temperance moderates the attraction of the pleasures of the
senses.[11]

One needs to be only slightly conversant with current military events to
know that character defects in wisdom, truthfulness, moral courage, and/
or moderation have been the undoing of numerous leaders, military and
civilian, in the past decade. As good as current service "core values" are,
such concepts as "candor" or "commitment" or "excellence in all we
do" are not *hinges* upon which conscience itself can be founded. Only
the bedrock ideas of the cardinal virtues provide such a groundwork.

My argument in this book can be simply put: soldiers deficient in
the cardinal virtues will have serious defects of character—and of conscience.[12] For conscience does not magically or mystically appear; it is
formed over the years, as a matter of conscious routine (habitus) and as
the outcome of good education, experience, and training. Conscience is
taught by wise teachers and by good books and films and conversations—and it is caught from sometimes hard experience and suffering.[13]
When we read that soldiers—people—of "ordinary sense and understanding" (or reasonable prudence) ought to be able to distinguish licit
and binding orders from illicit, and therefore not binding, orders, we
have embraced a natural-law argument with powerful application in what
Colonel Hartle regards, quite properly, as "the hardest place to maintain
our humanity"—war.[14] If we place soldiers in combat demanding disobedience of unlawful orders, those orders that people of "ordinary sense
and understanding" would refuse—and since the war crime tribunals at
Nuremberg, Tokyo, and Manila, we have indeed made that demand—
then we must train and *educate* our soldiers.

NATURAL LAW AND RIGHT REASON

The soldier who refuses an order in time of war may risk a court-martial, and conceivably his life, on the strength of "a judgment of reason"
or a "sense of right and wrong," which we identify, customarily rather
weakly, as conscience. There are two terms upon which that soldier's
legal defense—hence, his very life—might well depend. The first is

synderesis, which means "inborn knowledge of the primary principles of moral action" (according to Webster's *Third New International Dictionary*). Although *synderesis* is often used interchangeably with *conscience,* Saint Thomas Aquinas understood synderesis as "the quasi-habitual grasp of the most common principles of the moral order (i.e., natural law), whereas conscience is the application of such knowledge to fleeting and unrepeatable circumstances" (often called *syneidesis*).[15] If by synderesis we mean a "habitual knowledge of the first principles of practical reasoning . . . that are naturally known"[16] and by *syneidesis* we mean the "capacity to apply general principles of moral judgment to particular cases" (Webster's *Third New International Dictionary*), we are, in essence, concerned with natural law.[17]

For "ordinary sense and understanding" implicitly refers to synderesis and syneidesis. Why? In a crisis, where does the soldier turn for guidance when he thinks he has been given an unlawful order—as were the soldiers at My Lai? If his comrades are carrying out such orders, should he follow suit? But to whom, then and there, can he appeal? The chaplain? A Judge Advocate General (lawyer) officer? A higher-ranking officer? They are not there. The soldier has one place to seek a hurried answer—his "soul," or his "psyche," or his "conscience." Insofar as circumstances permit, he weighs his orders against whatever standards of decency and honor make him what he is. The military has helped to form his soldierly skills. Does the military owe him nothing—readings, classes, teachers—as he meets this terrible test at this terrible time? If "ordinary sense and understanding" is merely what the "crowd" says, then how is it that we hold Calley and his complaisantly homicidal platoon morally liable for a massacre? (They acted, after all, "together"; I almost write "*virtually* together.") Truth—and its manifestation in conscience—is not the product of, or limited to, a murderous platoon, a deformed culture, or an ethnocentric pride. There may be times when *ordinary* sense is truly extraordinary. And that is where natural law enters the picture.

Natural law is considered by some theologians and philosophers to be inherent in human nature, helping us to rightly order our conduct with respect to God and our neighbor.[18] Saint Thomas Aquinas defines natural law as "the participation of the rational creature in the eternal law of God" and contends that all men and women, through the light of reason, can arrive at a basic moral code, embracing at least the principle that good must be done and evil avoided.[19] One of the best and shortest explanations of the concept appeared more than thirty years ago in an excellent book about Edmund Burke: "Natural Law was an emanation of God's reason and will, revealed to all mankind. Since fundamental moral laws were self-evident, all normal men were capable through unaided 'right reason' of perceiving the difference between moral right and wrong. The Natural Law was an eternal, unchangeable, and universal ethical norm or standard, whose validity was independent of man's will; therefore, at all times, in all circumstances and everywhere it bound all individuals, races, nations, and governments.[20] True happiness for man consisted in living according to the Natural Law."[21]

That natural law—or "moral sense"—is no dream of idle (and medieval) theologians is attested to by James Q. Wilson, whose moving description of moral sense is quoted in chapter 3.

This is not a matter merely of philosophy, but of international and municipal (i.e., domestic) law. Natural law has "left its imprint upon international law with such concepts as justice, morality, rationality, and equality under law."[22] Natural law, if we accept Wilson's analogy, is a moral sense found in all rational people; its relationship to conscience is perhaps best explained in a recent papal encyclical: "Whereas the natural law discloses the objective and universal demands of the moral good, conscience is the application of the law to a particular case; this application of the law thus becomes an inner dictate for the individual, a summons to do what is good in this particular situation" (syneidesis).[23]

That quotation captures the precise difficulty of the soldier who receives what he regards as an unlawful order in a situation of stress. There is no time for appeal to anyone other than the one who has issued the order. The only recourse that the soldier has is to consult his conscience—which is to apply principles of the moral order (natural law) to the "fleeting and unrepeatable" circumstances in which he finds himself (synderesis and syneidesis). Rather like the character of Moliere's who was delighted to learn that he had been speaking prose all his life, very few soldiers are aware of the moral reasoning process they employ in weighing the courses of action open to them in moments of moral crisis. There is little reason to try to educate all soldiers about recondite philosophical concepts and vocabulary. What matters is that they be educated to understand the following fundamental points:

- The orders they receive are presumably legal and moral and therefore binding.

- They have the right and the duty to disobey illegal orders.
- Any order they receive that they regard as contrary to what soldiers of "ordinary sense and understanding" would do should very probably be disobeyed.
- No guidelines, checklists, "decision logic trees," or "option sheets" exist for them to consult in moments of stress, particularly in combat situations.
- Nevertheless, they have moral resources upon which they can, should, and must call if they find themselves in the exigent circumstances of perhaps refusing an order.

Among the moral resources available to soldiers, even in moments of great stress, are these: the treasury of their own spiritual, religious, and ethical constructs; the teachings of their parents and other family members; instruction from religious counselors, teachers, and coaches; their academic education and personal or professional experience; and their professional military education, whether it is at the level of war college or only basic training. (See the epilogue for more recommendations.)

HIGH ETHICAL EXPECTATIONS

If we are prepared to say that "ordinary sense and understanding" means conscience, then I think we must be prepared to meet, even if we cannot resolve, a most pressing problem. Is it reasonable to believe—and is there evidence to support—the notion that soldiers, enlisted or officers, can reason morally at the levels required to "follow their [well-formed] consciences"? The controversial work of Lawrence Kohlberg, for example, is troubling in this context. Kohlberg has distinguished six stages of cognitive moral development, each stage representing a certain manner of thought about moral problems. We begin at a preconventional level, stages one and two, where morality is wholly utilitarian—based on a calculus of pleasure and pain. By the age of about ten, we have moved on to the conventional stage, levels three and four, where we are aware of interpersonal relations and social systems. Obedience to authority comes from our desire for approval and our wish to maintain social coherence. Stages five and six constitute the postconventional level, where there is awareness of a social contract and of universal ethics—a principled level. Kohlberg has argued that very few people have reached even the *conventional* level by the time of high school graduation. From 5 percent to 10 percent of adults reach the sixth level.[24]

Kohlberg's theories are controversial and have been widely challenged, but that is not of immediate concern here. If there is any value to his thesis—and I am persuaded that there is—its importance to the armed forces lies in this: how can we reasonably expect young men and women, especially in combat, to look deep into the abyss of their own souls and consciences, perhaps refusing orders on grounds of conscience as "reasonable and prudent" people of "ordinary sense and understanding," when they simply do not have ordinary sense and understanding, do not know the cardinal virtues, and have little prospect of engaging in serious moral reasoning? The late Christopher Lasch offered this observation: "Many young people are morally at sea. They resent the ethical demands of 'society' as infringements of their personal freedom. They believe that their rights as individuals include the right to 'create their own values,' but they cannot explain what that means, aside from the right to do as they please. They cannot seem to grasp the idea that 'values' imply some principle of moral obligation. They insist that they owe nothing to 'society.'"[25]

The words of the Latin poet Juvenal explain further: "Consider it the greatest of crimes to prefer survival to honor and, out of love of physical life, to lose the very reason for living."[26] If our service members do not know that there are truths and powers beyond the immediate; if they do not know that there are the moral criteria of wisdom, temperance, courage, and justice; if they are not taught to reason morally; if they do not understand that conscience means participation in what is ethical rather than what is expedient—then they cannot be "reasonably prudent" people. Then there is no such thing as "ordinary sense and understanding." Then there is nothing left that is worthy of defense. Unless the cardinal virtues—leading to well-formed conscience and high moral character—are rediscovered, the profession of arms will be like Nero fiddling as Rome burns.[27] But our modern Nero may be excused by his invincible ignorance, for he will not know that he is fiddling and he will not know that Rome burns.

Of the seven deadly sins, we can make the case that five of them—gluttony, greed, lust, pride, and acedia or moral sloth—are so much a part of the political and ethical landscape today that we hardly notice them anymore. (The other sins, anger and envy, may apply as well but must be seen in their broadest definitions.) One is reminded of the frog in the laboratory. Only by degrees is the frog in the beaker heated until at last the frog, without a protest, is boiled to death. By degrees we have modified the political and ethical "heat" so that we hardly notice the changes around us. We go about our separate lives and our distinct professions—"fiddling"—while all around we run the increasing risk of self-incineration, of burning "Rome" to the ground. Like the doctor in the epigraph to this chapter, we think that right or wrong is the product of merely counting heads or of consulting political horoscopes.[28] In the end we have forgotten, as T.S. Eliot tried to tell us, where moral reasoning starts:[29]

> O weariness of men who turn from God
> To the grandeur of your mind and the glory of your action,
> To arts and inventions and daring enterprises,
> To schemes of human greatness thoroughly discredited,
> Binding the earth and the water to your service,
> Exploiting the seas and developing the mountains,
> Dividing the stars into common and preferred,
> Engaged in devising the perfect refrigerator,
> Engaged in working out a rational morality,
> . . . .
> Turning from your vacancy to fevered enthusiasm
> For nation or race or what you call humanity;
> Though you forget the way to the Temple,
> There is one who remembers the way to your door:
> Life you may evade, but Death you shall not.
> You shall not deny the Stranger.
>
> *Choruses from "The Rock"*

To reason well, we begin with the certain knowledge that we are souls. We have bodies, temporarily.

5

Prudence and the Profession of Arms

Wisdom comes alone through suffering.

—Aeschylus

Prudence is cause, root, mother, measure, precept, guide, and thus prototype of all ethical virtues; it acts in all of them, perfecting them to their true nature; all participate in it, and by virtue of this participation they are virtues.

—Josef Pieper, The Four Cardinal Virtues

In Chapter 4 we discussed synderesis and syneidesis, rather abstract terms that refer to one's ability to understand general principles of morality and apply them wisely and well to particular circumstances. The argument advanced there is that "ordinary sense and understanding" amounts to little more than conscience and that conscience is what synderesis and syneidesis are all about. There is another way to understand the argument advanced in chapter 4 that "ordinary sense and understanding" amounts to little more than conscience and that conscience is what synderesis and syneidesis are all about. That is to use the term *prudence.* Saint Augustine wrote that prudence is love choosing judiciously between the helpful and the harmful.[1] Prudence has been called a "rudder" virtue because it "steers" all other virtues. All the cardinal virtues— indeed all virtues—can be misunderstood, misapplied, misrepresented. As Aristotle and others have tried to teach through the centuries, virtue taken to the extreme can become vice; thus what is virtuous can become vicious. (It is an interesting evolution of language that the word *vicious* is generally understood to mean "savage" or "ferocious" and not "characterized by vice." In keeping with the argument of chapter 3, we might ask this question: what, if anything, in today's world *is* generally considered as being "characterized by vice"?)

The Old Meaning of the Old Word

The word *prudence* today conveys the notion of cautious good sense, even timidity, and perhaps shrewdness—as in a business deal. To the ancient Greeks, however, *prudence* had a different denotation and connotation. To the Greeks *phronesis* and *sophia* both meant *wisdom,* but the former referred to "practical wisdom" or "political wisdom" and the latter to "philosophical wisdom"; the first was a matter of "common sense" and the second a matter of speculative or theoretical education. The Romans, similarly, distinguished between *prudentia* (related to experience) and *sapientia* (related to science). Can the words be used interchangeably? Is prudence not just, well, prudence?

This is not simply a matter of etymology. In fact, one hears variations of this argument in many places—even in bars or at ball games. "I got my education in the College of Hard Knocks," some people like to say. "He just doesn't have any common sense," say others. "He's just plain overeducated" is another complaint. Can one be wise in the ways of the world—street-smart—and know little of sophia or sapientia? Of course. Conversely, we know that one may be superbly educated in theoretical sciences—book learning—and know little about everyday affairs.

To the ancient Greeks, there was no substitute for experience, which deals in particulars, whereas education deals with universals. Aristotle, for example, thought that young men could become wise as, say, mathematicians, but that the other kind of wisdom—phronesis—would come only with experience in practical matters. It is as if an engineer skilled in advanced automotive design were at a loss about how to change the oil in his car or how to rotate the tires.

Many years ago I worked in a plastics factory during the summers when I was in college. I ran machines. During my shift one evening, one of the plant bosses—the head of quality control—was strolling through the main work area when a piece of hot plastic became stuck in a die on one of the machines. A warning buzzer told us of the problem, something relatively easy to fix if one followed a simple mechanical procedure. The boss was standing near the machine when the buzzer sounded, and everyone looked at him, expecting him to unjam the machine. Sensing everyone's eyes on him, he tried to fix the problem, but it soon became obvious that he did not know what he was doing. One of my coworkers, barely suppressing a smirk, strode over to the machine, fixed it, and walked away, the boss having lost face. The boss knew "universals" (the big picture), but of the particulars of machine operation he was ignorant. That is, in essence, what the Greeks and Romans were talking about two thousand years ago or so.

Almost everyone who has done anything "practical" (blue-collar workers) will have similar stories about their bosses (white-collar supervisors). This kind of labor-management, enlisted-officer split seems to be part of the human condition. After some reflection, however, most of us reach the point of recognizing the need for both planners and practitioners. It really was not necessary for the boss in the plastics factory to know how to clear a jammed machine any more than it is necessary for the machinist to understand all the aspects of quality control in a factory. Smugness and conceit can be directed by the bosses toward the workers on the line because of their lack of education, or such arrogance can be directed by the workers toward the bosses in their offices "because they don't sweat for their bread."

I cannot resolve here the debate between those who compare and contrast book learning (sophia) with practical learning (phronesis). In the profession of arms, there is no question that both are important to all soldiers. The lowest-ranking enlisted persons must sometimes make difficult ethical judgments that may involve universals, suggesting one kind of wisdom or prudence. The highest-ranking officers may often make decisions based on their knowledge of details or particulars, suggesting a second type of prudence or wisdom. "It is impossible," said Aristotle, to be good in the full sense of the word without practical wisdom or to be a man of practical wisdom without moral excellence or virtue."[2] But whether one works primarily with the head or primarily with the hands, one should become, and strive to remain, a good person. We have arrived, then, in the arena of prudence, for prudence helps us to determine the right from the wrong, the helpful from the hurtful, the virtuous from the vicious. There are elements both of phronesis and sophia and of prudentia and sapientia in the cardinal virtue of prudence. But, understood most simply, prudence is about knowing and doing what is just, courageous, and temperate.

Saint Thomas Aquinas contended that in order to live ethically, one must know what a humanly good life is and have the ability to apply a well-formed understanding of universal moral norms to specific situations. Prudence refers to the capacity of discernment by which one translates the general demands of morality into concrete action.[3] Only the prudent man, observes Prof. Josef Pieper, "can be just, brave, and temperate, and the good man is good in so far as he is prudent." Modern man, he says, will too often call lies and cowardice prudent and term truthfulness and courageous sacrifice imprudent.[4]

THE KEY ARGUMENT ABOUT PRUDENCE

What is an antonym of *prudent*? Is it *hasty, impetuous, impulsive,* or *rash*? What is a synonym of *prudent*? Is it *cagey, clever, crafty,* or *cunning*? As the term is used informally, those words are correct. But as the term *prudence* is used in its philosophical sense, those terms are irrelevant and wrong. The prudent man is a good human being, one who tries his best to know and do what he *ought* to do. Not only the ancient Greeks and Romans, but also the ancient Jews had a concept of prudence: "You have been told, O man, what is good, and what the Lord requires of you: only to do right and to love goodness, and to walk humbly with your God" (Mic. 6:8).

Prudence is the ability to know right from wrong, but it is more: prudence is also the moral and physical bravery, the sense of mature justice and truthfulness, and the forbearance and self-control to "do right and to love goodness." There is nothing there of cunning or shrewdness or excessive caution, let alone egotism and self-centeredness. Similar to prudence, properly understood, are wisdom, informed conscience, ordinary sense and understanding, synderesis, and syneidesis. In modern times, however, the argument is not so simply made.

This understanding of prudence implies that there is a standard against which we can measure our conduct—and ourselves. Michael Gerson explains the argument: "There is no meaning . . . in democracy or human rights if there is no meaning in anything. And there is no meaning in anything unless there is an Author of human rights and moral truth. A skeptical relativism removes this source of dignity, reducing people to objects of commerce or power or pleasure, and leading to a 'culture of death' in which the strong exploit or destroy the vulnerable. George Weigel puts it this way: 'Human beings are more than meat, and when we start thinking of ourselves as simply ambulatory meat, then we start treating other people as meat. And that in a nutshell is the history of the horrors of the 20th century.'"[5]

In opposition to this, of course, one can consult the writings of Michel Foucault or Jacques Derrida or Richard Rorty, among many others, who insist that our moral vocabulary is always a product of our society or our customs—in short, that there is no overarching norm or standard or set of ethical universals to which we may appeal in our quest to know and do what is right. In fact, according to postmodernism there is no objective Truth, but only culturally derived "truths." Neither is there an enduring human nature, both spiritual and material, but human natures, functions of environment. Of course, there is no such thing as natural law, based upon right reason and revelation, because thinking is a social construct, language is arbitrary, and there is no Revealer. Besides that, western civilization is an oppressive culture (and it is a clear indication of the corruption in this book that this chapter includes references to the ancient Greeks, Romans, and Jews!). Declares Prof. Robert Nash: "The postmodernist asks (and I [Nash, that is] agree): Who, in an age of moral pluralism, indeterminacy, and incommensurability, knows for sure what is good or *a fortiori* how to make others good?"[6]

For Nash and the many like him on college campuses today, there is no prudence as the term is understood in philosophy, for there is no ultimate Authority and therefore no means of distinguishing right from wrong, with spiritual assurance and on the basis of objective standards. If right is merely what we conceive it to be on the basis of our personal convenience; if truth is a function only of our private taste; if justice is at heart simply what suits us or our group—then we are, indeed, pieces of meat. And meat does not concern itself with the prudent, the truthful and just, the morally and physically courageous, and the temperate. All those terms are, well, arbitrary and capricious, probably the products and property only of the wealthy class, and, furthermore, the ancient Greeks, Romans, and Jews are dead.

Philosophical prudence is indefensible, outmoded, and, frankly, silly if there is no way of recognizing the good and decent and the just and true. If all things are matters only of taste—and if there is nothing that is universally virtuous—then prudence will soon go the way of good manners.[7]

HUMAN GOODS

Conscience, and therefore prudence, may be understood as "one's awareness of moral truth." Two authors have put the matter simply. "For mature consciences, the fundamental question is: What is the good and
wise thing to do?"[8] There are some goods that are objectively demon-
strable. We all—whether in Japan, Bolivia, or Norway; whether female
or male; whether atheist, Methodist, or Mormon; whether black, white,
yellow, or red—have a natural interest in living, in being healthy, in
having knowledge, and in having friends. Certainly, there are people
who want to end their lives; people who are antisocial; people who will
harm their health through drugs or drink. But in almost every such case,
we can point to regrettable (and, we hope, rare) circumstances impel-
ling those people to choices that we regard as unfortunate or mistaken.
No rational person, for example, deliberately chooses sickness and ignorance. We ordinarily choose goods that will help us, not those that
will hurt us (consider Saint Augustine's definition of *prudence,* cited at
the beginning of this chapter). Such goods as health, knowledge, and
friendship are thus perfective of human beings. These goods "are
transcultural. It is true for all human beings that health and knowledge
perfect them while sickness and ignorance diminish them. This is because human beings have certain basic potentialities in common. We
pick out some entities in the universe and call them 'human beings'
precisely because they share a complex nature in common, that is, they
have certain basic potentialities in common."[9]

To continue this line of reasoning, Prof. J. Budziszewski of the
University of Texas, drawing upon both philosophy and theology, suggests that there is a new theory of natural law (although it clearly is
drawn from the Thomist tradition), advanced primarily in the work of
Germain Grisez. There are several forms of good that are mutually ex-
haustive and irreducible. Covering all the possibilities of human goodness, they are valuable in and of themselves, not as aspects of another.
These goods are

1. Self-integration: The elements of the self are at peace with
   one another—not being torn by reason leading in one way,
   passion treacherously leading in another.
2. Authenticity: There is harmony among one's abilities, judgments, choices, and behavior (practical reasonableness)—

determining what is good and acting resolutely on that knowledge.
3. Interpersonal harmony: As social beings we have justice and friendships in our relations with others.
4. Reverence, piety, and holiness: We have harmony with God.
5. Life and health: We have well-being and safety.
6. Knowledge and appreciation of beauty: We have intellectual and aesthetic fulfillment.
7. Skillful performance of work and play: Our lives are enriched by our fruitful labor and our revivifying recreation.
8. The human good of marriage.[10]

"Taken together," say Grisez and Shaw, "these eight goods tell us what human persons are capable of being, not only as individuals but in community."[11] The balanced, fulfilled life works toward realization of the reflexive or existential goods (harmony with oneself and one's decisions, with others, and with God) and the substantive goods (health, knowledge, work, and play—and for most people marriage and family).

Exactly how important these goods are is underscored by this observation: "It is in the light of the dignity of the human person—dignity which must be affirmed for its own sake—that reason grasps the specific moral value of certain goods towards which the person is naturally inclined." If we fail to live our lives in a coherent way, giving each of the eight forms of good its proper due, we court personal—and no doubt professional—distress. We must live in such a way as always to observe "the primordial requirement of loving and respecting the person as an end and never as a mere means"; that implies "respect for certain fundamental goods, without which one would fall into relativism and arbitrariness."[12] In other words, people are not pieces of meat. Prudent acts, therefore, help us to realize our human potential. Choices that are respectful of the basic human goods are morally worthy; choices disrespectful of the basic human goods are morally unworthy. Human beings in their private and in their professional lives can—and often do—have *dueling duties,* my term for conflicts in their responsibilities (see chapter 6). The listing of basic human goods does not, by itself, resolve our ethical problems. But it points us toward one ethical reality, one fundamental element of ethical reasoning, that we must never forget: there are standards and principles that we can and must consult as we seek to know and do right. As we are not pieces of meat, neither are we little gods whose ultimate source of truth looks back at us every time we glance at a mirror.

THE VIRTUOUS CIRCLE

If there are certain "goods" toward which we are oriented, we must nonetheless act in such a way that we are consistently oriented toward achieving those goods. Daily we find snippets of would-be wisdom—in fortune cookies, on tea bags, in cute proverbs, on greeting cards, even on bathroom walls. Genuine wisdom or prudence, I fear, comes to us, much as Aeschylus wrote (see the epigraph to this chapter), not in the homely sayings found at the bottom of pages in slick magazines, but through suffering. Prudence is purchased at a high price. We learn to be prudent through the heartaches and afflictions of living. Someone once suggested that there are three things that are "real": God, whom we can never fully understand; human error, which we can never fully eradicate; and a sense of humor, which allows us to get through life's trials.

All of us make decisions on the basis of rules, commandments, or philosophies. All of us have some criteria by which we sort out what we ought to do and what we do or forbear doing. As Socrates said, the unexamined life is not worth living. An essential element of wisdom, therefore, is self-examination (see chapter 9 for more on this). Self-examination is the purpose, or at least a purpose, of religious retreats, academic sabbaticals, and even some vacations, which are intended as means of re-creation. (The seventh human good, after all, involves not just fruitful work but also spirited play.)

But according to what principles do we seek out the human goods? Servais Pinckaers has this answer: "The beatitudes [found in the fifth chapter of Matthew] are still relevant at both the personal and social levels. It is not difficult to see in them questions which have constantly recurred throughout human history: problems of poverty and wealth, meekness and violence, pleasure and grief, hunger and thirst, justice and forgiveness, uprightness and purity of heart, war and peace, persecution. We can find in the beatitudes all the things that torment our world today." The Beatitudes, he says, "are realistic and true. They go deeper than words and ideas. They confront us with the aching realities of human existence and show us what lies in our own depths."[13] The Beatitudes have the advantage of being positive declarations—"Blessed are the merciful"—rather than restraints or injunctions (as are the Ten Commandments, however vital they are).

If we suppose, as I do, that there is for each of us an interior law that we can recognize and follow[14]—that we are in fact empowered to tell right from wrong—then if we fail to do what we should, we experience remorse. Unfortunately, according to Henry Fairlie, "we seem no longer able to admire, respect, or be grateful for what is nobler or lovelier or greater than ourselves. We must pull down—or put down—what is exceptional."[15] We should thus be ashamed of ourselves. Shame is not at all a bad thing, but remorseful people, those afflicted with guilt because they have committed sins of commission or omission, are unhappy. And ethics is rooted primarily in happiness, only secondarily in obligation.[16] Following the counsels of the Beatitudes forms us—and our conscience—in such a way that we see and hear and do the things we should; that way lies happiness.

The ancient Greeks declared that happiness consists in using our talents as they ought to be used. The shovel can cut; the knife can dig. But a shovel is not a cutting tool, and a knife is not a digging tool. Humans can impair their reason by drink or drugs, and we can lie, cheat, and steal. But we are "designed" to develop and to use our reason and to be honest. In doing what we should, we bring about our happiness. When I say that ethics is about "owing" (hence, about obligation), that is a shorthand way of saying that knowing and doing what is true results in our happiness. We are arrived at a *virtuous circle*—not the proverbial vicious circle: synderesis (knowing the first principles of human action) and a well-formed conscience (applying those principles wisely and well to particular cases) results in happiness—and in the fulfillment, the joy, that results from living as we should. The more we do what we should, the more we conform ourselves to incontrovertible ethical standards, the happier we become;[17] consequently, we perform our duties better. The more fulfilled we are as people, the more fulfilled we are as professionals. The better we understand and do our duty as people, the better we understand and do our duty as professionals. When we fail as people, we fail as professionals. By being good people, we know happiness; in knowing happiness, we are doing what we should; in doing what we should, we are being good people—without feelings of remorse.

Euripides put these words into the mouth of Agamemnon addressing Pyrrhus in *The Trojan Women:* "What the law does not forbid, then let shame forbid." The pitiful people who appear on daily television to confess, shamelessly, sins that ought to morally appall anyone watching—why anyone would watch in the first place we will not take under consideration here—have no doubt never read Euripedes or Jean Bethke Elshtain. It is Elshtain who says that "shame requires some set of standards, some set of norms. When people transgress these, it's appropriate to feel shame." If we have no ideal of shared values, no culture based upon fairly clear-cut notions of morality, we cannot expect to experience the medicine of shame. Writer Elizabeth Austin expresses the value of shame this way:

> We need to recognize that the opposite of shame is not shamelessness, but grace, and that grace's secular equivalent is community. That means shame cannot be an end in itself, but rather must begin a process of accepting blame for the wrongs we commit, admitting our own culpability, seeking forgiveness from those we've harmed, making restitution whenever possible—and granting that same forgiveness to those around us.
>
> In a culture of grace, shame is a perilous gift. Shame is the mirror to our secret souls; when we look into that reflection, we have the choice of smashing the mirror or reshaping ourselves.[18]

For good reason, this sounds very much like the Beatitudes. Austin thus confirms the point: there is a standard of right and wrong beyond our own skins. When we serve it well, we are fulfilled. When we ignore the transcendent standard and seek the false happiness of self-indulgence, we will, in time, reflect morosely that we have failed. Pleasure before principle; diversion before duty; revelry before reverence—these are prescriptions not for happiness but for the kind of tawdry television in which people without shame unknowingly—and literally—*disgrace* themselves.

PRESCRIPTIONS FOR PRUDENCE

What or whose "standard of right and wrong" are we to follow? Which religion, which philosophy, which set of guidelines do we embrace—especially when we talk about the profession of arms, a secular enterprise? I think an answer appears in the form of what Germain Grisez

calls "Modes of Responsibility."[19] Although these prescriptions for prudence are derived from the Christian tradition and make reference to a
Supreme Being (as do the officer's and the enlisted member's oath of
office),[20] they can serve all well, I believe, as wise moral guidance, ob-
jectionable to none but extreme postmodernists. Each of the prescriptions incorporates one of the Beatitudes, and seven of the eight modes of
responsibility incorporate an "antonym" (one of the traditional seven
deadly sins).

Modes of Responsibility

1. Be energetic, diligent, ambitious, and creative. We accept the
   fruits of our own good work, and use them beneficently.
   Humility means gratefully accepting, developing, and
   employing our talents wisely and well (cf. Luke 11:33–36).
   Blessed are the poor in spirit. Pride (in the sense of arrogance and selfishness) is wrong.
2. Build community, and work with others. Although we have
   talents, we know we cannot accomplish a great deal by
   ourselves. We accept our limited roles and do the best we
   can with them. Blessed are the meek. Pride is the appropriate "antonym" here as well.
3. Act reasonably, not just to satisfy mindless cravings. Accepting and living out one's vocation involves a measure of
   sorrow and "mourning." We put aside or avoid everything
   (except for needed recreation) that is not necessary or
   useful in the fulfillment of our personal vocations. Blessed
   are those who mourn (for we know that we can never fully
   be satisfied). Gluttony is wrong.
4. Do what you ought to do even when it is disagreeable. Do not
   let the fear of suffering rule your life. We must cultivate a
   proper sense of detachment. Blessed are those who hunger
   and thirst for righteousness. Sloth is wrong.
5. Never discriminate unreasonably. We must be merciful, not
   just fair. "Friends," Budziszewski concludes, "should be
   treated differently from nonfriends but only in matters that
   pertain to friendship alone."[21] Blessed are the merciful.
   Mercy shares reasonably; avarice, which does not, is
   wrong.

6. Act in the light of moral truth, not just to keep up appearances. Problems must be charitably confronted; mere "sincerity," superficiality, and frivolousness cannot replace our need, as Grisez says, "to do what is right [rather] than [merely] to feel good." Blessed are the pure in heart. Moral cowardice (not a traditional deadly sin) is wrong. The desire for moral truth is transcendent and spiritual; lust, the desire only for the carnal and material, is wrong.

7. Be patient and long-suffering, wherever possible. Revenge and the destruction or damage or impeding of any human good are counterproductive. Blessed are the peacemakers. Willing harm and destruction, which is wrath or anger, is wrong.

8. Do what is right, but do not try to get the best results at *any* price. Never do evil that good may result.[22] Blessed are those who are persecuted for righteousness' sake. (On the idea of doing the greater good *up to a point,* see chapter 6.) We must make reasoned choices in the light of the truth of principle, not the shadow of preference. Envy, in the sense of desiring something at any price, is wrong.

[Although I use Germain Grisez's term "Modes of Responsibility," the list is based upon several sources.]

The eight human goods and the eight modes of responsibility are not checklists we can consult to ascertain invariably virtuous behavior. But I believe that knowledge and wise application of these ideas can help us to achieve the kind of prudence we require to be better people and better professionals. The eight modes of responsibility, condensed to apothegms, are these: (1) be energetic and committed; (2) build teams and partnerships; (3) prioritize, doing the necessary first and the trivial, if at all, only afterward; (4) be resolute in doing what must be done despite concomitant unpleasantness; (5) be impartial, and normally judge as you would wish to be judged; (6) prefer substance to shadow, choosing real accomplishment over the appearance of accomplishment; (7) be forgiving and not vengeful, trying to respect the eight reflexive and substantive human goods in all that you do; and (8) do not do what is wrong in order to achieve what is right; it rarely, if ever, works that way. From a study of the abstract notion of prudence comes a remarkably down-to-earth listing of items for leadership—wise and prudent leadership.

GOD, PRUDENCE, AND THE PROFESSION OF ARMS

The three moral cardinal virtues of justice, courage, and temperance are driven by the intellectual cardinal virtue of prudence. Religious scholars would agree that only prudence can assure that God's eternal law "duly informs each just, brave, and temperate action through the medium of correct moral reasoning." This correct reasoning results in what Saint Thomas Aquinas called a "rectified appetite," a state in which our emotions and appetites remain suitably disposed to achieve their proper ends or goals. Romanus Cessario explains: "Prudence promises that when correct moral reasoning combines with rectified appetite for good ends, a virtuous action inevitably results."[23] For Aquinas, virtue is a habitus, understandably translated "habit." But knowing and doing the virtuous act are rarely a matter of unreflective, hence customary, action.[24] (Again, that is why we use the word *habitus,* meaning a settled, but reflective, moral disposition). It is certainly true that by repetitively and thoughtfully doing good, we build our character (see chapter 9). But Aristotle and Aquinas taught that the virtues must be grounded in a reasoned understanding of what it means to live a good life. If one discusses "the good life" at any length, he will find himself at the door of theological speculation.

I have argued in this chapter that ethics begins with a concern for the happiness we experience when we do the good or right thing. Virtue is therefore more than obedience to law, for virtue is, in the end, good character. And character is habitus, that is, the ability and desire to discern overarching principles of good (synderesis) and then, by means of prudence, to apply them conscientiously to particular circumstances (syneidesis). To make what appears to be an abstract philosophical idea more concrete, we have the eight human goods and the eight modes of responsibility to aid us in our moral calculus. We expect good people to be able to distinguish between right and wrong. That task is harder by far than we like to admit.

In 1843 Daniel M'Naghten was a woodworker who believed that he was the target of a conspiracy involving British prime minister Robert Peel and Pope Gregory XVI. He tried to shoot Peel but mistakenly shot and killed Peel's secretary. When he was declared delusional, a jury found him not guilty by reason of insanity. An angered public protest led to the creation of a panel that developed the M'Naghten Rule: Defendants may be acquitted only if they labored "under such defect of reason from disease of the mind" as not to realize that what they were doing was wrong or criminal. A more recent concept, the Durham Rule (introduced into federal jurisprudence by Judge David Bazelon in 1954), holds that "an accused is not criminally responsible if his unlawful act was the product of a mental disease or mental defect." In favoring the Durham Rule, a prominent psychiatrist says of the M'Naghten Rule that "it requires an incalculable degree of presumption to say whether *another* individual 'knows' right from wrong, especially when few of us could truly say (except in utter naivete or ignorance) what our own degree of expertise is in this distinction." The psychiatrist continued: "The M'Naghten Rule . . . demands too much of human beings, by assuming that all but 'delirious and demented' individuals know right from wrong, and, having that knowledge, are capable of guiding their conduct in its light."[25]

Argues Prof. David Schaefer: we should question the wisdom of replacing the strict M'Naghten Rule with the rather broad Durham Rule or others like it. Who among us, he asks, does not have some defect of mind or emotion that sometimes affects his behavior? "Moreover, if we assert that the criminal is responsible for his conduct only if it is not the product of a mental defect, are we not implying that crime *per se* may be the product of a simply healthy psyche? And does not this implication contradict the fundamental moral assumption that evil actions are, by definition, the result and sign of a defective character?"[26]

Something is right or wrong only within a certain context, only by reference to a certain standard. What happens to the concept of crime, to the idea of character, to the meaning of morality, to the philosophy of the cardinal virtues if we surrender to the argument that evil actions are the product only of mental disease or maladjustment? Do we agree, thereby, that the definition of goodness is the concern, principally or exclusively, of psychiatrists? Might we agree that crime flows only from social structures, class antagonisms, and financial deprivation? Is "criminal conduct" therefore a manifestation, principally or only, of economic oppression, and must juries forevermore be comprised exclusively of financial analysts?

Or is there an overarching set of fundamental truths that human beings can discern and, discerning, act in the light thereof. We speak of values; we speak of virtues; and now we speak of verities—truths that cannot reasonably and fairly be denied.[27] Eric Voegelin observes that "the truth of man and the truth of God are inseparably one. Man will be in the truth of his existence when he has opened his psyche to the truth of God; and the truth of God will become manifest in history when it has formed the psyche of man."[28] If there are transcendent truths, then there are both spiritual and political duties; and these duties can be known to people of "*ordinary sense and understanding*" (see chapter 4). Despite the mental and emotional conflicts we are heir to, we can and must know and do what is right—do it as a matter of habitus, as a matter of prudence, as a matter of conscience. We are responsible because we are ethical; we are ethical because we are responsible. Ethics is about happiness and about obligation, a thought captured in this ancient proverb, "Happy is the man who keeps God's law" (Prov. 29:18b).

If all of this is generally understandable and acceptable to most religious people, what of the nonreligious person, especially in the profession of arms? The cardinal virtues can be traced, as we have said, to the ancient Greeks and Jews, and they were established in the Christian church by Thomas Aquinas and others. Does that mean or imply that cardinal virtues, human goods, and modes of responsibility are "religious" or "sectarian"? Not without reason have a number of officers and Department of Defense civilians raised the alarm that, in their view, much of what passes for "core values instruction" (let alone the cardinal virtues) is little more than an attempt to proselytize.

To be sure, there are instances of discrimination in the armed forces by theists against atheists; the reverse no doubt occurs as well. This is true in the sense that one often hears charges of favoritism by federal academy graduates (West Point, Air Force Academy, Annapolis, etc.) for fellow graduates over ROTC and Officer Candidate School (OCS) graduates. Such religious or "academic" discrimination is not only unethical; it is also illegal. In the case of religion, no officer has either the duty or the right to employ his military powers or properties to proselytize on behalf of his spiritual convictions. The fear that the higher echelons of command in the armed forces will eventually become bastions or cliques of Baptists or Mormons or Jews or Methodists or Catholics is surely as misplaced as the fear that the federal government will become a citadel of atheism.[29] On the basis of a decade of teaching at a war college, I can say that I have met a number of deeply religious officers and a number of officers unconcerned with matters of the spirit. I know civil servants who are unreligious and civil servants who are religious. I see no evidence of a conspiracy afoot by either group.

That said, I want to be clear that the core values of the military and the cardinal virtues do have religious roots. As Robert Bork has pointed out, "we all know persons without religious belief who nevertheless display all the virtues we associate with religious teaching. . . . such people are living on the moral capital of prior religious generations."[30] But the air force is correct in saying in its pamphlet *Core Values* that the U.S. Air Force "attempts no explanation of the origin of the Values except to say that all of us, regardless of our religious views, must recognize their fundamental importance and accept them for that reason. Infusing the Core Values is necessary for successful mission accomplishment." In saying that, the U.S. Air Force is in very good company: As Saint Thomas Aquinas said: "Prudence not only helps us to be of good counsel, but also to judge and command well."[31]

CASE STUDY

At about 2:00 P.M. on 24 June 1994, a B-52 bomber took off from Fairchild Air Force Base in Washington State on a practice run for a coming air show. About fifteen minutes later, the aircraft, while attempting to circle the air tower in a tight turn, lost altitude and crashed. The crew of four officers perished.[32] The pilot of the B-52 was Lt. Col. Arthur "Bud" Holland, who had a reputation as an extraordinarily talented "stick" (pilot). There were stories about Holland, however, that suggested that he was reckless to the point of endangering the lives of his crewmen and people on the ground. He once climbed so steeply that fuel flowed out of the vent holes on top of the B-52's wings. He is thought to have popped five hundred rivets during one prohibited climb. He put his bomber into a "death spiral" once over one of his daughter's softball games. He once flew so low over a change-of-command ceremony that "people practically jumped out of their salutes." Holland had talked about "rolling" a B-52—something that has never been done. In one case, at a 1992 air show at Fairchild, Holland flew so dangerously in exceeding standard operating procedures that his enraged superior promised that Holland would never fly in another air show. But in May 1993 that officer was reassigned, and no record of the reprimand was left.

One of Holland's copilots, Capt. Eric Jones, said that Holland once flew so close to a ridgeline that he (Jones) had to yank back hard on his wheel to keep the aircraft from smashing into the ridge. Afterward, Holland just laughed. Jones found no humor in the incident. He reported the matter to the commander of the 325th Bomb Squadron, Lt. Col. Mark

McGeehan, who promised to take action. McGeehan, in turn, went to Col. William Pellerin, commander of the 92d Operations Group, to make a complaint about Holland. McGeehan said he did not want his crews flying with Holland, whom he considered unsafe.

Colonel Pellerin later said this was the first time he had heard about Holland's excesses. He wanted "to get Bud's side of the story." Twelve prior commanders of Bud Holland had allowed him to keep flying. There was no question that he was a brave and highly talented air force pilot. No commander wants to be the one who throws a "wet blanket" over daring, dauntless flying. Little progress will be recorded in any field where the pioneers are reined in. Bud Holland, in his own way, was a "pioneer," a crack pilot with top-notch flying skills. Was he brave or foolhardy? Was he heroic or self-destructive? What was Pellerin's duty to the air force, to the 92d Operations Group, to McGeehan and his squadron, to Holland himself? What, in this case, did prudence, the human goods, and the modes of responsibility require?[33]

Pellerin subsequently said that he had reprimanded Holland but had chosen not to curb his flying. "Bud," said Pellerin, "was Mr. Airshow." McGeehan, according to one report, was "humiliated and infuriated." The air show was scheduled for Sunday, 26 June. One more practice flight was planned. So, on the 24th, Holland, McGeehan, Lt. Col. Kenneth Huston (operations officer of the 325th), and Col. Robert Wolff, the wing vice commander (flying in place of Pellerin, who was called away at the last minute) climbed into the B-52 and took off. Fifteen minutes later, they were dead.[34]

Colonel Pellerin was subsequently court-martialed for dereliction of duty. He pleaded guilty. It was 1995. In 1270 Saint Thomas Aquinas had written, "Prudence not only helps us to be of good counsel but also to judge and command well."

6

Justice and the Profession of Arms

Charity is no substitute for justice withheld.

—Saint Augustine

In every generation there has to be some fool who will speak the truth as he sees it.

—Boris Pasternak

Deuterocanonical Scripture refers to books in the Greek translation of the Old Testament that do not appear in the Hebrew Scriptures. Jews and Protestants designate the deuterocanonical books collectively as the Apocrypha and do not include them in their Bibles; they are a part of the Catholic Bible, however. Among these books is the first book of Esdras, which contains an extraordinary "debate." The emperor Darius holds a great banquet. After all the guests have left, three bodyguards decide to debate the issue of what is the strongest thing in the world. They write down their answers, submitting them for decision to Darius, who will surely reward the wisest guard. When he wakes, Darius reads the notes thus sent to him and calls the guards in so that they may further explain their positions. The first guard says the strongest thing in the world is wine, for "it confuses the mind of everyone who drinks it . . . [whether] king or orphan, slave or free, rich or poor" (3:18–19). The second guard declares that "nothing in the world is stronger than men, since they rule over land and sea and, in fact, over everything in the world. But the emperor is the strongest of them all" (4:2–3) (could this guard have been the first sycophant in history?). The third guard, Zerubbabel, proposes a different view: "Men may accumulate silver or gold or other beautiful things, but if they see a woman with a pretty face or a good figure, they will leave it all to gape and stare, and they will desire her more than their wealth" (4:18–19). Indeed, he argues, some men "have been put to death, have ruined their lives, or have committed crimes because of a woman" (4:27). Even the emperor, he dares to suggest, can be browbeaten by a woman; once, he says, he saw a woman slap the emperor with impunity. Zerubbabel is not finished, though. His conclusion is that truth is the real victor:

> There is not the slightest injustice in truth. You will find injustice in wine, the emperor, women, all human beings, in all they do, and in everything else. There is no truth in them; they are unjust and they will perish. But truth endures and is always strong; it will continue to live and reign forever. Truth shows no partiality or favoritism; it does what is right, rather than what is unjust or evil. Everyone approves what truth does; its decisions are always fair. Truth is strong, royal, powerful, and majestic forever. Let all things praise the God of truth! (4:36b–40)

Darius proclaims Zerubbabel the winner and rewards him appropriately.

THE DEATH OF NEW YORK CITY

Justice and truth are apparently inseparable. But can one ever serve the cause of the cardinal virtue of justice by lying? What are absolutism, relativism, and universalism? What do we do when we are placed in circumstances that make prudence appear impossible? How do we do what is just when we encounter a problem like the following one, which I take from the film and book *Fail-Safe*, by Eugene Burdick and Harvey Wheeler? During the darkest days of the Cold War, the United States has launched a nuclear bomber attack on the Soviet Union, by mistake. The American president, horrified by this terrible error, appeals by telephone to the Soviet leader to absorb the nuclear strike on Moscow without retaliation. The Soviet leader informs the president that such a course is politically and militarily impossible; he must and will retaliate. World War III has begun—by mistake. The president telephones an old friend, a U.S. Air Force officer, and gives him a macabre command. The air force officer is to fly an American bomber over New York City and drop one nuclear weapon on the city, killing millions of his countrymen. In the process, however, World War III will be averted because this will be evidence to the Soviet leader that the strike on Moscow was, in fact, a mistake. The American officer follows the order and drops the bomb, killing millions (including the president's beloved wife who is visiting New York City that day). The officer drops the bomb without help from anyone else in the aircraft, then turns control of the plane over to his copilot and swallows deadly poison. New York City and Moscow are gone in nuclear bursts, but World War III is averted (for a few more years). Did the president act prudently? justly? truthfully? Did the air force officer follow a legal order? What was his duty? Zerubbabel, what now is the most powerful thing in the world?

As discussed in chapter 5, human goods and modes of responsibility can serve as moral lamps for us as we seek out the path of prudence and wisdom. Although I think the case can be made that these "lamps" are matters of reason and practical experience, not only of religious revelation, postmodern society, in shunning all expressions of Truth, will likely also eschew these concepts. The Ten Commandments are probably the best example of the "divine command theory," which contends that God has made known to humanity certain moral concepts, which we choose to ignore at our spiritual peril. In *Veritatis Splendor,* Pope John Paul II states that Christ's directive to keep the Commandments (Matt. 19:17) is "not so much about rules to be followed, but *about the full meaning of life.*"[1] That is precisely what the cardinal virtues concern: a full life, one rooted in knowing and doing what we should.

But the word *should* implies that there are things we must do, things that we have a duty to do. Ignore those basic duties, we can reason, and we will bear the burden of ethical failure and moral cowardice. But what duties are "basic"? There are principles or prescriptions regarded by some as prima facie (immediately plain or clear). The philosopher W.D. Ross, for example, argued in the 1930s that *right* and *good* are empirically undefinable terms that name objective properties known intuitively by mature, educated persons. We deal with particular circumstances, arriving at general principles by what he called "intuitive deduction." According to Ross, there are certain obligations that are reasonably self-evident to people of "ordinary sense and understanding" (as discussed in chapter 4). Keeping promises, for example, is a matter of fundamental fairness. But any prima facie duty is a requirement only if there is no stronger prima facie duty. When duties conflict—and the conflict of duties is the very basis of military ethics—we must do what best satisfies all our obligations. This, in turn, is a function of judgment.[2] What Ross was saying, in essence, is that justice (doing what is right) is a matter of prudence. The cardinal virtues are inseparable, and to have a full life in any meaningful sense, we are free only insofar as we know the truth and do what truth teaches and directs.[3]

"Doing Ethics"

In ethics, the school of thought known as *intuitionism* holds that in every situation of moral consequence, we must consult our conscience in order to discover the ethically right thing to do. Military ethics *cannot* be based solely upon flashes of ethical insight, however important intuition may be. Over the course of years, the ethical insights that we human beings have tend to become rules, norms, or principles. These are the tried and true concepts that we know in such forms as "Honesty is the best policy"; "Don't lie, cheat, or steal"; "Let your word be your bond." These nostrums amount to the moral currency with which we deal every day. There is a symbiosis, then, between the "flashes of insight" known to intuitionists and rules of conduct favored by deontologists (who customarily resort to such rules as tests of goodness).

Certain scholars have told us that there are no facts but only interpretations. Despite that glib and mistaken notion, however, we understand that in moral science, as in physical science, there are some foundational truths. If the law of gravity is a given in physical science, so is the law of truth-telling in moral science.[4] But just as gravity can be overcome, so can truth-telling. (To overcome the law does not mean that it is "canceled.") Are there times when we should lie? (Remember the arguments in chapter 1, in which I proposed lying as a frequently acceptable course of action—a position renounced and refuted in chapter 2.) This argument is so critical to this book—and to the field of military ethics—that I want to take it slowly, step by step.

1. Over the course of centuries, the thinking and living of the human race have produced for us a treasury of moral knowledge, ethical principles, and guides to rightful conduct, which we ignore at our peril. The moral intuitions (and some would add religious revelation) of our

forebears have created this deposit of moral knowledge, this corpus of rules.

2. From the body of rules has developed a school of ethics known as deontology, which in essence holds that we have a duty to perform certain tasks measured by these rules or principles, regardless of the consequences.[5]

3. The school of ethics known as teleology holds that one must determine what to do on the basis of the probable consequences of one's choice. Utilitarians are teleologists.[6] After teaching at a war college for ten years, I know that most military officers determine right from wrong on the basis of a utilitarian, cost-benefit analysis. I regard this approach as perhaps occasionally necessary as a kind of moral shorthand but never sufficient by itself.

4. If all ethical matters can be reduced to analysis of the basic political science question *Cui bono?* (whose good?—that is, who stands to benefit, and who stands to lose?), then ethics is a function of arithmetic. Justice amounts to little more than the interest of the stronger, as Thrasymachus (in the *Republic*) told the classical Greeks before the birth of Christ. But if ethics is *more* than figuring out who wins and loses in particular circumstances—if ethics is a matter of knowing and applying the right *rules,* regardless of circumstances—are there any rules that *always* apply?

5. My answer is yes, there are some rules that always apply,[7] among them these: one must always try to do good and to avoid evil, and one must always seek to reason well. There are and can be *no exceptions* to those precepts. To virtually every other rule that one can stipulate, however, there are exceptions, exemptions, or overrides.[8] Absolutism insists that there are transcendent principles that answer every possible situation in life regardless of culture or consequence. Ethical or cultural relativism, by contrast, insists that truth and moral conduct depend upon one's society, station in life, or situation—and that "principles" are relative to time and place. Here I propose a new term—*universalism*—to describe the view of one who leans toward absolutism (as all religious believers must) but who nevertheless understands that certain events may compel departure from principles that would otherwise be binding.[9] Let us look again at an example from chapter 1: suppose you are Polish and a Warsaw resident in 1939, and you are harboring two Jews in your basement. An SS officer knocks on the door and asks you whether you have seen any Jews. May you lie to protect the Jews?

- The relativist—or utilitarian—will lie. Circumstances and probable outcomes dictate his course of action.
- The absolutist—knowing that lying is wrong—will tell the truth, because lying is *always wrong*. Circumstances and probable outcomes are irrelevant.
- The universalist will lie, reasoning that, in this troubling circumstance in which (W.D. Ross's) prima facie duties conflict, he must resolve the conflict in the most discriminating manner possible.

The relativist chooses as his circumstances may require; the absolutist chooses as a flash of insight or as a universal rule may require; the universalist chooses according to circumstance, intuition and insight, rules, and reasoned judgment. Notice that the just decision flows from wisdom or prudence. That is why, among the cardinal virtues, prudence is first, and justice is second. Circumstances and outcomes matter; there are flashes of insight and "gut reactions" that should not be discounted; we do know some things and we have developed some rules. But all of these must be filtered through our education, our experience, our reason, our faith. For universalists ethical decisions can be wrenching and painful; but universalists are not released from taking action. "Paralysis by analysis" is not an option. When action is required and decisions are needed, universalists deliberate about what to do based upon the underlying principle of military ethics: *Always choose the greatest good for the greatest number—up to a point.*

But this is *not* an appeal to or on behalf of utilitarianism. Military officers—indeed, most of us—can sometimes wisely use the idea of choosing between alternatives on the basis of "the good of the many outweighs the good of the few or of the one." But there are some things so solemn and so sacred that such efforts at arithmetic ethics or mathematical morality are, by themselves, inadequate. I believe that there are times when we can and must say that, regardless of the consequences, I cannot do this or that action. In other words, there are points beyond which I will not go and certain lines that I will not cross.

6. Universalism (the ability to choose well in situations where obligations conflict) allows us to speak not only of good outcomes and judicious rules but of *good people* (see chapter 9). People do not exist for rules; rules exist for people.[10]

Dueling Duties

In the profession of arms, soldiers frequently, and sometimes dramatically, encounter conflicting obligations. What obligation, after all, can carry greater significance than the command "Thou shalt not kill"? Yet the soldier, when not killing the enemy, is preparing to do precisely that. How, therefore, can soldiers be just or participate in justice? Soldiers must constantly weigh and balance competing claims upon their consciences. I call these competing claims "dueling duties."

But the very notion of competing or dueling duties suggests that there are no absolutes having unrivaled ownership of the soldier's conscience. Some people, reacting to this statement that there are few if any absolute obligations upon the soldier, will dismiss what I write as mere relativism. That assessment is mistaken. A number of years ago, Malham M. Wakin suggested that "the more human actions we attempt to incorporate under a single principle, the less specific the principle can be; absolute moral principles are necessarily vague." He then made a critical point: "We should note that if principles really are absolute . . . , they could never be in conflict with each other since each must be obeyed in *all* possible circumstances." In language that W.D. Ross would no doubt approve, Wakin says:

> Clearly, those moral obligations dealing with human act-types, like truth-telling, promise-keeping, preservation of life, respect for the property of others, and so on, are not absolute obligations. Does that mean that they are relative obligations to be observed only when we find it expedient to do so? Certainly not.[11] Rather it is the case that we could best refer to these types of moral obligations by use of another term; . . . let us call them "universal" obligations. . . . Ought they always to be observed? No. Then they cannot be absolutes.[12] Can they conflict? Yes. Then they cannot be absolutes. Are they sufficiently arbitrary to be ignored whenever one is in a different society or whenever it is convenient or expedient to do so? No. Then they cannot be relative principles in either the cultural or most subjective sense. Universal obligations of this sort hold for all human beings (they are not subjectively or culturally relative) but not in all possible circumstances (they are not absolute).

They hold in analogous sets of circumstances and they may conflict with each other.[13]

Let us return to Warsaw and the citizen deciding whether he should tell the Nazis the truth about the Jews he is harboring in his basement. If telling the truth is an absolute ("free from *any* restriction, limitation, or exception"), then his duty is to give away the Jews. Now listen to the counsel of a religious text: "The *right to the communication* of the truth is not unconditional." And "No one is bound to reveal the truth to someone who does not have the right to know it."[14] Now imagine—in a scene from Victor Hugo—a miserable, starving man desperate for food for his family and for himself. As a parent, he must try to feed his family, but there is no work and no one will give him so much as a crumb. He steals a loaf of bread, which is wrong. Should he be severely punished? Again the religious text tells us, "There is no theft if . . . refusal is contrary to reason and the universal destination of goods. This is the case in obvious and urgent necessity when the only way to provide for immediate, essential needs (food, shelter, clothing . . .) is to put at one's disposal the property of others."[15]

Universalism counsels us that when action is necessary, one must act to serve the greater good insofar as he is able to discern it. The greater good in Warsaw is to lie. The greater good for Hugo's character is to steal. But to say "Always do the greater good," though I think that is necessary advice, is not sufficient and is morally dangerous on that account.

First, I am not sure we have ways to measure well when we weigh alternatives. Second, even if we can choose the greater good, there must be some things we would be unwilling to do even after making our utilitarian assessment. When I spoke recently about military ethics to the class of 1999 at the Naval War College, I used the following example to make a point. On vacation in a Latin American country, you are hiking in the mountains when you stumble across a band of revolutionaries who seize you. You are glad to learn that they "like Americans" and are prepared to let you go unharmed after you perform a duty for them. The revolutionaries have captured a dozen government soldiers, all of whom they plan to execute. But if you will shoot one of those soldiers in the head with a weapon having one bullet, they will promptly release the other eleven. The soldiers themselves are willing to accept this, fearing that all twelve of them will be shot if you do not comply and believing that the revolutionaries will in fact keep their word, letting you and them (at least eleven of them) go free after you have shot one of their number. They are also willing, via a gambling procedure, to choose the one soldier to die.[16] "Always do the greater good!" Therefore, you shoot one soldier. Right?

Wrong. "You may not shoot the soldier," I told the Naval War College class. One naval officer became quite adamant, insisting that she would, in fact, kill one hostage to save eleven others. "They will all die unless you have the courage to kill one of them," she insisted. I was equally adamant: "You are choosing to commit an act of cold-blooded murder." She argued, "This is not murder; it's killing. It's what we in the military have to be ready to do all the time."

I could not—and I do not—agree. Let me argue by analogy, then by principle, then by belief. From *M*A*S*H*, the television show, comes this case. A group of American soldiers and South Korean civilians in the Korean War are on a bus, which for some reason is behind enemy lines. North Korean soldiers are known to be in the area. The bus is camouflaged, waiting for enemy patrols to pass by so that they can restart the bus and find their way back to friendly forces. But a South Korean woman has a crying baby, whose noise will give away their position. "Shut the baby up! Shut the baby up!" An American doctor on the bus, understandably anxious not to be captured, is desperately hoping the baby will be silenced. Then the baby stops its crying. The enemy patrols pass. The bus returns to friendly lines. The South Korean woman has suffocated her baby, and the doctor, horrified at the incident and at his own reactions on the bus, has a nervous breakdown. If the South Korean woman deliberately killed her child, was that not the right course of action? No.

Surely over the centuries we have learned that to deliberately take the life of an innocent person is simply wrong. (The baby is clearly innocent, and the soldier in the mountains is innocent, too, in the context explained.) I am willing to do the greater good—but only up to a certain point. I am confronted with "dueling duties": kill the baby (or the soldier) to save the bus passengers (or the other soldiers), or do not kill the baby or the soldier but thereby risk the capture of the passengers or the execution of the other soldiers. I will not commit an act of murder.

The religious concept is found in Romans: one may not do evil that good may come of it—the people who do such are "justly condemned" (3:8). Says a religious text, "It is . . . an error to judge the morality of human acts by considering only the intention that inspires them or the circumstances (environment, social pressure, duress or emergency, etc.) which supply their context. There are acts which, in and of themselves, independently of circumstances and intentions, are always gravely illicit by reason of their object[—]such as blasphemy and perjury, murder and adultery. One may not do evil so that good may result from it."[17]

Not convincing enough? One more analogy, then. A state trooper is called to the scene of an accident. The driver of a large truck is pinned helplessly in the cab with no chance whatsoever of immediate extrication. The truck is on fire, and the flames are spreading with no prospect of being extinguished. Known fire trucks are many miles away. The driver, who does not want to burn to death, pleads with the trooper to shoot him. The trooper removes his weapon from its holster and thinks. He puts it back. The driver's screams cause the trooper once more to remove his pistol—and once again he replaces it. Should he shoot the man?[18]

Military ethics is all about dueling duties. It is all about competing claims. And it will never be easy to make clear moral choices. On an intelligence trip behind enemy lines, you and your patrol are spotted by a civilian teenager—or an enemy soldier. Your work is compromised unless you kill him. Can you? No.[19] You need information about enemy positions and strength. You have two prisoners. Can you torture or kill one to make the other talk? A qualified no.[20] You are on a bombing raid and there is the prospect of "collateral damage" (meaning destruction or death visited upon innocent people as you bomb legitimate targets). Can you proceed? Probably yes, according to the principle of double effect.[21]

By the way, could the president's friend, the air force officer mentioned at the beginning of this chapter, morally drop the nuclear weapon on New York City? Was it a legal order? Probably. Did the president mean well, trying to avert World War III. Certainly. Good intentions, however, are not enough to justify unethical action. The relativist *might* condone dropping the bomb on New York City on utilitarian grounds. The universalist must condemn the action.[22]

THE NATURE OF JUSTICE . . . AND OF EVIL

"No one can escape from the fundamental questions: *What must I do? How do I distinguish good from evil?*"[23] Distinguishing the wise from the foolish, the just from the unjust, the virtuous from the vicious requires more than personal or idiosyncratic knowledge. If the only frame of reference I have is my own background and experience, my viewpoint will necessarily be limited and egotistical.[24] That is one reason we talk of the liberal arts as broadening, for good education should inculcate respect for moral tradition.[25] Edmund Burke in his *Reflections on the Revolution in France* put it this way: "People will not look forward to posterity who never look backward to their ancestors." The historical amnesiac will invariably be a moral illiterate; that is, those who have not read history forgo a great deal of knowledge and, presumably, wisdom that can be a helpful guide to present and future action. But those who have little knowledge of history and little knowledge of ethics (and there are so many today of whom that is true) can hardly hope to distinguish justice from injustice. As the philosopher John Kekes says: "If we know what our moral tradition and conception of the good life call for, then we know how to evaluate and judge complex situations. And then the exercise of courage [see chapter 7], moderation, and justice becomes a matter of applying our knowledge to make the right effort, in the right circumstances, in the right way."[26]

When postmodernist thought tells us that there is no Truth, it unavoidably contributes to a victory of the gutter. After all, if there is no Truth, then there is no Evil. And Evil—utter, unredeemed hate—surely exists. We shrink from identifying evil as such because we are afraid of being called self-righteousness or intolerant or old fashioned. Moral cowardice so often equates with the fear of not being "cool." Roger Shattuck sees four kinds of evil: natural evil (such as earthquakes), moral evil (harmful actions that contravene accepted moral principles), radical evil ("immoral behavior so pervasive in a person or society that scruples and restraints have been utterly abandoned"), and metaphysical evil (which confers honor upon evil—as in the respect given to Nietzsche).[27] In chapter 3 we traced the moral dissolution of American society, from its entertainment industry to its abortion industry; in many ways we have come to the point of celebrating evil. Notice that evil gets more laughs at a party.

Susan Sontag has written that "we have a sense of evil," but we no longer have "the religious or philosophical language to talk intelligently about evil."[28] Hannah Arendt, whose book about Nazi murderer Adolf Eichmann made famous the phrase "the banality of evil," understood neither Eichmann nor evil, contends Stephen Miller. Arendt wrote that Eichmann was a Nazi bureaucrat, mindlessly, if enthusiastically, following orders to murder millions of human beings. Miller objects, contending that "there is a common denominator in Arendt's attempts to clarify the nature of evil, which is that evil is less a choice than the outcome of certain circumstances." One of Arendt's critics, for example, wrote to her and complained that "what you are saying is that Eichmann lacks an inherent human quality: the capacity for thought, consciousness—conscience."[29] Conscience demands an understanding of moral tradition, ethical principle, and Truth (see chapter 4). No truth, no conscience; no conscience, no evil; no evil, no dilemma in bombing either Moscow or New York City; no dilemmas, no limitations in the conduct of war; therefore, justice does not exist, and war need have no limitations.

From Plato through John Rawls, philosophers have attempted to define justice. Frequently, they settle upon the formula that justice is giving everyone his due. Responding to that view, the writer Anatole France observed, "Justice is made to give everyone his due; to the rich his richness, to the poor his poverty."[30] As is so often true, words that suggest ideas of fundamental, eternal importance are inadequate in conveying the essence of their subject. *Justice,* as a word, hardly conveys the full meaning of justice as a cardinal virtue. Perhaps both term and concept can be understood better by looking briefly at the three basic forms of justice: commutative, distributive, and legal.

Commutative justice refers to fairness in exchanges or contracts between people (in such areas as wages and prices). As the philosopher Josef Pieper wrote, "Every phase of man's communal life, in the family as well as in the state, is a compromise between the interests of individuals with equal rights."[31] Distributive justice refers to the allocation of social resources, such as power and wealth. General or legal or contributive justice pertains to what the citizen owes in fairness to the community. We might think of these three types of justice as, first, what we owe to one another (fulfilling obligations and paying debts), what the community owes its citizens in accordance with their contributions and needs, and what we owe our society. Note that we are back to the fundamental concept of ethics: owing. We cannot be happy, fulfilled people leading lives of purpose and meaning unless we know and do what we ought to, unless we justly discharge our duties. The problem, as we have seen, is that duties can conflict. For example, we know that we must return property in good order to those from whom we borrow. Would that apply to returning a car promptly to its owner, even though he might be inebriated at the time, or to returning a hunting rifle to its owner at a time when he is momentarily enraged at a neighbor? What is the just thing to do?

The three basic types of justice[32] are reminiscent of the three types of liberty discussed by Mortimer Adler, who refers to "circumstantial freedom" (having means), natural freedom (being intellectually able to choose), and moral or acquired freedom (the ability to choose habitually as we ought to choose). (The only freedom that must be regulated by justice, he says, is the circumstantial, which has to do with money.)[33] Liberty and justice are complementary. As Adler explains, "when just laws are enforced, they enlarge the liberty of the individual. Quite the contrary is the condition of persons living under the tyranny of unjust laws, the rule of might rather than right. Compelled by coercive force or by duress to act neither as they please nor as they ought, their freedom is severely limited. What they have lost by such limitation is true liberty, not license."[34] Justice is personal (commutative), economic (distributive), and political (legal); freedom is personal (natural), economic (circumstantial), and political (moral or acquired). Because we are members of a state (a country or a polis), we learn a cultural and moral tradition. If that tradition is wise and just, we are likely, but of course not certain, to be increasingly wise and just. So much of who we are depends upon where we have come from (thus the dedication of this book). No one has put this better than Alasdair MacIntyre: "I inherit from the past of my family, my city, my tribe, my nation, a variety of debts, inheritances, rightful expectations and obligations. These constitute the given of my life, my moral starting point. This is in part what gives my life its own moral particularity."[35] We cannot expect to be reasonably just or truly free unless we are well educated about the problems of the past, the promises of the future, and the perils involved in both.

All ethics is about *perspective*—being able to see both distance and depth. Perspective demands that we examine issues from many standpoints, not just one. Perspective demands broad vision. As we learn from art, which informs us about illusion and the conflict of interpretation, we learn from perspective. We are reminded of "dueling duties," of universalism, of the need to choose wisely and justly. We are members of a country; we may be members of the profession of arms—both shape and influence us. They give us a "moral particularity." We owe our country; we owe our profession and colleagues. But we owe only *up to a point*. There are things we cannot do for family, for profession, for country. If they ask us to cross the line, there are things (such as bombing New York City, killing innocent hostages, shooting trapped truckers) that we must refuse to do.

One hundred years ago, on 17 October 1899, Carl Schurz, an American editor, gave a speech in Chicago to the Anti-Imperialist Conference: "Our country, right or wrong," he said. "When right to be kept right; when wrong to be put right." Our country—its laws, traditions, and customs—gives us our moral starting point. But we must have the perspective, the ethical power of discrimination, and the prudence to know that standards exist according to which we can judge our country and its political and military officers, its politics and diplomacy, and its national security policies and decisions. We must remember that keeping and putting our country "right" requires an understanding of what *right* means. Zerubbabel was correct, after all: there is no injustice in truth. Our task, politically and morally, is to ensure that justice and truth always coincide.

BRIDGES, POINTS, AND LINES

In the next section of the book, I want to offer a few "Obiter Dicta" about education. Many of those comments, however, can be collapsed into a few observations about ethics and "plane geometry." There is a way to explain, briefly and pointedly, much of what I have written above. Imagine a bridge. On one side of the bridge are our beliefs. On the other side of the bridge are our actions. We know that, to be just, our actions should be consistent with our beliefs. If they are not, we have failed. We have been either moral cowards or hypocrites. Therefore (1), we have to cross the bridge, "connecting" our beliefs with our actions. But that is not enough.

There are gravitational (and occasional transportational) pressures on the bridge, and it will collapse unless it has certain supports. The supports for our ethical bridge are our faith, family, customs, laws, friends, associations, education, and so on. Suppose the supports are rotting or already rotten. We have a poor education or no family to speak of, or we are surrounded by unjust laws or evil friends. The supports of the bridge will not hold it up when we must walk from the side of (wise) beliefs to the side of actions. So (2) we must have strong supports under our "ethical bridge," and the supports must be continually refreshed and renewed, even as physical bridge supports must occasionally be reworked to maintain their strength. But that is not enough.

In (1) and (2) I assume "good" beliefs. As physical bridges forbid the passage of certain unwanted traffic for various engineering reasons, so our metaphorical bridge must forbid the passage of certain beliefs for ethical reasons. The "bridgekeepers" are wise parents, family, friends, teachers, colleagues, and so on, who continually counsel us. The connection of evil beliefs with evil actions—and the celebration of philosophical monsters such as Nietzsche—result only in a "bridge" over which pass convoys headed to death camps. Thus (3), a good bridge between beliefs and actions demands prudent "bridgekeepers," who know the difference between wise and foolish, just and unjust, virtuous and vicious. But that is probably not enough.

Most people, after all, do not have the temperament or the time for advanced theological and philosophical study.[36] Much of what passes for wisdom often amounts to undigested morsels of folklore, parading as eternal truth. That is not always bad, but it is by its nature at least unconsidered, and it may be ill considered. Stephen Carter first made the point that honesty is not the same as integrity, for honest and sincere people, if unreflective, may serve the cause of evil (see chapter 7). The general approach to ethics of most people is consequentialist or utilitarian. Justice amounts to acting upon the answer to a simple, single question: what offers the greatest benefit to the greatest number? So (4) one must do what brings about the most good to the most people. But that is not enough.

Here is where "ethical plane geometry" enters the picture. "Do what offers the most good to the most people" makes great sense *up to a point.* There must be a point beyond which we would be unwilling to go in some actions. Are we willing to do *anything* to achieve *something*? Or are there some things so important, so fundamental, so *sacred* that we will not—we must not—transgress them to achieve something else? Then (5) one must do what offers the most good to the most people, up to a point. But that is not good enough.

"In everything we do, however great or small," writes Tom Morris, "we should always be asking ourselves, 'In doing this, am I becoming the kind of person I want to be?'" For "whenever you make a decision, whenever you act, you are never just doing, you are always becoming."[37] The decisions we make reflect the truth of this bit of folklore— "We are what we do; we do what we are." Making one good decision, establishing one point beyond which we will not go, is fine; but it is something we must continually do. In making numerous decisions, and in establishing numerous points beyond which we will not go, we effectively create a *line* (a series of points). That line is an assembly of the sacred and solemn points—*the habitus*—of our life.[38] That line reminds us that there are principles we will not betray, people we will not abandon, things we will not do, concessions we will not make to achieve some goal. Our lives are spent creating a line we will not cross. And in drawing that line, we recognize the universal need to discriminate: there are wrong things and "wronger" things (which is why we may commit the wrong thing of killing in just war in order to prevent the "wronger" thing of letting the Nazis conquer Europe and kill millions of innocents); and we recognize, too, the power of Truth, in which no injustice resides. Therefore (6), the ethical line we draw, with the help of those who have gone before and in order to help those who will come after, is our bridge between conscientious belief and courageous action. We have informed our conscience and thus formed our values on the basis of virtue. We understand what Abraham Lincoln said in February 1860: "Let us have faith that right makes might, and in that faith let us to the end dare to do our duty as we understand it."[39] The bridge of justice, built upon the support of prudence, will carry virtuous beliefs into courageous action.

CASE STUDY

On 1 August 1971, Gen. John D. Lavelle assumed command of the U.S. Seventh Air Force during the Vietnam War. He found himself in a dilemma. Rules of Engagement (ROE) are military orders ordinarily providing detailed instructions to commanders and subordinates about authorized combat or other operational procedures. ROE are not normally to be ignored, compromised, or rescinded without proper chain-of-command approval. The ROE were explicit in authorizing U.S. fighter aircraft to strike targets in North Vietnam only if they were fired upon or if Surface-to-Air Missile or Anti-Aircraft Artillery radars were activated against them.

According to writer George C. Wilson, Lavelle felt deep frustration about the restrictions on his airmen and about the fact that airmen were killed because of the ROE.[40] Meanwhile, the air war in Vietnam was intense, and the North Vietnamese—aware of the restrictions on American aircraft—were building up. Lavelle had three choices: (1) to monitor the buildup but take few, if any, actions against it; (2) to send U.S. aircraft in dangerously low over enemy installations to provoke the North Vietnamese to fire upon them, thus permitting an authorized "protective reaction bombing"; or (3) simply to ignore, or to "bend," the rules, conducting air war operations according to his best judgment.

General Lavelle had "dueling duties." First, he had to obey orders; but he also had a clear duty to protect his men insofar as he was able to do so. As the general subsequently told the Senate Armed Services Committee, "In your deliberations I ask that you bear in mind one underlying consideration which I believe to be of the most paramount importance. That consideration is simply this: that all of my judgments were made as a field commander acutely mindful of my often anguishing responsibility for the protection of the lives and safety of thousands of courageous young airmen under my command. It was the central consideration which was at the heart of my motivation with respect to every operational judgment I was ever called upon to make in Southeast Asia."[41]

Lavelle therefore took aggressive action (during twenty-four bombing missions over about four months), contending that military circumstances justified tactical operations that the ROE had formerly restricted or forbidden. According to Lavelle's operations officer, Maj. Gen. Alton D. Slay, Lavelle commanded subordinates to write two sets of records on missions that he ordered to attack enemy buildups. One set of records was true and was filed; the other records were falsified and were sent up the chain.[42] Lavelle maintained that he never deliberately ordered his officers to falsify reports on a regular basis. He admitted that on one occasion he told his staff that they could not report "no enemy reaction" as the pilot had done. After that, Lavelle said, "the word apparently got distorted," and somehow the air force bureaucracy took it to be standard procedure to falsify reports on all subsequent "protective reaction" raids. Lavelle denied knowledge of continued falsifications.[43] Of course, either Slay or Lavelle was lying. During congressional hearings, Sen. Harold Hughes of Iowa asked General Slay why he "didn't question more than [he] did the orders that [he] had been given." Responded General Slay: *"Sir, I [have] spent all my life since 17 in the military service and that is all I know."*[44]

An air force sergeant, Lonnie Franks, had written a letter to one of his senators, explaining the falsifications. Franks said, "Everybody we knew were [*sic*] falsifying these reports." When Franks asked why, he was told, "That's the way we do it."[45] The air force chief of staff, Gen. John Ryan, sent his inspector general to Lavelle's headquarters to determine the legitimacy of Franks's charges. On 7 April 1972, General Lavelle retired, having been demoted one grade.[46]

On 1 November 1972, General Ryan issued a terse policy letter to air force commanders. He said, in part:

> Integrity—which includes full and accurate disclosure—is the keystone of military service. . . .
>
> Therefore, we may not compromise our integrity—our truthfulness. To do so is not only unlawful but also degrading. False reporting is a clear example of a failure of integrity. Any order to compromise integrity is not a lawful order.
>
> Integrity is the most important responsibility of command.[47]

Although Zerubbabel would understood Gen. John Ryan's policy letter, he would have been at a loss to understand General Slay's troublesome and weak-kneed remark that military service "is all I know." Such an ethical bridge is too feeble, too low, too treacherous.

At this writing, the chief of staff of the U.S. Air Force is Gen. Michael Ryan, the son of John Ryan.[48]

Obiter Dicta

The first duty of a lecturer—to hand you after an hour's discourse a nugget of pure truth to wrap up between the pages of your notebook and keep on the mantelpiece for ever.

—Virginia Woolf

One father is more than 100 schoolmasters.

—George Herbert

VALUES AND EDUCATION

An obiter dictum is an incidental or passing remark or opinion; it is a tangent. In this brief tangent, I offer a few remarks about teaching, which is my life's work. *Teaching, directly or indirectly, is also the life's work of all armed forces officers.* All officers teach, by deed if not by word, in all that they do or fail to do. As a college professor dealing now principally with highly successful military officers and high-ranking government civilians, I think I am unusual in that I have also dealt over the years with thousands of students in undergraduate colleges and high schools.[1]

Over the past two or three decades, a spate of books has appeared to condemn the decline in education.[2] As accurate as most of these analyses are about the deterioration of higher learning in recent years, that is not my focus here. Nor do I want to discuss at great length "values clarification," the attempt by certain self-styled educators to help students define "their own" values.[3] In the scheme of values clarification, a student's reaction to issues of war, capital punishment, or abortion is as much "a personal choice" as his or her favorite color or favorite flavor of ice cream.

The idea of modes of responsibility would be anathema to those enmeshed in values clarification. To them, what matters is process, not product. The very notion of classical or cardinal virtues seems absurd, hopelessly outdated. That is because, as Christopher Lasch puts it, the great majority of college students, "relegated to institutions that have given up even the pretense of a liberal education, study business, accounting, physical education, public relations, and other practical subjects. They get little training in writing (unless 'Commercial English' is an acceptable substitute), seldom read a book, and graduate without exposure to history, philosophy, or literature."[4] By 1990, students could graduate from 68 percent of American colleges and universities without taking a course in the history of western civilization. And as Yale history professor emeritus C. Vann Woodward has pointed out, high school students could "satisfy their social studies requirements by taking courses in current events, drug education, and sex education, and no history course whatever." By the middle of the 1990s, 57 percent of U.S. high school seniors were scoring below "basic" in their knowledge of American history in the National Assessment of Educational Progress. It is not possible to score lower than that.[5] Without the perspective of history, comparative literature, and philosophy, students can hardly hope to discern well and to differentiate wisely among competing values. Choosing is thought by some to be all that matters; the choice itself is unimportant. He likes chocolate ice cream; she likes the idea of dropping nuclear weapons on Baghdad. On the one hand, we have Abraham Lincoln; on the other, we have Stalin; who is to decide whose policies were "better"? The word *better*, after all, implies a "value judgment," and we are to shun such judgmental thinking.

Is lying wrong? Is cheating wrong? Is stealing wrong? If one's logic leads him or her to believe that the murder of millions of Jews—or even the murder of one Jew—by the Nazis was somehow morally correct, then the person is morally disordered. It may be true that there is no point in arguing about taste *(De gustibus non est disputandum)*, but about matters of truth, argument is important and indispensable *(De veritate disputandum est)*. That is the point of chapter 1, an exercise in values confusion; the point of chapter 3 is to suggest that the cardinal virtues can point us toward sound moral reasoning. If lying, cheating, and stealing depend upon the ethical inclinations and the emotions of the one deciding, then all is isolation and despair.

Jean-Paul Sartre, a Marxist and an atheist, creates truth for himself; therefore, education to him is a means of helping people to engage with the problems and prospects of life in order to define themselves. But the cardinal virtues tell us that Truth must be discovered and, once discovered, accepted. Christ's remark "You shall know the truth, and the truth will set you free" (John 8:32) must confound the Sartrean existentialist. Even more exasperating to Sartre would be the Pauline notion that we are not to conform ourselves to the world but instead to determine God's will and follow that (Rom. 12:2). Nonetheless, therein lies genuine education, which is the recognition of the sacred and obedience to its requirements.

Sacred Education in a Secular World

This may be very well for students in religious high schools and colleges. But can students in public high schools and colleges deal with "the sacred"? In a quarter-century of teaching, I have integrated virtue ethics (see chapter 8) into almost all of my classes and lectures, whether at public, private, or parochial institutions. Although my own views are shaped by my Christian moral inheritance and convictions, I hope that I have always respected the diverse perspectives of my students (and colleagues), while remaining true to my own beliefs. Some years ago at a National Endowment for the Humanities summer institute at the University of Massachusetts, I met a professor from a small Pennsylvania college who taught—and strongly believed in—Marxist principles. He told me that he insisted that his students prove to him (for example, on their final examination), not only that they understood the fundamentals of Marxism, but that they had *become* Marxists. I thought then and think now that this is as unforgivable as a conservative professor's insistence that students demonstrate their conversion to conservatism in order to pass a course. Bullies can be found behind lecterns (with doctorates in hand) as well as in the third grade on the playground at recess. Unless a student is enrolled in a seminary, he should not be expected to demonstrate conversion to any creed.

There are many moral values that, although rooted in and nourished by the sacred (that is, they come to us from religion), are nonetheless "profane" (that is, they apply to the secular realm as well as to the sacred). Without doubt, the best example of that is the U.S. Military Academy at West Point, where the honor code forbidding lying, cheating, and stealing has helped to form cadets into officers for generations.

Is that code "religious"? In a sense it is; its roots clearly can be traced to a religious heritage. But men and women of decency and moral discretion, regardless of whether they are personally religious, can and should embrace that code. Thus, what is sacred has valuable secular purposes without becoming sectarian (pertaining to a particular religious denomination). Another example is the core values movement in the military services and in much of contemporary industry. The U.S. Air Force, for instance, says of its core values of integrity, excellence, and service before self that it "attempts no explanation of the origin of the Values except to say that all of us, regardless of our religious views, must recognize their functional importance and accept them for that reason." These values, maintains the air force, are "necessary for mission accomplishment."[6]

High schools and colleges, too, have "missions," the most important of which is the development of men and women of character and competence. It is possible—and indeed desirable—for every school and college to have a code of honor that should be inculcated into its student body. It should go practically without saying that religious high schools and colleges should have such codes. My wife has been teaching theology for several years at a Catholic high school in Alabama. That high school did not have an honor code. I therefore proposed to the principal the following two codes.

Code of Honor: As a member of a Catholic High School community, I will neither lie, nor cheat, nor steal, nor seek to deceive.

Code of Conduct: Knowing that Jesus is the reason for my high school, I will act in such a way as to reflect credit upon my Church, civic community, school, family, and self.

The codes, although apparently thought highly of by administrators and teachers, were not adopted. One high-ranking administrator said that it would be unfortunate to have such good codes ignored by students; therefore they should not be adopted. Should such logic dominate the educational scene, I hate to think of what would happen to the Commandments and Beatitudes! Indeed, of the colleges from which I earned degrees, only one—a public university (the College of William and Mary)—had an honor code; the two Catholic institutions I attended (St. Anselm College in New Hampshire and the University of Notre

Dame in Indiana) did not have honor codes. The notion that honor codes are only for religious or for military schools is clearly mistaken.

The idea of a clause in faculty contracts about "moral turpitude" is ordinarily seen as outrageous today. What administrator, after all, can "dictate" moral codes to his or her faculty members? Suppose a faculty member receives a parking ticket. Should he be fired? Suppose a teacher runs a red light. Do we terminate his contract? These are the kinds of issues normally brought up to lampoon the idea of moral turpitude. Certainly the issue can be complex in a democratic republic. Universities exist to accommodate a *universe* of views and to encourage critical thinking. The idea of "virtue police" on campus is anathema to anyone who believes in university education. Many years ago, Bertrand Russell, a strong critic of Christianity and a proponent of open sexuality, received a faculty appointment to teach at City College in New York. The appointment brought a firestorm of criticism from conservatives. During a civil suit, at one hearing Russell was described as "lecherous, salacious, libidinous, lustful, venerous, erotomaniac, aphrodisiac, atheistic, irreverent, narrow-minded, bigoted, and untruthful." The judge, a Catholic, ruled that Russell was morally unfit for the position.[7] Is there a danger that academic freedom may be destroyed by intellectual inquisition?

Yes. The danger of closed-mindedness always lurks in the corridors of academe. Those on the political left have been turned into pariahs—insulted and silenced—by "McCarthyites" of the right. But those on the political right have similarly been turned into pariahs—insulted and silenced—by "Jacobins" of the left. Hard cases make bad law, and extreme examples rarely serve well the cause of serious argument. Having an open mind does not, however, mean having an empty head. There are some beliefs and convictions so transparently evil that men and women of what used to be known as common courtesy and ordinary decency must rise up and forbid them. Would it be "closed-minded," for example, for a campus to refuse to hire faculty who espouse pederasty, who advocate spouse beating, who support the resurrection of slavery, or who champion racial hatred? Is there not a cluster of fundamental values upon which we can (still) agree? Is there no understanding of those values and virtues that make up the lady or gentleman? Is there no agreement upon the basic manners and morals of our society?

I think such common agreement is in evidence, despite the too-frequent lapses into barbarism around us—for example, the ubiquitous car back-window decal of a cartoon character urinating on various people or things. These elements of common conduct and decency are what can and must be taught. We cannot long maintain a society in which lying, cheating, and stealing are the norm. Is one "left-wing" or "right-wing" because he thinks these are wrong? We cannot long maintain a society in which monstrous and grotesque behavior is applauded or endorsed. A society does not deserve respect if it condones such things as dragging a man to death behind a car because he is African American, beating a man to death because he is homosexual, or throwing a newborn into a dumpster because the child is unplanned. "'Judgment,' wrote William Bennett, "is a word that is out of favor these days, but it remains a cornerstone of democratic self-government. It is what enables us to hold ourselves, and our leaders, to high standards. It is how we distinguish between right and wrong, noble and base, honor and dishonor."[8]

In any serious university, there will always be disagreement about what adjectives such as *monstrous* or *grotesque* mean. But I submit and believe that the best teachers are generally kind and decent people. They may well agree to disagree on many issues, but in the most pressing cases they will, sometimes surprisingly, agree. For example, I think empirical data would confirm that almost all teachers would reject the Soviet Communist and Nazi creeds; reject cruelty to children, the elderly, and animals; believe in truth-telling and promise-keeping; advocate sound reason, honesty, industry, punctuality, cleanliness, and geniality; and condemn plagiarism and other forms of theft, as well as brutality, sadism, and savage treatment of others. From such common convictions as these education can and must take its collective virtues.

The Failure of Teachers

Unfortunately, there are also incompetent and indolent teachers. After four years at Harvard University in Massachusetts, for example, a graduating senior said in his commencement address: "I believe that there is one idea, one sentiment, which we have all acquired at some point in our Harvard careers; and that, ladies and gentlemen, is, in a word, confusion. They tell us that it is heresy to suggest the superiority of some value, fantasy to believe in moral argument, slavery to submit to a judgment sounder than your own. The freedom of our day is the freedom to devote ourselves to any values we please, on the mere condition that we do not believe them to be true."[9] And who are "they"? "They" are faculty members—we used to say *teachers*—who sow the seeds of moral confusion in the name of values clarification, open-mindedness, relativism, nihilism, hedonism, and assorted other ethical detritus.

Why is it, ask Hanson and Heath, that our nation's elite "now have no morals"? Why do "our lawyers, doctors, politicians, journalists, and corporate magnates equate the accumulation of data with knowledge, frankness with truth, inherited power with justice, titles and suits with dignity, and capital with talent"? They lay the blame, I think correctly, on teachers themselves. For teachers and scholars have embraced the corporate world with relish: "Our administrators ('officers,' no longer scholars) now justified their enormous raises on the basis of running a 'business' (no longer a university) with a 'payroll' (salaried professors) in the millions, of supervising a 'physical plant' and real estate (no longer the gym, library, or open ag. field) worth millions, and offering a 'product' in high demand by its 'consumers' (so much for degrees and students)."[10]

There is no question that educational institutions require money for salaries and buildings and the like. But it is not readings, discussions, and lectures (however useful) that create men and women of conscience; it is not libraries and laboratories (however important) that form people of character; it is not big endowments or beautiful buildings or lovely grounds (however desirable they may be) that turn out extraordinary people. What matters more than anything else is the good teachers met daily by the students. And it is precisely good teaching that has been ignored, dismissed, ridiculed, and devalued over the past two or three decades. What so often matters is *how many* students are "taught," how many publications are produced, and how many grants are obtained. Scholars compete *not* to be teachers. In many institutions, the best scholars are rewarded by not having to teach freshmen. I recently taught for a semester at a large public university where graduate assistants routinely taught almost all the introductory courses in many disciplines.

Good teaching, some seem to believe, drives out good scholarship. It is an old debate whether one can teach well—which involves counseling, writing recommendations, serving on faculty committees, helping to recruit new faculty, and the like—and also be a productive scholar. I do not know how one can be effective in the classroom without finding time to read, study, and reflect. To be sure, there are scholars who do not teach; but there cannot be good teachers who do not regularly read, perform research, and meditate. (I must concede, however, that they may not have time to publish extensively.) Nonetheless, good teachers can and should, whenever practicable, take part in "professional development" by speaking to student groups, to faculty forums, and to community and church groups. The idea is for faculty members to keep ideas alive—and bubbling—in their minds. The good teacher is always a good learner and, moreover, represents commitment to and enthusiasm for the life of the mind.

The good teacher, I believe, is characterized by four virtues: wisdom, justice, moral courage, and temperance. Readers of this book will not be surprised by the four virtues I have chosen.

- A good teacher is reflective, thoughtful, and considerate (in the truest sense of that term) and transmits not just knowledge, but also appreciation for and analysis of that knowledge. (How many would-be teachers, in high school and college, think their education is finished when they are hired or tenured?)
- A good teacher is just, truthful, and fair and demonstrates these qualities both personally and professionally. (How many would-be teachers abuse their power by distorting information to their own ideological ends, by failure to admit honestly their own ignorance on certain matters [and then correcting it] or by unfairly discriminating in one form or another against students?)
- A good teacher is diligent and morally courageous in upholding reasonable standards and being willing to speak truth to power, whether the "power" is that of administrators, fellow faculty members, student opinion, or community leaders. (How many would-be teachers cater to prevailing opinion or coddle students by desiring academic popularity at the price of professionalism or high standards?)
- A good teacher is "intemperate" (that is, exhilarated) in presenting his or her material but temperate in personal manners and behavior. (How many would-be teachers abuse liquor, drugs, or food, forgetting that "a sound mind in a sound body" should be a goal of educated people?)

The cardinal virtues tell us that teachers should be, insofar as possible, masters of their subject matter, for learning never ceases; scrupulously fair in all dealings; organized and industrious; and enthusiastic about the power and purpose of teaching. *All true professional people are teachers.* Every priest, minister, or rabbi; every doctor, nurse, or lawyer; every engineer or architect; every military officer—all of them teach as well or as poorly as they carry out the details and routines of their craft. But teaching is the whole substance of the life of the teacher. Everything the teacher does or fails to do is about teaching. Those who want only to research, to write, to make their fortune, to travel to conventions, to see their name in lights—such as these may be professional in every way except one: they are not teachers.

ANNA DALTON

Many years ago in the small western Massachusetts town of Monson, I had an eighth-grade English teacher named Miss Anna Dalton. Although she was at that time an older woman, she was a firm disciplinarian. She believed strongly in the value of diagramming sentences, an exercise we in her class did innumerable times that year. I remember her as an entirely competent and concerned teacher. But the greatest lesson she was to teach me occurred many years later when we were "colleagues." Armed with Miss Dalton's English instruction, I went on to the public high school, then to college, and finally into the army. After my military tour, I returned to Monson for a few months before entering graduate school. During my time there, I substituted in area schools. One day, I was asked to substitute teach at my old high school in Monson. One of the other subs that day was Miss Dalton, retired but still occasionally substituting.

There was nothing exceptional about the school day until about midmorning. Someone called in a bomb threat, and the principal had no choice except to order everyone out of the building while the school was checked. There was no time to get coats or sweaters. All the classes immediately filed out with their teachers—into a windy, bitterly cold March day. The teachers told their classes to stand out in the cold (to facilitate a subsequent head count), awaiting the word to return to class. Before long, all the teachers I saw had left their kids to get into their warm cars. (In this public high school, few students had cars, and they were forbidden to use them in any way during school hours.) I had just come from being an infantry officer and had learned, if nothing else, that officers do not leave their men. I was about twenty-six, in good shape, and able to tolerate the cold day. The only other teacher who stayed resolutely with her class (for about an hour, after which we were told it was safe to reenter the high school) was Miss Dalton. Indomitably standing with her kids, the wind whipping around her, was this elderly woman—a substitute teacher. The regular teachers were nowhere to be seen. The one *real* teacher stood with her kids. I believe that Miss Dalton taught me well that day; she taught her kids; and she taught the younger teachers who, I hope, had the sense to be shamed by this elderly woman whose life was about teaching—even outside on a cold, windy day.

Years later, after I finished my dissertation and before I started my first college teaching job, I substitute taught in the schools in South Bend, Indiana. One day, in the faculty lounge at a South Bend high school, I was alone with a teacher who was about my age. We had little in common, but I was able to talk with him about teaching. His response to my question about whether he enjoyed teaching at that school was unforgettable to me. He had no use for teaching or for the kids, but the work was easy and he "got off work" at about 2:30 every day, so he could tolerate it. Of course, people joke around about such things, but he was entirely serious. My mind flashed to Miss Dalton, standing in the cold at another high school, years before. How much of what I had learned did I owe to Miss Dalton and to others like her? I do not know that. But I do know this: I was glad and grateful that I had had few teachers such as this lout in South Bend who had the temerity to claim the proud title of "teacher." Perhaps he had once been one, but I doubt it.

Hiring Secondary School Teachers

Very rarely do we read material about how to hire teachers. There are times when school systems, desperate for teachers, will hire practically anyone, even people whose sole credential is a degree in "education." There are, I am sure, earnest and eager people who have majored in education, desiring to be teachers; but courses in education—as mindless as so many of them are—cannot be a substitute for substantial courses in history and mathematics and English and so on. Whenever possible, teachers should major in an academic subject at a serious university, known for requiring serious intellectual work. Those who hire teachers should ask to see not college catalogs but syllabi of some of the major courses taken by the candidate. All teaching candidates, during their interview, should be asked to do two things:

- Orally respond to this question: name two books (exclusive of religious works) that have influenced your intellectual and moral development. These may be novels, works of history, biographies or autobiographies, and the like. The interviewers should discuss the candidates' answers to this question to be sure that those interviewed are not merely naming books without understanding the theme or thesis of the book.
- Respond in writing to this request: please write three paragraphs, right now, on this subject—"I admire _____ because [he or she] . . . ." All teachers should be able to write clear, coherent prose.

Other questions that candidates should respond to are these: Why do you want to teach? Who was your best teacher and why? Which course in college did you like the least and why? Which college course did you like the most and why? What is your chief strength (or weakness) as a teacher? Finally, if practicable, every aspiring teacher should present a lesson, or part of a lesson, either to the interviewers or to a real class with an experienced teacher present to evaluate.

If my experience is any guide, I think many aspiring teachers would be unable to name two books that have influenced them. In fact, sad to say, many of them would be unable to name two unassigned books they have read in the past few years. They would go blank. It is safe to conclude that ideas and concepts are not "bubbling" in their minds. How can we expect them to be competent and enthusiastic teachers if they are apathetic themselves about learning? Experienced teachers can watch a tyro for only a short while and tell whether the new teacher has a command of language and of subject matter, coupled with a desire to communicate with students, equal to the challenge at hand. Tests like these can be used—should be used—much more frequently by those who hire teachers.

Hiring College Teachers

There can be no question that college teachers—professors—must be hired on the principal basis of scholarship. Ordinarily, that means that candidates are judged first on where they did their graduate work; second on who directed their dissertations; and third on their publications to date or their promise of future publications. Only rarely is very serious attention given to candidates' ability to inspire undergraduates. The verb *inspire* would cause snickering by most faculty members, many of whom long ago abandoned any desire to be inspirational teachers. The simple, if sad, fact of the matter is that in academically competitive institutions (in the sense of gaining admission), teaching is an irrelevant enterprise; at academically noncompetitive institutions, teaching is frequently impossible because teachers are badly overworked (and seriously underpaid). In the former case, many gifted students are exposed to lethargic and perfunctory teaching by professors whose goal is publication and grantsmanship (or by teaching assistants understandably anxious to get their own dissertations done). In the latter case, many students of average academic ability are exposed to apathetic teaching by professors teaching four, five, or more preparations per semester and whose goal is to get through the semester without a nervous breakdown.

Professors at the "best" colleges must again start to *teach*. Professors at less prestigious colleges must have time for reading, research, and the presentation of their efforts to appropriate academic, student, or civic audiences.[11] But I despair. I know a number of teachers at "less prestigious" colleges who tell me that the money simply is not available to reduce their burdensome teaching load. The brightest and most industrious scholar would have trouble trying to teach well with four or five preparations per semester, keep up with grading and advising responsibilities, remain current in journal and book reading, and have the time to *talk with students*. The other side of this can best be told by relating a recruiting story of my own.

A few years ago, I was at the University of Notre Dame to attend a conference on good teaching named after Notre Dame's "Mr. Chips," Francis J. O'Malley.[12] Always on the lookout for good teachers who can serve as visiting professors at the Air War College, where I now teach, I met a Notre Dame professor, a recently tenured economist, with whom I had lunch. As I talked to her about opportunities for teaching a year at the war college, she told me about her tenure process at Notre Dame. When she first took the job at Notre Dame, she told me, a colleague visited her office and "clued her in." She was told not to spend much time preparing for her classes and to spend no time with students (lest they get the idea that she would be available to them), because none of that would help her gain tenure. What mattered, first and only, was publication of articles in the "right" journals and publication of a book with a "good" press. As part of her tenure package, there was a separate folder containing syllabi, evaluations, and so on. But this folder was not even taken to the tenure meeting by her advocate, the economist told me. I was struck by the great irony of hearing these comments while attending a conference to promote good teaching.[13]

In hiring the college teacher, search committees should look, of course, for highly competent scholars. But competence must be complemented by sound character. ("How are we to measure *that*?" comes the question.) What else has the candidate done besides proving scholarly excellence? Has the person served honorably in the armed forces, job corps, or peace corps; worked at various jobs; taught previously? How generally well educated is the person? Does the candidate communicate a desire to teach as well as to write? Has the candidate taken the time to research the institution where he or she is applying for a job? Does the candidate evince a good sense of humor? Does the candidate speak genially to secretaries and janitors and not just to members of the search committee? An interview stretched over three days, whenever practicable, will reveal much about the person hired by a college to teach its future alumni. Most contemporary professors, I believe, would be literally horrified by the remarks of Josiah Bunting about the qualifications of soul, mind, and body he wants in his professors, but I think that is an indictment more of the modern professor than of Bunting, who is the head of Virginia Military Institute.[14]

"The business of undergraduate education," writes Bunting in his recent fascinating novel, "remains the cultivation of character and mind, of instinct and ability of leadership and service. It is the way that men should live and behave in our culture and our country that is the proper business of our colleges."[15] If we desire good people, we must have good teachers. As simple as that sentence is, too many administrators at too many colleges have forgotten it.

A NOTE ABOUT RELIGIOUS COLLEGES

Federal service academies such as the Air Force Academy and West Point have long insisted that their teachers should be officers who can represent the profession of arms to the cadets. Recent legislation, however, has mandated that about half of the faculty members at these institutions be civilians—an excessive number and a mistake, in my judgment. Religious schools and colleges have a similar problem. Baptist, Lutheran,

Mormon, and other schools want to have believers on their faculty. Should there be a religious test? What form should that test take? Catholic colleges, in the decade ahead, will face a similar, and stern, problem. Are Catholic colleges Catholic any more? Many, clearly, are not.[16] In order to keep the *Catholic* in Catholic colleges, Pope John Paul II published the Apostolic Constitution *Ex Corde Ecclesiae (From the Heart of the Church)* in 1990, and in July 1998 he issued the apostolic letter "Ad Tuendam Fidem" (To defend the faith). The norms require that presidents of institutions, teachers of theology, and a majority on the boards of trustees be "faithful Catholics." *Ex Corde Ecclesiae* is clear that "in order not to endanger the Catholic identity of the University . . . , the number of non-Catholic teachers should not be allowed to constitute a majority." *America* says: "For Catholic colleges and universities that live in a world of accrediting associations and government regulation, the adoption of such norms would reverse three decades of development." The editors of *America,* a well-known Catholic publication, are saying that implementing the Pope's norms would be "disastrous." Responds Father Richard John Neuhaus, in one word, "Precisely."[17]

Administrators of well-known Catholic universities are eager to compete for celebrity, status, money, and grants with many of their Ivy League rivals.[18] I have heard administrators at federal service academies make similar suggestions, arguing that, say, West Point should be able to "compete" with Cornell. I have heard a number of university presidents dismiss with a smile the college rankings of such publications as *U.S. News & World Report,* but they are nonetheless eager to trumpet their own listing, if their institution is included or is high in the ratings. I think I understand the public relations aspect of the ratings, and having a high rating is certainly not bad. But if the rating, the prestige, the money, and the fame are purchased at the price of their raison d'être, their "life," it is a tragic trade, a Faustian bargain. Military academies exist to produce competent military leaders, not to compete with Cornell. Religious universities exist to produce men and women of conscience and character, not to have their graduates say, as the previously quoted Harvard graduate did, that they have learned only moral "confusion." That military colleges ought to have mostly military officers on their faculties, that religious colleges ought to have mostly believers on their faculties—these goals seem neither unreasonable nor unattainable. But suppose the rankings of the Catholic colleges suffer because they attempt to abide by the instruction of the Pope. It matters, I think, very little, for the Catholic college is *supposed* to answer to a higher author-ity. In the meantime, administrators of Catholic colleges intent upon defying the Pope might practice composing an answer to another, older question: "What profit would there be for one to gain the whole world and forfeit his life?" (Matt. 16:26).[19]

The First and Best Teachers

The first and best teachers should be our parents, grandparents, and great-grandparents. It is a national catastrophe that families are so strained today. Parents are never perfect, and our children see all the imperfec-tions to which we are heir. In public, we can perhaps pretend to be what we are not; it is impossible to do so at home. I shudder to think of the many errors and the bad examples I set for my own children. I wish— sad words, are they not?—I could change much of what I said or did or failed to say or do. I have the consolation, and maybe my children have the consolation, of knowing that I did my best, despite my sins and short-comings. I know that is true, as well, of my parents, who were my first and best teachers. Every parent is a teacher, and parents teach more by what they are than by what they say. The father who tells his daughter to go to church but does not go himself, who tells his son not to smoke but does so himself, who tells his daughter always to vote but ignores poli-tics himself, who tells his son to read but incessantly watches television himself—all these fathers have taught their children the lessons of ac-tions over words.

In the end, teaching is all about one of the great commands: follow Me.[20] The best teachers are kind and decent people, ardent learners, and competent and conscientious professionals. "A teacher," wrote Henry Brooks Adams, "affects eternity; he can never tell where his influence stops."[21] For the sake of our country, let us hope that we are speaking of *good* teachers[22] and of good parents—and that their influence will never stop.

If we believe that loving parents and good teachers are necessary for the development of good people, and that good people make the best leaders, and that good leadership is critical in the armed forces (as in every profession)—then a wise, just, courageous, and temperate profes-sion of arms begins in the classrooms of our country. Perhaps this sec-tion of "Obiter Dicta"—passing or incidental remarks—is not tangential after all. Perhaps it is at the heart of all ethical concerns.

7

Courage and the Profession of Arms

Courage is fear holding on a minute longer.

—George Patton

O God, give us the serenity to accept what cannot be changed; courage to change what should be changed; and wisdom to distinguish the one from the other.

—Reinhold Niebuhr

Bravery in battle; courage in combat; fortitude in fighting—is that not what the profession of arms is all about? Yes, for the armed services exist to win our country's wars. But what is courage and how is it nurtured? Where does courage begin? How is it developed and sustained?

COURAGE: CHARACTER IN ACTION

We know that courage is unique to human beings. Animals may be daring by instinct, but they are not brave—if we consider bravery (a word I will use interchangeably with *fortitude* and *courage*) to be a calculated, chivalrous response to danger. A person, like a beast, may respond instinctively and intrepidly to perilous circumstances, but as admirable as that response may be, it is not true bravery unless the person in distress has the opportunity to assess the situation and act knowingly in the face of danger. That is, an act may be objectively brave without the actor's being subjectively brave. This is in no way intended to demean the one who acts; it is rather to suggest that unique and unconsidered spontaneous action, however noble, does not necessarily mean that the actor is courageous.

Thus, robotlike, conditioned response to danger, unless it is a consequence of pattern (which suggests time for consideration), may be commendable but is likely not courageous. For courage implies consideration—one's assessment of risk to himself before acting. The soldier in a just cause on the battlefield, exposed day after day to the mortal dangers of combat, who one day performs a particularly heroic act, is truly courageous, for he has had time to think about the ubiquitous perils around him. The man who sees a speeding car bearing down upon a child playing in the street and impulsively dives at the child, pushing him out of the automobile's path, has certainly performed a very brave act. He deserves great praise for doing a noble deed, but the single, unreflective act does not necessarily indicate the sustained quality of courage.

Courage is character in action; it is a pattern; it is a settled disposition (a habitus) formed, fashioned, and developed over many years. If, by chance, an otherwise ignorant man might know the answer to a trivial question—which U.S. president was in office on 1 January 1901? (McKinley)—such an answer to a single question hardly suggests a sound education in American history. Education is a product of years of reading, study, and reflection. Beginning philosophy students sometimes argue which is true: we do what we are, or we are what we do.[1] In fact, the dichotomy makes little sense. Do we think as we act, or do we act as we think?[2] Of course, it is both: at any moment we both are (that is, we are the product, the being, of all we have thought and done), and we are becoming (that is, we are in the process of developing). It is precisely in that sense that the bumper-sticker slogan, "Today is the first day of the rest of your life" has it right. (Of course comedian George Carlin says that "The day after tomorrow is the third day of the rest of your life.") We are "being" (product) and "becoming" (process) simultaneously. Our character is never *finally* formed.[3] Therefore, courage is not episodic but enduring; it is not a note but a melody; it is not a matter of a heroic minute but of a gallant life.

The topic of bravery in battle "comes with the territory" of discussing the profession of arms. I have had the honor over the years of speaking with many brave men. Most recently, at the University of San Diego, I talked with Vice Adm. James B. Stockdale, who spent seven and a half years as a prisoner of war during the Vietnam War, including four years in solitary confinement.[4] Heroes do not flinch from saying that they have been afraid, exhausted, melancholy; they admit to instances of defeat, depression, and despair. But the true heroes seem to have a remarkable quality of resilience, a powerful ability to resurrect themselves and reestablish the pattern of courage from which torture, pain, fatigue, and physical and mental anguish may momentarily divert them. Stockdale has taught those with the ears to hear many invaluable lessons, but among the most important, I believe, has been this: brutal and inhuman circumstances may cause the brave man temporarily to fail, but because of that man's core qualities, he will surely reconstruct himself and his circumstances.[5] Courage does not mean that people never fail or never sin; it means that they have the spiritual resources to try again and again and again and again, never admitting final defeat or ultimate subjugation. Courage, then, is for the long haul, not the short ride.

THE PURPOSE OF COURAGE

Aristotle believed that we become brave by doing brave acts. At the time of an act, *we are;* we do the act and *we become.* What we become, we are. The next time we encounter a challenge, we are better than we were before. This is a virtuous circle in much the same way that a vicious circle means failure leading to failure, resulting over time in a character of failure. "Now, the courageous man is dauntless as a human being," wrote Aristotle. "Hence he will fear what is fearful; but he will endure it in the right way and as reason directs for the sake of acting nobly." We return to the important idea that courage not does mean fearlessness; it means, rather, the resolve to deal with natural fear. "Accordingly, he is courageous who endures and fears the right things, for the right motive, in the right manner, and at the right time, and who displays confidence in a similar way. For a courageous man feels and acts according to the merits of each case and as reason guides him. . . . Thus it is for a noble end that a courageous man endures and acts as courage demands." Aristotle tells us that a reckless man is excessive (and foolish), and a coward defective, whereas a courageous man has the proper degree of courage.[6]

Aristotle's *good teacher* was Plato. In Plato's dialogue *The Apology,* Socrates (Plato's *good teacher*) appears before a jury of Athenians to defend himself against nonsense charges that he is corrupting Athenian youth. The unexamined life, Socrates tells his accusers and jurors, is not worth living. Perhaps, by pleading for mercy and admitting his "guilt," Socrates says, he might gain leniency. But that he cannot do:

> Neither in court nor in war ought I or anyone else to do anything and everything to contrive an escape from death. In battle [Socrates had been a brave soldier for Athens] it is often clear that a man might escape by throwing away his arms and by begging mercy from his pursuers; and there are many other means in every danger, for escaping death, if a man can bring himself to do and say anything and everything. No, gentlemen, the difficult thing is not to escape death, I think, but to escape wickedness—that is much more difficult, for that runs faster than death.

Condemned to death, Socrates asks of society only one thing:

> Punish my sons, gentlemen, when they grow up; give them this same pain I gave you, if you think they care for money or anything else before virtue; and if they have the reputation of being something when they are nothing, reproach them, as I reproach you, that they do not take care for what they should, and think they are something when they are nothing. . . .
> And now it is time to go, I to die, and you to live; but which of us goes to a better thing is unknown to all but God.[7]

It is in this sense that the book of Proverbs warns us, "The beginning of wisdom is the fear of the Lord" (9:10). Christianity tells us that perfect contrition for sin derives from love of God and sorrow from having offended Him; imperfect contrition, still desirable, derives from fear of eternal punishment. By the same token, courage is thus related to ends, to ultimate purposes, to higher standards beyond those of the moment. Can a criminal be courageous? I think the common response would be yes, a murderer in a shoot-out with police can demonstrate bravery. I disagree with that conclusion. Aristotle states that "many qualities have no name,"[8] and we encounter such a situation here. The murderer in a shoot-out with police may demonstrate a kind of *bravado* (a word that does not adequately capture the quality we seek to define), but not bravery; for bravery is related to noble ends and to virtue.

Courage helps us to act heroically and thus to escape wickedness (which we are to fear more than death). But it is good education and conscientious teachers, it is justice, and it is prudence and wisdom that enable us to understand wickedness. The murderer is wicked; consequently his apparently brave act in fighting police to the death is corrupt and vicious. It cannot be bravery because it serves an evil end. Did German soldiers in World War II lack bravery because they, if only indirectly, served the Nazi cause? Had the German army triumphed over the British, Russians, and Americans, Hitler's vile cause would have been advanced. We must conclude, therefore, that German soldiers, though often demonstrating competence, skill, and perhaps valor, could not demonstrate bravery in the sense understood by Aristotle. "Thus it is for a noble end that a courageous man endures and acts as courage demands."[9]

In 1978 in Guyana, the "Reverend" Jim Jones, whose flock had created Jonestown, were investigated by Rep. Leo J. Ryan of California. Cult members soon killed Ryan, three journalists, and one defecting cult member. Shortly afterward, Jones ordered the members of his cult to commit suicide. More than nine hundred persons, including Jones, died. Was Jones a leader? Was he to be revered (as in the word *reverend*)? Can we correctly describe Hitler as a heroic leader?[10] We can use the term *dictator* for Hitler and perhaps *tyrant* for Jones. We know that Jones and Hitler were false leaders because they pursued evil policies. We must similarly conclude that what appears to be bravery but is exhibited in an evil cause cannot be described as bravery, for bravery requires the wisdom and justice of moral discernment before valiant action. We conclude with Saint Thomas Aquinas that "the praise of fortitude is dependent upon justice."[11]

Honesty—in the sense of sincerity—may not be enough to mark the virtuous man, who must take the pains to enlighten his honesty (see the next section, "Moral Courage"). When one acts on the advice of conscience, it is not enough unless the conscience is well formed (see chapter 4). Valor that serves ignoble or base ends cannot accurately be described as courage in the classical sense. Here we encounter a difficult practical problem. Are we arguing that the average soldier, or even the young officer, acting heroically in the service of disgraceful ends, cannot be said to be brave? Every person, civilian or military, has the irrefrangible duty of seeking truth and applying its counsels. Soldiers have a clear legal and religious responsibility to obey higher authorities until that obedience transgresses the moral law.[12] If the state or one's superiors violate the moral or natural law, one must say no; to say yes with courage to a corrupt order (such as Calley's orders to his men at My Lai) does not alter the fact that one has consented to evil. The defense of following superior orders in the service of depravity is ordinarily no defense if one can reasonably be expected to discern the good (see chapter 4).

At the same time, there is in moral theology what is called *invincible ignorance,* which is "lack of knowledge, either of fact or law, for which a person is not morally responsible. This may be due to the difficulty of the object of the knowledge, or scarcity of evidence, or insufficient time or talent in the person, or any other factor for which he is not culpable."[13] The soldier on line, perhaps even the government civilian, may not be able to discover truth. In such cases, their resolute and valiant efforts to promote ends that are objectively in error cannot be said to be subjectively wrong, wicked, or sinful. Therefore, if a German officer knew Hitler was monstrous and followed orders valiantly, there is no bravery in his act.[14] But if a German soldier could not reasonably have known about the barbaric nature of the Nazi regime, we may accurately describe his valiant action in combat as brave.

The cardinal virtues of prudence or wisdom, justice or truthfulness, fortitude or courage, and temperance are truly one. That is what leads Josef Pieper to this judgment: "Prudence and justice precede fortitude. And that means, categorically: without prudence, without justice, there is no fortitude; only he who is just and prudent can also be brave; to be really brave is quite impossible without at the same time being prudent and just also."[15] "Fortitude without justice," remarked Saint Ambrose, "is a lever of evil."[16] Courage is not an end in itself but is a means of bringing about virtuous ends.

MORAL COURAGE

It is customary to recognize two kinds of courage, physical and moral. But the argument we have made is that all courage must be moral courage. The soldier trained to respond bravely on the battlefield may be, in fact, a "lever of evil" unless he is serving a good cause. Physical courage, unless it is consonant with high purpose, cannot be moral courage.

Moral courage may even prohibit physical courage. The bravest soldiers in Hitler's army may have been those who refused to fight.[17] This is hardly a blanket endorsement of pacifism, which I in fact reject, but it is a recognition of the fundamental duty we have of seeking truth and then conforming our actions to it. Both the seeking and the conforming may require great courage. Probably all of us have found ourselves in circumstances where our convictions demanded that we speak out for or against certain statements or policies, although we know that by doing so we may anger the group we are with. Such things happen in the councils of government, and they happen on high school sports teams. They happen when we confront racist remarks; they happen when we are with people who support positions we regard as immoral; they happen when our bosses tell us to do things that we believe are wrong. And often, too often, we sigh and go along. Over the course of time, the small concessions we make to please our friends (at the price of our principles) develop into a routine, a pattern, a character. People who "habitually violate moral norms often reach the point of *not* knowing what is right, because they are likely to resort to rationalization and close their eyes to the truth in order to subdue their guilt feelings without reforming their lives," point out ethicists Grisez and Shaw.[18]

Most of us betray the truth only by degrees. A few years ago, I learned of a federal prisoner who was at one time a judge in Louisiana. A criminal crowd approached him, asking him only to reduce a sentence he was about to give one of their gang and saying that there would be a great deal of money in the deal for him. They certainly did not expect him to try any legal tactics to get the criminal off, they told him, just to reduce the sentence a bit. The judge had a mortgage, car payments, tuition bills, and so on to pay. What was the harm? The pattern persisted for a few years until one day, the criminals told the judge to try to get somebody off the legal hook altogether. The judge protested, saying that he had never before been asked to do such a thing. "That was before," he was peremptorily told. Now he was owned by the gang—and he had better follow orders. In short course, he was caught, tried, and jailed. He had sold out a little at a time until he hardly knew right from wrong any more. The judge had not had any moral courage.[19] (That is not to say, however, that he is beyond redemption through the "corrections" process over which he once presided himself.)

Many years ago as an undergraduate student, I was in a fairly large course with a difficult final examination. I prepared assiduously for the exam. An unprepared friend of mine, sitting near me, asked me for help in the exam's objective portion. I hesitated. Then I helped him all I could, all the time knowing I was every bit as wrong as he was. I had had a presentiment of returning to the dorm, having refused my friend any help, only to be regarded as "selfish," a "do-gooder," and the like. Father Thomas Merton was entirely correct, I learned, when he said, "We are quite capable of being happy in the life [God] has provided for us, in which we can contentedly make our own way, helped by His grace. We are ashamed to do so. For we need one thing more than happiness: we need approval. And the need for approval destroys our capacity for happiness."[20] I lacked the moral courage at that time to do what I should have done—refuse my friend the "help" he unjustly sought. That exam—that experience—taught me a lesson that I have tried to put into practice ever since.

U.S. Army general Matthew B. Ridgway once explained this concept by saying that "physical courage is never in short supply in a fighting army. Moral courage sometimes is."[21] The ability to say what we mean and to mean what we say seems to shrink in the presence of our dissenting friends or our glowering boss. To get along, we go along. Stephen Carter has pointed out that "a person may be entirely honest without ever engaging in the hard work of discernment that integrity requires." He means that one can speak the truth as one sees it without bothering to determine whether it is true. Sincerity is necessary but not sufficient (there were sincere Nazis). Carter contends that integrity demands that we discern what is right from what is wrong; that we act on that discernment, regardless of personal cost; and that we say openly that we are acting from conviction.[22] That is the process of moral courage. In my own lectures, I have explained this process as "ponder, practice, and proclaim." Ridgway and Carter are saying essentially the same thing: in order to act virtuously, which is to say bravely, one must first ponder or discern or establish moral parameters. But going along is cheaper and easier and much less painful than thinking. It also can be chronic and addictive, leading to what Scripture terms "hardness of heart."[23] In any hierarchy—such as the armed services, industry, or even the ministry—people have a tendency to want to please colleagues and bosses, to say yes. There are times, however, when the modes of responsibility require us to say no. Again, Thomas Merton: "You must know when, how, and to whom to say 'no.' This involves considerable difficulty at times. You must not hurt people, or want to hurt them, yet you must not placate them at the price of infidelity to higher and more essential values."[24]

"Lives, Fortunes, and Sacred Honor"

When in 1776 the signers of the Declaration of Independence "mutually pledge[d] to each other [their] lives, [their] Fortunes, and [their] sacred Honor," they were promising to see their fight against English tyranny through until the end—to hang together, as Franklin put it, lest they all hang separately. Sacred honor is what moral courage is all about. The term *sacred honor* rings rather hollow today, however. It seems mawkish, maudlin, mushy. Today we talk little about such things—and are indeed suspicious of people who do. No one doubts for a moment the physical courage of the chiefs of staff who served the Vietnam-era presidents. But if H.R. McMaster is right, the chiefs, for mistaken reasons both personal and professional, could not bring themselves to say no when geostrategic reality required them to. President Johnson was lying to the American people, and the chiefs had a duty not to withhold the truth from Congress when they testified there. There were, in McMaster's apt and censorious phrase, "five silent men":

> The president's plan of deception depended on tacit approval or silence from the JCS [Joint Chiefs of Staff]. LBJ had misrepresented the mission of U.S. ground forces in Vietnam, distorted the views of the Chiefs to lend credibility to his decision against mobilization, grossly understated the numbers of troops General Westmoreland had requested, and lied to the congress about the monetary cost of actions already approved and of those awaiting final decision. The Chiefs did not disappoint the president. In the days before the president made his duplicitous public announcement concerning Westmoreland's request, the Chiefs, with the exception of commandant of the Marine Corps Greene, withheld from congressmen their estimates of the amount of force that would be needed in Vietnam. As he had during the Gulf of Tonkin hearings, Wheeler lent his support to the president's deception of congress. The "five silent men" on the Joint Chiefs made possible the way the United States went to war in Vietnam.[25]

Of these four-star generals and admirals, physical courage was no longer required, and most had doubtless demonstrated their valor in other places in other days. Now a higher order of courage was required, moral courage—the courage of "sacred honor"—and the ability to say no when circumstances required. In the powerful book *The Nightingale's Song,* Robert Timberg writes of five other men (John McCain, Jim Webb, Oliver North, Bud McFarlane, and John Poindexter), all of whom were graduates of the U.S. Naval Academy. Most of them demonstrated great physical courage—particularly McCain—but as the Iran-Contra scandal unfolded, "the Academy training that had helped propel North, McFarlane, and Poindexter into the White House had played a powerful role in landing them in the dock." Timberg perceptively writes, "At Annapolis and throughout their military careers they had been ingrained with the dictum that the wish of a superior officer was their command. Somewhere along the line, though, probably at the White House, a venue that has turned lesser men to fools, their common sense [moral courage?] deserted them. They knew there were times when a subordinate must say no to a superior, but as the Iran-Contra affair makes clear, their threshold was appallingly high." Timberg wanted them to ask, to keep asking, one main question: "We're not going to do anything stupid here, are we?"[26] That this is not confined to Vietnam or Iran-Contra is testified to by David McCormick, who suggests that the downsizing atmosphere of today's army is creating "junior and mid-career officers less willing to show initiative or to take well-conceived risks." In an era of smaller sizes in personnel and budgets, soldiers "feel competing pressures between flawless performance and moral and ethical behavior."[27]

Soldiers are trained—and expected—to be physically courageous.[28] But as Vietnam and Iran-Contra indicate, the lack of moral courage is likely to result in greater death and destruction than the want of physical courage. Unless the cardinal virtues of wisdom, justice, moral courage, and temperance are part of the soldier's education, the soldier courts disaster for himself or herself and for the republic.

But the same applies to civilian leaders. Our founding fathers knew the importance of moral courage. Walter Lippmann spoke perhaps more presciently than he knew when, almost fifty years ago, he wrote:

> With exceptions so rare that they are regarded as miracles
> and freaks of nature, successful democratic politicians are
> insecure and intimidated men. They advance politically

only as they placate, appease, bribe, seduce, bamboozle, or otherwise manage to manipulate the demanding and threatening elements in their constituencies. The decisive consideration is not whether the proposition is good but whether it is popular—not whether it will work well and prove itself but whether the active talking constituents like it immediately. Politicians rationalize this servitude by saying that in a democracy public men are the servants of the people.[29]

The courage to choose the ethical over the expedient, to serve the cause of principle over the desire of being popular—these are the heart and soul of sacred honor. "Having the numbers" may be important in business or athletics, but, as Fulton J. Sheen once pointed out,

The majority is not always right. Majority is right in the field of the relative, but not in the absolute. Majority is a legitimate test so long as voting is based on conscience and not on propaganda. Truth does not win when numbers alone become decisive. Numbers alone can decide a beauty queen, but not justice. Beauty is a matter of taste, but justice is tasteless. Right is still right if nobody is right, and wrong is still wrong if everybody is wrong. The first poll in the history of Christianity [in the choice of Barabbas (Matt. 27:15–26)] was wrong![30]

It was an American president (Andrew Jackson) who said that "one man with courage makes a majority." When I teach my course on core values at the Air War College, I have the officers in the seminar begin the course by reading the play *An Enemy of the People* by the Norwegian Henrik Ibsen. They wonder, at first, why I would choose such an old play, and one set in Scandinavia. It concerns a doctor who discovers that the town waters, popular among tourists and therefore a lucrative industry to the town's people, are polluted. The doctor is intent upon exposing the problem to save the health of people drinking the water. He meets strong resistance—even from his own brother. Although he expects truth to win out, he learns that polls and finances can seemingly subvert the truth. Doing what is right can often result in great personal sacrifice. The students also read Robert Bolt's fine play *A Man for All Seasons* about Sir Thomas More, who went to the gallows rather than accept King Henry VIII as the head of the church. "I die the king's good servant, but God's first," More is supposed to have said just before he was beheaded. Understanding the order of values in the context of virtue: is that not what sacred honor is all about?[31]

HABITUS

As we have seen, the Latin word *habitus* can be translated "habit," meaning repetitious and largely automatic behavior. There is, however, a subtle but important distinction between *habit,* as we ordinarily use the term, and *habitus* (which I use both in the singular and the plural, according to context), by which moral theologians refer to interior and "stable dispositions that develop the power of our faculties and render us capable of performing actions of high quality." The habitus should not "be confused with our ordinary understanding of habits—psychological mechanisms that diminish the moral commitment to an action."[32] A habit suggests a mechanized and inveterate reaction; we might say that a second baseman in baseball has a habit of pivoting in a certain way. *Habitus,* however, communicates the idea that the moral life, as Father Cessario explains it, "involves an educative and developmental process." Further: "The theologian, when he speaks about habitus as a quality, understands that quality refers to a real modification of a person's moral character."[33] The following quotation from ethicist Servais Pinckaers makes the point clearly: "Virtue is not a habitual way of acting, formed by the repetition of material acts and engendering in us a psychological mechanism. It is a personal capacity for action, the fruit of a series of fine actions, a power for progress and perfection." It is referred to by Pinckaers as "freedom for excellence." "At the heart of continuity and in its perfection, through the power of virtue, a man achieves works bearing the stamp of his unique quality as a moral person."[34]

The idea of habitus is, I think, critical to understanding the cardinal virtue of courage. An act of courage requires consideration. A mechanical or unreflective act of "courage"—a conditioned response like the baseball player's pivot at second base—may be a worthy effort, but it is not, properly speaking, courageous until it is (1) the fruit of judgment and (2) consistent with noble ends and standards. Habitus are dispositions, not regimented habits; these dispositions, or moral arrangements, are developed over time as a result of contemplation (and, some would add, grace). The virtuous man has not simple habits but an ethical constitution, which, like our written Constitution, is founded in fundamental principles but cautiously evolves over time. There are certain automatic procedures—often called checklists or SOPs (standard operating procedures)—that armed forces personnel can use for everything from clearing a jammed M16 rifle to resolving a problem in the cockpit of an F-16. In a sense, referring to these checklists is taught as a matter of habit. But aside from the Commandments, the Beatitudes, the modes of responsibility, and the human goods (which may be seen as "constitutional" ethical principles), the same person does not have a checklist to consult when making moral decisions. He must rely on his interior moral compass or habitus.

In one of the verses of the old and beautiful hymn "Faith of Our Fathers" by Frederick W. Faber (1814-1863), we read

> Our fathers chained in prisons dark
> Were still in heart and conscience free.
> And truly blessed would be our fate
> If we, like them, should die for thee.

Vice Admiral Stockdale and other political and religious prisoners over the centuries were, odd to say, truly free although "chained in prisons dark." They were still developing their habitus—"still in heart and conscience free." We have the habit of breathing; habitus—the stable disposition of our heart and conscience—leads us to ask why we breathe, what meaning is there for our suffering, for our lives, for the causes we embrace. Moral courage, then, is truly teleological. That is, we are courageous insofar as what we do is calculated—despite danger, pain, or estrangement—to bring about virtuous ends. "Truly blessed would be our fate [despite imprisonment, suffering, and death] if we, like [our fathers] should die for thee." If by "thee" is meant Jim Jones's pseudoreligion in Guyana, we have only pity for the nine hundred people who consumed Jones's poison. If by "thee," however, we are referring to the various genuine religions that people have died for or, indeed, to responsible political movements over the centuries, we have respect and reverence. When we speak of the soil upon which Jim Jones's charges died in 1978, we fairly cringe, recalling the terrible pictures. When we think of Lincoln's reference at Gettysburg in 1863 to the ground "consecrated" by "the brave men, living and dead, who struggled here," we think of that reference as being entirely appropriate and highly eloquent. If we live and die for genuine virtue, we develop the stable disposition, the cast of mind, and the character to say no when no must be said.

Lord Charles Moran, who fought in World War I and served later as Winston Churchill's physician, offers this analysis of courage on the strength of his experience, and no paraphrasing of mine can do it justice:

> I contend that fortitude in war has its roots in morality . . . and that war itself is but one more test—the supreme and final test if you will—of character. Courage can be judged apart from danger only if the social significance and meaning of courage is known to us, namely that a man of character in peace becomes a man of courage in war. He cannot be selfish in peace and yet be unselfish in war. Character as Aristotle taught is a habit [here he should use the term *habitus*], the daily choice of right instead of wrong; it is a moral quality which grows to maturity in peace and is not suddenly developed on the outbreak of war. For war . . . has no power to transform[;] it merely exaggerates the good and evil that are in us, till it is plain for all to read; it cannot change, it exposes. Man's fate in battle is worked out before war begins. For his acts in war are dictated not by courage, nor by fear, but by conscience, of which war is the final test. The man whose quick conscience is the secret of his success in battle has the same clear cut feelings about right and wrong before war makes them obvious to all. If you know a man in peace, you know him in war.[35]

CASE STUDY

On the morning of 16 March 1968, U.S. Army warrant officer Hugh Thompson, crew chief Spec. 4 Glenn Andreotta, and door gunner Spec. 4 Lawrence Colburn were flying their helicopter over the Vietnamese village of My Lai. They were to witness one of the most barbaric acts ever committed by American forces, the massacre at My Lai, in which more than five hundred Vietnamese civilians were mercilessly slaughtered.[36] Thompson and his two enlisted men saw a teenage Vietnamese girl lying wounded in a rice paddy. Thompson popped green smoke to mark her position and radioed for help. On the ground an American soldier ran to her. Thompson expected the soldier to administer first aid; instead, to Thompson's horror, the soldier killed her. As Thompson, Andreotta, and Colburn watched the butchery of My Lai—with not a single enemy soldier in sight—Thompson decided to act. He saw a group of U.S. soldiers chasing about ten Vietnamese who were fleeing to a makeshift bunker. Thompson set his helicopter down in front of the advancing Americans and gave his gunner a simple, direct order. If the Americans attempted to harm the villagers, Colburn was to shoot the Americans. The group of Vietnamese was saved. As Thompson took off, he passed over a heap of bodies. Andreotta saw something move in the pile of carnage. Thompson landed, and Andreotta walked into the virtual charnel house, pulling to safety a bloodied but unhurt three-year-old boy. (Andreotta was killed in battle three weeks later.)[37]

The Pentagon's final report on the massacre praised the actions of Thompson and his men. Awarded the distinguished Flying Cross for his actions at My Lai, Thompson refused it, believing that the army was trying to buy his silence. The citation to accompany the award was cryptically worded, failing, in the words of one reporter, "to note that the uniforms worn by the hostiles confronted by Thompson and his crew were American."[38]

Thompson subsequently testified against Lieutenant Calley, the commander of troops responsible for the massacre at My Lai. Colburn later said, "We were dishonored for telling the truth [in the hearings]." In 1998 Thompson and Colburn returned to Vietnam for ceremonies and to meet the little boy, now fully grown, whom Andreotta had pulled out of the pile of corpses. The American ambassador to Vietnam, by the way, declined the opportunity to participate in the ceremony: "Neither the policy objectives of the United States nor the current relations between the U.S. and Socialist Republic of Vietnam would be served by Embassy participation."[39]

A Clemson University professor and former army officer, David Egan, had begun a personal campaign to have Thompson and Colburn properly recognized and rewarded for their moral (and physical) bravery in Vietnam.[40] Such officers as Col. Anthony Hartle and Lt. Col. Kevin Clement of the army resolutely supported the Egan initiative. Army leaders agreed, if reluctantly, to the award. The official suggestion was that Thompson and Colburn receive their medals in private, thus not drawing attention to My Lai all over again. Frustrated, Lieutenant Colonel Clement E-mailed his superiors, "I thought the criteria [*sic*] we applied was supposed to [be] . . . 'Is it fair to the soldier?'—not, 'How will this play in the press?'"[41] Thompson wanted the award to be presented at the Vietnam Memorial in Washington, D.C. "They denied the request. They said it would be too cold to stand outside in the winter."[42]

Finally, the army relented. On 6 March 1998 Hugh Thompson and Lawrence Colburn were publicly honored with the Soldier's Medal at the Vietnam Memorial in Washington, D.C. Said Chaplain Donald Shea at the emotional ceremony, "Remembering a dark point in time, we are now a richer nation as their personal heroic service is woven into the fabric of our history."[43] Engraved on the wall at the site of the medal presentation was the name of Spec 4 Glenn Andreotta, who had waded into the carnage of My Lai and carried a child to safety. The U.S. Army now uses the story of Thompson, Colburn, and Andreotta to teach its soldiers about the meaning of courage.

8

Temperance and the Profession of Arms

Moderation is an ostentatious proof of our strength of character.
—*La Rochefoucauld*

[The people] have a right, an indisputable, unalienable,
indefeasible right to that most dreaded and envied kind of
knowledge—I mean of the character and conduct of their rulers.
—*John Adams*

"Temperance," we are solemnly instructed, "is the moral virtue that moderates the attraction of pleasures and provides balance in the use of created goods. It ensures the will's mastery over instincts and keeps desires within the limits of what is honorable. The temperate person directs the sensitive appetites toward what is good and maintains a healthy discretion."[1] One dictionary defines *temperance* as "moderation in action, thought, or feeling: restraint" and as "habitual moderation in the indulgence of the appetites or passions: self-control."[2] One of the chief difficulties we encounter in discussing the word *temperance* is determining what it means, who agrees with that definition, and under what conditions the word has the agreed-upon definition. Thus the world was confronted recently by the appalling spectacle of the president of the United States questioning what the word *is* means.[3] One is reminded of Lewis Carroll's *Through the Looking Glass,* in which we read: "'When *I* use a word,' Humpty Dumpty said, in a rather scornful tone, 'it means just what I choose it to mean—neither more nor less.'"[4] Thus, what is a temptation to me is of little moment to you; what is gluttony to you is merely gustatory satisfaction to me; what is lust to you is merely natural sexual desire to me. And who is to differentiate the one from the other?

APPETITES AND STANDARDS

Let us imagine a society in which lying—even under oath—is either common or, in fact, the norm. Chaos would reign: there would be no way of telling truth from falsity, fact from fiction. The expectation of truth-telling enables a society to conduct not only the affairs of state but also the ordinary matters of everyday business and personal interaction. This is not to say, of course, that lies do not occur or even that lying is not a frequent occurrence in politics and in personal affairs. But we may nonetheless confidently assert that lying is generally regarded as an exception to the norm of truth-telling; even a gang of criminals must be able to count upon one another in the execution of an illegal scheme. The norm, the expectation, the standard of truth-telling, is fundamental to human organization.

In much the same way, as the philosopher Alasdair MacIntyre has written, "it is a logically necessary condition for any group of beings to be recognized as a human society that they should possess a language . . . [with] shared rules."[5] If, for example, someone says "It is snowing," we have a common understanding of what that means. Now one may say "snowing" when I think a blizzard has begun; another might say "snowing" when you perceive only a few frozen flakes falling from the sky. But *snowing* conjures up a fairly uniform meteorological expectation. If one announced "It is snowing" on a blistering hot July afternoon in Alabama, we would conclude that the person was joking or really had no understanding of the word *snowing*.

So it is with many of the concepts associated with the virtue of temperance. Sybarites or hedonists (those whose sole concern is their own sensual pleasure) can do many things, but being a reliable military officer is not among them. If one's sole reference point for determining good from evil is one's stomach or genitalia, we may be confident that such a person cannot well and wisely serve in the profession of arms. The profession of arms—like any human society—has certain arrangements and accommodations of language that help us to quickly and reliably sort out the virtuous and the vicious, the honorable and the shameful.

A spate of recent cases, well known to anyone who reads a daily newspaper, testifies to the problems that intemperance—in this case, the subordination of one's reason to one's genitalia—has caused. The most infamous example, of course, is the 1991 Tailhook Association meeting at the Hilton Hotel in Las Vegas, during which numerous women were sexually harassed, groped, and otherwise mistreated by drunken male officers. The scandal affected even the retirement of Adm. Frank Kelso, the chief of Naval Operations, when the Senate voted 54-43 to permit Kelso to retire with four stars instead of the three stars demanded by some who alleged that Kelso had witnessed misconduct at the hotel but had done nothing about it.[6] At the army's Aberdeen Proving Ground in Maryland, at least fifty women soldiers filed official complaints of sexual abuse, implicating one officer and twenty noncommissioned officers. Five women subsequently said that military investigators tried to coerce statements from them. On 29 April 1997, Staff Sgt. Delmar Simpson was convicted of raping six women trainees under his command in 1995 and 1996. Abuses by other drill sergeants at the post were described as "rampant." The Speaker of the U.S. House of Representatives ordered a review of sexual harassment prevention programs in all the services.[7] These are only two tragic and criminal illustrations of what happens when reason yields to illicit passion. Other examples abound[8]—including the case study with which this chapter concludes—and involve flag-rank officers such as Rear Adm. R.M. Mitchell Jr. (relieved for allegedly making repeated advances to a female subordinate), Brig. Gen. Stephen Xenakis (removed from command of army medical operations in the Southwest after being accused of an "improper relationship" with a civilian nurse who was taking care of his ailing wife),[9] Brig. Gen. Robert T. Newell (demoted to colonel after being accused of inappropriate contact with a female subordinate), and others such as the male guards at an army post who harassed a woman guard (the army settled by paying the woman $60,000) and a male navy chief petty officer who groped a female sailor (the male sailor was jailed, fined, demoted, and then discharged).[10]

There cannot be the slightest doubt that intemperance ruins careers, marriages, and lives and that its impact on national security itself is palpable.[11] The soldier, sailor, airman, or marine who is interested in his own illicit and selfish sexual gratification is a failed officer because he or she is, first, a failed human being. That does not necessarily mean, however, that such people are beyond military, let alone personal, redemption and rehabilitation.

Three officers whose careers suffered or ended because of indiscretions or, in one case, guilt by association include Gen. Joseph Ralston of the air force, Maj. Gen. John Longhouser of the army, and Cmdr. Robert E. Stumpf of the navy. In 1993 Commander Stumpf was cleared of any wrongdoing in the Tailhook scandal. In May 1994, the Senate committee approved his promotion to captain, but the navy mistakenly failed to send his Tailhook file to the armed services committee. The panel later reviewed Stumpf's file and asked Navy Secretary John Dalton to strike Stumpf's name, which Dalton did. A navy selection board in March 1996 renominated Stumpf for captain, and Dalton supported the promotion. On 8 November 1996, however, Stumpf, former leader of the Blue Angels, resigned.[12] Longhouser, commander of the Aberdeen Proving Ground, had had an affair in 1992 while separated from his wife; questioned about the affair, he resigned.[13] Ralston, virtually assured of being the next chairman of the Joint Chiefs of Staff, removed himself from consideration for that position after admitting that he had had an affair with a civilian woman at the CIA in 1984.[14] At this writing, General Ralston continues to serve on active duty. Were Ralston, Longhouser, and Stumpf victims, or did their punishments fit their "crimes"?

On the basis of available evidence, one seems justified in concluding that Commander Stumpf had been unfairly tainted by the broad brush of Tailhook. Although adultery is clearly wrong, one can argue that the punishment of Longhouser and Ralston was inconsistent with the offense. There is, in traditional Christian morality, a three-part formula for forgiveness and rehabilitation: confession to the appropriate person, contrition, and firm purpose of amendment. In the cases of Longhouser and Ralston, there is no evidence of which I am aware that they lied, disobeyed orders, or exhibited a pattern of infidelity reckless beyond measure. This is not to excuse the adultery. It is to say that where the national security or command integrity is not affected; where such instances are clearly family matters; and where the offense is limited to a single and short-term occurrence (and not habitual and seemingly endless adulterous assignations), we can perhaps believe that the truly repentant might be well instructed to "go and sin no more."

About drunkenness, there should be little debate. Recently, for example, a marine corporal on Okinawa was arrested for drunken driving in a traffic accident during which he is alleged to have knocked a woman off her motor bike. The woman subsequently died because of injuries sustained in the accident. This episode occurred about three years after three American servicemen on that island gang raped a twelve-year-old girl.[15] Crimes of this sort make all the more vital the teaching of such values as these, taken from the "Little Blue Book" of U.S. Air Force core values: "Those who allow their appetites to drive them to make sexual overtures to subordinates [and twelve-year-old girls] are unfit for military service. Likewise, the excessive consumption of alcohol casts doubt on an individual's fitness, and when such persons are found to be drunk and disorderly, all doubts are removed."[16]

Although we must concede that there may be differences in degree when we discuss, say, gluttony, there are unlikely to be differences in kind. That is, overeating may simply be that—overeating; some may, not without good reason, call overeating gluttony. Others would reserve *gluttony* to describe a pattern of overeating resulting, predictably, in being seriously overweight. But almost all of us would agree that when we observe the following, we know it is defective or wrong (or disgusting): "Watch a gluttonous man at his food. . . . Only occasionally does he look up at his companions with a glazed look. His mouth has only one function, as an orifice into which to push his food. Now and then he may grunt at what someone has said. Otherwise he stuffs. He is like a hog at its swill. . . . He crams, gorges, wolfs, and bolts. He might as well be alone. As with all the sins, Gluttony makes us solitary. We place ourselves apart, even at a table of sharing."[17]

There is likely to be difference of opinion, too, about when erotic craving constitutes lust. At what point does natural and normal sexual desire turn into disordered, frenetic, and insatiable sexual urge? We might disagree on the number of instances required for us to call a pattern of activity lust—once again, this is a disagreement about degree. But I think we can reach consensus about what lust is (agreement about kind). Those who are governed by their gonads are filled with lust. Lust is defined by one source as the "disordered desire for or inordinate enjoyment of sexual pleasure."[18] Words, as always, are imperfect means of communication. What is "disordered"? What is "inordinate"? Although there would be strong dispute in today's world about the exact nature of lust, there is little question that expressions of lust such as rape must be universally condemned. That is, in essence, the principal point I want to make here: we may well disagree over the precise meanings of what is temperate or intemperate. But in the case of clear and extensive departures from the norm, we remain capable of saying, "This action is clearly contrary to restraint and to self-control; it is disordered and inordinate. It is wrong."

In a powerful essay that first appeared early in 1968, the philosopher Will Herberg asked, "What is the moral crisis of our time?" He answered: "Briefly, I should say that the moral crisis of our time consists primarily not in the widespread violation of accepted moral standards— . . . when has any age been free of that?—but in the repudiation of those very moral standards themselves."[19] Peter Kreeft subsequently agreed: "We have lost objective moral law for the first time in history. The philosophies of moral positivism (that morality is posited or made by man), moral relativism, and subjectivism have become for the first time not a heresy for rebels but the reigning orthodoxy of the intellectual establishment. University faculty and media personnel overwhelmingly reject belief in the notion of any universal and objective morality."[20] If there is no standard for judging the temperate as against the intemperate, then temperance is a wholly meaningless concept.

Imagine a Hollywood where no movie approvingly featured fornication (sexual intercourse between unmarried people); imagine a college campus where drunkenness was publicly held up to scorn as an intemperate, disordered use of alcoholic beverage. Movies—even "family" movies—routinely feature fornication; it is practically de rigueur on many campuses to drink to excess after sporting events or during social activities. The sole purpose of many nonprescription drugs is to achieve a state of intoxication. But consider these two paragraphs, for example, from a religious text:

> The virtue of temperance disposes us *to avoid every kind of excess:* the abuse of food, alcohol, tobacco, or medicine. Those incur grave guilt who, by drunkenness or a love of speed, endanger their own and others' safety on the road, at sea, or in the air.
>
> The *use of drugs* inflicts very grave damage on human health and life. Their use, except on strictly therapeutic grounds, is a grave offense. Clandestine production of and trafficking in drugs are scandalous practices . . . gravely contrary to the moral law.[21]

Is that the "moral law" to which Professor Herberg was implicitly referring? Is there a standard, a norm, an expectation that certain types of conduct—or the use or abuse of certain goods or substances—may be wrong, or even shameful?

AN "END" TO GUILT AND SHAME

In a recent book about shame, James Twitchell explains how the erosion of language indicates a deterioration of morality in the United States. Thus "relief" becomes "welfare," which in turn becomes "entitlement." "Wrong" becomes "inappropriate." "Bad habits" become "lifestyle choices," and "illegitimacy" turns into "nonmarital childbearing." "Promiscuous" becomes "sexually active" and "heinous killer" becomes "victim of an abusive family." Twitchell makes a point that is critically important: "Make shameful acts repeatedly public and they soon become shameless." Of the argument that calling an act shameful makes the accused person uncomfortable, Twitchell writes: "Of course it makes the individual feel bad. But it does so in the name of a higher social good. Shame is the basis of individual responsibility and the beginnings of social conscience. It is where decency comes from."[22] Temperance is concerned with shame. There can be no temperance if there is no shame, for shame is concerned with how one feels after recognizing that his or her actions have transgressed an established moral norm. For example, if there is no permanent moral order—no Commandments, for example— there is no sin. If we can dispose of the idea of a moral order, then we can do what we please, so long as we do not wind up in jail because of our choices. (There is still the matter of public law to be dealt with.) As Fyodor Dostoyevsky had one of his characters in *The Brothers Karamazov* say, if there were nothing eternal, then "everything would be lawful, even cannibalism."[23] In short, the ideas of shame and sin are based squarely upon the idea of responsibility; abolish it and the notion that we have a duty to something beyond our own pleasure is simultaneously destroyed.

If, as Charles Sykes has written, we are becoming a nation of "victims," then responsibility and shame, the moral order and sin, and the very idea of temperance are outmoded and rather silly. Writes Sykes, "As it becomes increasingly clear that misbehavior can be redefined as disease, growing numbers of the newly diseased have flocked to groups like Gamblers Anonymous, Pill Addicts Anonymous, S-Anon ('relatives and friends of sex addicts'), Nicotine Anonymous, Youth Emotions Anonymous, Unwed Parents Anonymous, Emotional Health Anonymous,

Debtors Anonymous, Workaholics Anonymous, Dual Disorders Anonymous, Batterers Anonymous, Victims Anonymous, and Families of Sex Offenders Anonymous."[24] Perhaps, if we truly are a nation of victims, then the ministrations of the clergy amount to no more than so much superstitious nonsense. It is past time, some might argue, to replace priest with psychiatrist, to substitute mental health clinics for ministers' homilies. We do not have to deal with evil and sin but with psychiatric maladjustment and psychic infirmity. Thus we are barraged with terms such as "posttraumatic stress disorder, antisocial personality, identity crisis, libido, repressed, obsessive-compulsive, sadomasochistic, castration complex, acting out, introversion, phallic symbol, Oedipus complex, psychopathic deviate, seasonal affective disorder, penis envy, defense mechanism, inferiority complex, midlife crisis, authoritarian personality, sublimation, transference, death wish, projection, accident-prone, social maladjustment, transient situational disturbances, sleep disorders, the immature personality."[25]

On the shelves of practically any bookstore today, one can find a bevy of "New Age" writings utterly free of such notions as the Ten Commandments, the Sermon on the Mount, the Spiritual and Corporal Works of Mercy, and the like. One writer reports that his students, working together in one class at a well-known Catholic university, were unable to list the Ten Commandments; none of the students had ever heard of the Seven Corporal Works of Mercy;[26] and to many of the students *abstinence* and *chastity* were new words.[27] These days, we substitute psychiatric nostrums that comfort us with the knowledge that we are not responsible for our urges and appetites; that we are the victims of society; that we cannot help ourselves—and that we should feel no guilt for our transgressions (if there are any transgressions).

THE PROFANE OVER THE SACRED

The well-known sociologist Alan Wolfe contends in a recent book that "middle-class Americans have never let God command them in ways seriously in conflict with modern beliefs." He says that today "middle-class Americans no longer believe that right and wrong provide unerring guidelines for informing them about how to lead their lives."[28] A more devastating ethical indictment of our country I can scarcely imagine. "In the whole of philosophy," wrote Prof. E.F. Schumacher, "there is no subject in greater disarray than ethics. Anyone asking the professors for the bread of guidance or how to conduct himself, will receive not even a stone but just a torrent of 'opinion.'"[29] If we have fully and finally entered a time when the only real guide we have toward the understanding of right and wrong is the appeasement of our appetites and the satiation of our urges, all that we can say of temperance is that it is so much drivel.

"A shame rule of thumb [writes Twitchell]: if you do it in private, if covering/uncovering it is important, or if the act is surrounded by a lexicon of expletives and euphemisms, you can guess that shame is near. When shame fails, disgust ensues."[30] That captures a key to understanding temperance. If an action is one that decent people would deplore, it is no doubt intemperate. But of course that is a circular argument. It says little more than that decency is temperance and temperance is decency. And whose notion of either *decency* or *temperance* is to prevail in this age in which everyone defines his own virtue? "There is one thing a professor can be absolutely certain of: almost every student entering the university believes, or says he believes, that truth is relative," wrote the late Allan Bloom.[31] If all virtue depends upon private tastes and personal pleasures, and if there are no universal moral norms, standards, or criteria, then there is no temperance.

But all that is good and decent and honorable and true cannot be vanquished, for it is the essence of genuine learning, which persists on some campuses today in much the same way that the monasteries preserved learning during the Dark Ages. "Whatever is true, whatever is honorable, whatever is just, whatever is pure, whatever is lovely, whatever is gracious, if there is any excellence, if there is anything worthy of praise, think about these things" (Phil. 4:8). These are the things that constitute temperance, and their contemplation and execution are what liberal learning was once about—and must again be about. For temperance has to do with knowing and doing what is right.

Temperance tells us that we have limitations and that in learning the nature of those limitations, we have both divine and human guidance. The idea of temperance reaches to the ancient Greeks, who understood the idea of temperance as being "of sound mind." The Delphic Code instructed the Greeks "Know thyself," do or have "nothing in excess," and "Think mortal [not self-aggrandizing] thoughts." Temperate heroes of classical Greek drama observed the limits imposed by social and religious guides; catastrophe awaited the man whose self-assertion led him to ignore those limits. Aeschylus and Sophocles, for example, observed that defects in temperance led to both personal and political disaster. Euripides, as Helen North tells us, saw the basic meaning of temperance as "self-restraint"; "only now does it regularly have such connotations as chastity, sobriety, continence, in preference to the older implications—good sense, soundness of mind, sanity—although these are by no means forgotten."[32]

Plato saw Socrates as the embodiment of temperance (especially in the dialogue *Charmides*) and discussed the four cardinal virtues in *The Laws* (1.631C). Aristotle saw temperance as the mean between excess and defect. Certain traditional Roman values—chastity or modesty, moderation, frugality or economy—resembled the Greek notion of temperance, and Cicero helped to transplant the Greek notion to Rome. Christianity similarly embraced temperance, rooting it in the ideas of purity, chastity, sobriety, and self-denial and in "the recognition of the example of Christ and His Blessed Mother as the supreme justification for the practice of temperance."[33]

NOBLE THINGS THAT WE KNOW

There are those who might question that understanding of temperance. Who says we should refrain from orgies of lust, drugs, drink, and the like? Who says that they are "indecent"? Church and biblical sources will be dismissed by some; the record of history that says depravity leads to destruction will be dismissed by others; a few will contend, with the twisted logic of moral anarchy, that "anything goes" and that every man makes his own truth. As the philosopher Ed. L. Miller has written, "From a purely logical standpoint not everything can be argued or there would never be an end to the arguing. A long time ago Aristotle pointed out that every argument finally rests on something that cannot be proved, and that it is the mark of an uneducated person not to realize that. There must be . . . a last outpost or final court of appeal." Miller calls this *foundationalism.*[34] There are some good and kind and decent and noble things that we know.

As Professor Budziszewski of the University of Texas has written, natural law "*is* written on the heart, for that makes it a standard for believers and unbelievers alike; not only is it right for all, but at some level it is known to all."[35] There are very many ethical issues of great importance, for instance, that I am happy to discuss and debate with friends, colleagues, and students. But among them is not the issue of whether child pornography ought to be legal or permissible. That is not a conversation that I will have, for the very subject is so morally indefensible that it does not merit the dignity of discussion. Much the same may be said about rape. Is there someone who will defend the practice—except, of course, for the twisted souls who want to appear on daytime television shows to gain a fleeting moment of fame at any cost? Liberal education rightly calls upon us to have open minds; but liberal education never insists upon empty heads—or blighted souls. Merely because we do not know everything does not mean that we do not know some things. When one hears that "lust is good," "drugs are mind-expanding," "date-rape is acceptable here," or "truth is what you make it," we are listening to the mantra of a sickness of the soul.

One may reasonably argue, moreover, that widespread personal and political departure from temperance is among the chief causes for the ultimate failure of the Roman republic. A nation that is rotting on the inside cannot long resist pressures exerted against it from the outside. By the same token, a person whose character is flawed by intemperance will not long be able to resist the temptations to which the flesh is heir. Many problems in contemporary political and military affairs derive from personal defects in what is best understood as temperance. When one drinks to excess, engages in gluttony, fornicates, and commits adultery, his actions will almost certainly lead to undesired consequences. The excuse that "everybody does it" is demonstrably untrue; and not everyone who fails morally cavalierly excuses himself or herself, claiming to be a "victim." One aspect of leadership is always the setting of a decent, if not noble, example. And drunkenness, gluttony, and lust are, after all, indecent behavior; they disqualify people—or most certainly should—from positions of power, authority, and influence.

Personal and Private Morality

An officer who is intemperate will almost inevitably find himself in circumstances that call into question his character. Is it true that one can have a "character defect" but still be a good commander, a good leader, or a good professional person? Let us take the case of a surgeon who routinely commits adultery. What is the impact, if any, of his adulterous relationships upon his surgical or medical skills? Suppose a military leader is similarly intemperate; does that suggest that his military judgment is somehow impaired? Is history not filled with examples of bad men who were good commanders? Actually, this question is rooted in an old philosophical debate about the unity of virtues.[36] Does a defect in one virtue spill over into others? Or is there a division between "private" virtue and "public" virtue?

Some philosophers hold that there is indeed such a distinction and argue that it is well that there is. For how can anyone be expected to be excellent at everything? The good teacher may be only a modest success as a parent and even worse as a shade-tree mechanic or home carpenter. The man who is a great golfer may not be a good driver of cars or may not be talented at bridge or chess. The good college lecturer may make up terrible exams or be inept at personally counseling students. Philosopher Thomas Nagel, regretting what he terms a "condition of total publicity," argues that one can be noble in public life even as he is weak or cruel in private life. Some point out that leaders with scrupulous characters may be the enemies of effective politics, which often requires seemingly unprincipled action. But Garry Wills insists that a "leader's inner life is a crucible in which he creates a will for public use." And journalist Miriam Horn asserts that "a politics steeped in the personal is reduced to gossip, but severed entirely from the personal, it becomes nothing but meaningless poses."[37]

We are not discussing skills, either personal or professional; we are concerned with virtue itself. There is a clear difference between not being comfortable or particularly competent with, say, academic counseling (in which case the professor may work hard to improve his skill or refer students to better counselors) and attempting to seduce students when they seek academic advice. If one has no wisdom or courage, one is unlikely to be able to resist the temptations of too much liquor, too much food, or illicit sex. If one has no sense of justice or truthfulness, one is unlikely to deal with such sins, make restitution, and have a firm purpose of amendment. Instead, we may expect self-rationalization, lies, and continued duplicities. I think it is possible, perhaps even probable, that the doctor with the defective character will perform a brilliant surgical operation today—or tomorrow, or perhaps even next month or next year. But over the course of time, his moral cancer will metastasize; the corruption will spread. Unless the doctor takes his own moral medicine, his prospects for improvement are slim. That his character corrosion will sooner or later spill over into his professional practice is almost certain. Philosopher Tom Morris told of a man who, in conversation with him, said that there was, on the one hand, private virtue and, on the other, public virtue, arguing, "I wear one hat at the office and another at home." Morris responded, "Yes, but you wear them both on the same head." Says Morris: "One of the great dangers we face in the modern world is an inappropriate compartmentalization of our lives. We can draw a distinction between the public and the private, between what is professional and what is personal, but I've come to believe that the most fundamental virtues and principles are the same."[38]

By the same token, the military officer who is a liar or a cheat or a thief may well be a strategic genius. I argue, however, that these are exceptions to the rule. What we continually do is what we essentially are; correlatively, what we essentially are will express itself in what we continually do. The officer who is a personal degenerate either is, or will soon become, a professional degenerate. This point was made many years ago by Hans J. Morgenthau, the noted professor of international politics, who was shocked to learn the reaction of students at Columbia University when one of their professors (Charles Van Doren) was fired for participating in a national TV quiz show scam. Professor Van Doren had received answers to the questions he was being asked but put on a charade, pretending to agonize over the question and sometimes answering it correctly with only seconds remaining until his time ran out. Discovered, Van Doren excused himself by contending that he had been involved in an entertainment enterprise; Columbia saw the matter differently and terminated his contract. Van Doren's students were outraged and wrote a bitter letter of complaint about his having been fired. Morgenthau responded to the students by telling them that a teacher represents truth all the time, not just during an hour-long class.

> The arguments of the good teacher and of teaching not being concerned with substantive truth go together. You [Columbia students] assume . . . that the teacher is a kind of intellectual mechanic who fills your head with conventionally approved and required knowledge, as a filling-station attendant fills a tank with gas. You don't care what the teacher does from 10 A.M. to 9 A.M. as long as he gives you from 9 to 10 A.M. the knowledge he has been paid to transmit. You recognize no relation between a teacher's general attitude toward the truth and his way of transmitting knowledge, because you do not recognize an organic relation between transmitted knowledge and an objective,

immutable truth. . . . The teacher . . . is not only the re-
corder and transmitter of what goes by the name of knowledge in a particular time and place, but he is also and
foremost the guardian and augmentor of a permanent
treasure. This is not a part-time job to be performed during
certain hours without relation to what goes on before and
after. . . . this is a profession which requires the dedication
and ethos of the whole man. Of such a man, it must be
expected that he be truthful not only between 9 and 10 A.M.
when he teaches, but always.[39]

WHEN TOLERANCE IS INTOLERABLE

G.K. Chesterton once suggested that tolerance is the virtue of those who
believe in nothing. To many, there is little to choose between being tolerant and being indifferent. It is, in fact, our responsibility to judge. But
William Bennett contends that *judgment* is a word that is "out of favor
these days." Nonetheless, "it remains a cornerstone of democratic self-
government. It is what enables us to hold ourselves, and our leaders, to
high standards. It is how we distinguish between right and wrong, noble
and base, honor and dishonor." With regard to the erosion of the standards we need in order to pass wise judgment, he warns that "if we do
not confront the soft relativism that is now described as a virtue, we will
find ourselves morally and intellectually disarmed."[40] We must not excuse the inexcusable, pardon the unpardonable, or accept the unaccept-
able in the name of tolerance.[41] "True tolerance is not the act of tolerating;
it is the art of knowing when and how to tolerate. It is not forbearance
from judgment, but the fruit of judgment," writes J. Budziszewski.[42]

     With regard to temperance, there are certain practical standards
that may be applied in particular cases. Is one driving under the influence of drugs or alcohol? There is a blood alcohol test that supplies an
answer. Is one so given to gustatory pleasure that he is seriously overweight? There are certain weight and measurement standards employed
by the insurance industry and by the armed forces that give an answer. Is
one so consumed by sexual urges and appetites that he cannot act within
national customary codes of conduct? But all of these things are subject
to challenge. Perhaps some actually can drive without impairment even
after having several drinks. Perhaps being "overweight" is a matter only

of subjective and prejudiced opinion. Perhaps marital fidelity is anachronous and inconsistent with "progressive" values. Are there truly transhistorical or metacultural standards? Of course, there is disagreement on that question, but for the profession of arms at least the answer is clear.[43] There is an ultimate criterion by which to judge private tastes and personal actions: combat readiness and combat effectiveness. The profession of arms exists to deter and, if necessary, to wage and win wars. Actions of service members that detract from that imperative are intolerable. Drunkenness, gluttony, adultery, and similar sins—I will not shy away from the term—substantially depreciate and decrease combat readiness. Thus, their prosecution is not a matter of a commander's "religious agenda" but of his legal responsibility to ensure that his command is ready for combat or for combat support operations.

By law commanders not only must be good examples of "virtue, honor, patriotism, and subordination"; they are also required to be "vigilant" in monitoring the conduct of their subordinates and to "suppress all dissolute and immoral practices."[44] Writes James Kitfield, "From their first day at a service academy, for instance, cadets are still indoctrinated in the traditional military values of duty, honor and integrity. They sign honor pledges—'I will not lie, cheat or steal, or tolerate those who do'— and accept a moral code that harks back to the Old Testament, condemning adultery, homosexual behavior, drunkenness and other 'conduct unbecoming an officer' as grounds for dismissal."[45] Groups of greedy, self-indulgent, and pleasure-seeking service members will not only fail to be good people; they will fail to be successful warriors. The intemperate person is ipso facto the failed soldier.

None of this means that we human beings will not make mistakes or that we will be free from sin. In sadness but in honest self-judgment, we must all admit in the privacy of our hearts and souls that we have failed in too many ways to be what we should. The decent person, however, has the integrity—the temperance—to recognize his errors, to make up for them as best he can, and to try never to repeat them. Good people do not expect never to make mistakes; but good people expect always to learn from their mistakes. Remorse, restitution, and recommitment are the hallmarks of the decent man. If it is at all true that we are what we habitually do and that we habitually do what we are—and Aristotle told us essentially that more than two thousand years ago—the surgeon or the officer who is viscerally corrupt in one major area of his personal life can be expected soon to be so in his professional life. Were it otherwise, service academies, ROTC, and Officer Candidate School could easily dispense with teaching lessons in character.

In his book *The Virtues,* philosopher Peter Geach has argued that temperance is "a humdrum, common-sense matter."[46] And so it should be; but it is not. Moral theologian Romanus Cessario tells us that "authentic virtue exists only when the human person possesses a certain interior conformity of both the cognitive and the appetitive powers to the purposes or goals of a virtuous life." In simpler language, when one is ruled by one's urges and desires, there is no prospect for virtue. Saint Augustine wrote that prudence is love choosing wisely between the helpful and the harmful.[47] Intemperance, then, may be considered as a destructive and excessive form of self-love; intemperance, at its heart, is self-indulgence. Intemperance is essentially egotism unchained. When one is intemperate, he is saying, either implicitly or explicitly, that there is one standard that governs my conduct: my stomach or my genitalia; all that matters to me is that I satisfy my urges and appetites. Everything may be excused in the name of my personal cupidity or my private craving. I am a law unto myself. I recognize no authority outside my own experience, beyond my own skin. Such people may be effective comedians or efficient consumers in a materialistic society. But there is in such people precious little sense of responsibility, an insignificant amount of integrity, and only a starved or starving sense of what piety, duty, or honor are all about. Who among us wants such a person as his doctor or his teacher—let alone as his commander? There is something of the intemperate in all of us. But if we believe that professionals care more about their own selfish pleasures than about their obligations, we rightly will have little or no faith in what they say or do. We can be professional only to the extent that we establish temperance in our private and our public lives.

Case Study

Air force first lieutenant Kelly Flinn had graduated from the U.S. Air Force Academy and had gone on to graduate at the top of her class from B-52 flight training. She subsequently appeared in promotional videos for the air force. In 1996 she was chosen to fly with the secretary of the air force, Dr. Sheila Widnall, in a B-52 demonstration flight. In June 1996, however, Flinn violated military regulations (and, some would hold, spiritual ones) by fornicating with an enlisted man. The next month she began an affair with Marc Zigo, a civilian soccer coach at Minot Air Force Base in North Dakota. Zigo was married to an air force enlisted woman. The affair continued until January 1997. During an investigation of the affair—termed "a witch hunt" by Flinn—she lied to air force examiners about her affair with Zigo, whom she subsequently labeled "a real con artist." Ordered to stay away from Zigo, Flinn disobeyed the order, later saying she was afraid of Zigo, who was then living with her. (Gen. Ronald Fogleman, then the air force chief of staff, contended, however, that after Flinn's commander ordered her to stay away from Zigo, "she didn't stop seeing her boyfriend—he moved in with her.")[48] By May 1997 the Flinn case was making national headlines. Democratic senator Tom Harkin of Iowa contended that in prosecuting Flinn, "the Air Force is looking ridiculous." Republican senator Trent Lott of Mississippi said, "Get real. I'll tell you, the Pentagon is not in touch with reality on this so-called question of fraternization." Flinn appeared on *60 Minutes,* and a number of editorials leaped to her defense. On 22 May 1997, for example, the *Philadelphia Inquirer* ran a three-panel cartoon showing Flinn in her uniform wearing the letter *A* and asking, "What does the scarlet letter 'A' stand for?" In a second panel is a grizzled, unkempt air force general officer answering, "Adultery." In the third panel is a woman, said to represent the "rest of the world," answering, "Air Farce."

On 21 May 1997 Representatives Nancy Johnson (R-Conn.) and Nita Lowey (D-N.Y.) called upon the air force to review its policies on fraternization and adultery. Johnson contended that the charges against Flinn stemmed "directly from the lack of clear, contemporary policy addressing sexuality in a way that respects the personal lives of professional soldiers." Grilled on the Flinn case before Congress, Gen. Ronald Fogleman said that the issue was "about an officer entrusted to fly nuclear weapons who disobeyed an order, who lied." On 22 May Secretary of the Air Force Widnall refused to grant Flinn an honorable discharge; Flinn accepted a general discharge.[49]

Whether, as part of her undergraduate education, Kelly Flinn ever read Plato's dialogue *Phaedrus,* we cannot be sure.[50] Had she read, learned, and applied it, perhaps she would not have come to the end she did. In that work one meets the idea of the charioteer (reason) guiding two horses, one of spirited nature ("an executive faculty somewhat resembling the will"[51] and loving "honour with temperance and modesty")[52] and one of appetitive nature (desire for physical and financial gratifications). As Father Copleston explains, "While the good horse is easily driven according to the directions of the charioteer, the bad horse is unruly and tends to obey the voice of sensual passion, so that it must be restrained by the whip."[53] Lieutenant Flinn, by all accounts an accomplished pilot of a B-52 "chariot," was unable to restrain the horse that led her, against good reason, to a sorry end.[54]

9

Character and the Profession of Arms

What you are speaks so loud that I cannot hear what you say.
—Ralph Waldo Emerson

Character is what God and the angels know of us; reputation is what men and women think of us.
—Horace Mann

A common dictionary definition of *character* is this: "the aggregate of features and traits that form the individual nature of some person or thing." I have five definitions of my own:

- Character is the inventory of choices, made by a person during the course of his life, which influences current and future moral judgments.
- Character is the persistent effort to apply one's concept of simple truth to moral complexity.
- Character is the settled ability to do what one's well-formed conscience whispers despite the opposing noise of the crowd.
- Character is the range of the whole person, the person's experience and education, as it displays itself on a given moral issue at a given time.
- Character is the process by which, in an active/reactive manner, one makes a present moral decision on the basis of his experience.

These definitions fail, however, because character escapes simple explanation. Saint Augustine once said of time that everyone knows what it is until he is asked to define it. Much the same is true of character. It is certainly true, as army colonel Anthony Hartle has written, that "persons of strong character are the ultimate resource for any military [or other] organization."[1] But even Colonel Hartle does not advance a simple definition of the word. Joel Kupperman, in his book *Character*, suggests that character "is what a person is, especially in the areas of her or his life that concern major choices." He adds that character is a "normal pattern of thought and action . . . most especially in relation to moral choice."[2] Character is wise, just, brave, temperate moral choice.

James Q. Wilson may be the closest to explaining character when he writes that "moral virtue is the same as good character, and a good character is formed not through moral instruction or personal self-discovery but through the regular repetition of right actions. These habits are formed chiefly in the family." Wilson points out, quoting Aristotle (which is de rigueur whenever one talks of "building character"), that moral virtue "is the product of habituation." "Ethics," Wilson says, comes from the Greek word *ethos,* which means "habit."[3] Character is about habitus, settled dispositions toward the good that are open to truth and grace (see chapter 7).

If the reader has been patient and persevering, he has plowed through a hoax chapter, a chapter repudiating that chapter, a chapter outlining a view of the moral disease with which we now find ourselves afflicted, a chapter explaining conscience and synderesis, and then four chapters on the cardinal virtues. At the end of all this, are we to conclude only that "we aren't really sure how to define *character,* but we know it when we see it"? Precisely. Character is not a definition; character is people who are constant to worthy purpose.

Some years ago, substitute teaching in secondary schools in Indiana, I used to play a verbal game with my students. I would say that I could prove to them that God did not exist. Unaccustomed to such unvarnished atheism, the students were momentarily diverted from their plans to torch the school and torture their teachers; they actually paid a bit of attention. I would explain that God is omnipotent, and then explain that term. Then I would suggest that if God cannot do something, He cannot do everything. Therefore He is not omnipotent or perfect; therefore there is no God. I would then ask them whether God could make a rock so big that He could not lift it. They would concede that God could not do that—Q.E.D.

The next day, having been "converted," I would demonstrate to them that God must exist by employing (rather loosely, I admit) the ontological proof. I would explain that our minds are finite. God is infinite. Therefore, how could we conceive of God unless He has suggested His existence to us? By explaining these concepts slowly and carefully, I was able to exhaust almost all of the normal high school period.

I would try to explain to my high school students what I regard as a foundational truth—most of the values, virtues, and verities we know as "character" resist simple definition. We cannot compress God into language. We can define *hypotenuse,* or *rose,* or *table,* or *carburetor;* but verbal definitions of *love, honor, justice, integrity,* or even of the four cardinal virtues, seem both inelegant and inadequate. Nonetheless, we know them when we see them. Art and music and poetry come closest, I think, to helping us understand the meanings of these words, which are, after all, only alphabetical representations of noble ideals. Character is well-formed conscience in action; when we see it, we know it.

About Not Being a Bum

When I was in college, I worked one summer in the public cemeteries in Monson, Massachusetts. I worked with an elderly man named Mr. Beckwith, who had been employed for many years by the Town Cemetery Commission; he truly knew where many of the bones were buried. As a twenty-year-old, I was fascinated by Mr. Beckwith's knowledge of the history and personalities of the town where my family had lived for a hundred years. The difficulty was that Mr. Beckwith liked to take a drink or two from his flask, especially at lunch. The boss forbade drinking, so Mr. Beckwith, in order to have his illicit libation, would walk through the graveyard. I would often accompany him, asking what must have seemed to him endless and importunate questions. He had the practice of walking near a grave of someone who had died perhaps in 1935 (which then seemed to me to be sometime during the Peloponnesian War) and capturing the deceased's life in a word or two. He would almost inaudibly mumble "nice fella" about this long-dead man; or he would mutter "bum!" about another person. It occurred to me that, in a sense, this might be as close to truly understanding character as I would ever come. One day, if only metaphorically, people we know, respect, and love will walk near our graves and capture who we were in a word or two. I do not want that description to be "bum."[4]

Thirty years after my summer work in a Massachusetts cemetery, I was lecturing to a class at San Diego State University. My point was that moral strength in the United States had been sapped by widespread ethical confusion approaching epidemic proportions. For the most part, the students disagreed, contending that all times have had their problems. I readily conceded that point but replied that I believe the extent of the moral rot today, and our willingness to tolerate it, are greater by far than was true in earlier periods. I then said something that seemed to puzzle my interlocutors: crime statistics aside, I could not prove my thesis. It was a function of impression and of intuition. I *know* that from 1960 to 2000 there has been a decline in what I call *character*. That decline has upset practically every facet of professional life—the various professions, the churches, the academy, industry, and so on.[5] That may be the reason there has been a nationwide movement toward character education, which involves (or should involve) teaching people to do what is right when doing wrong is easier, more popular, or less painful.[6]

That my reaction is not merely the personal worry of a middle-aged, conservative, religious believer is testified to by private, public, and parochial school character education programs. Even the federal service academies such as West Point, which have taught character since their founding, are establishing character education centers on their campuses. Businesses routinely invite ethics lecturers to visit. Seminarians receive more instruction in ethics. Colleges attempt to implement ethics-across-the-curriculum programs. We worry, quite properly, about the character of our leaders, debating whether private sexual peccadilloes affect public political decision making (in chapter 8 I tried to make that connection). One senses, indeed one hopes, that we are on the verge of a great ethical pendulum movement from the libertinism of the 1960s and 1970s (the remnants of which we see today) to a return of the values and virtues of an earlier day when people were concerned about being called "bums." As our World War II generation passes, we begin to appreciate what they take with them to the grave and what heritage they have given us, if we will but see.[7] Character is about being able to say thank you to those truly deserving gratitude.

We live at a time when fewer than 6 percent of Americans under the age of 65 have served in the military, and in Congress the proportion of veterans has dwindled from two-thirds to barely one-third.[8] Is the idea of service eroding before our eyes? What duty do we have to others and to our country? There is a famous "Peanuts" cartoon in which Lucy says, "It's mankind I love; it's people I can't stand." Character is about service to real people, not love of a meaningless abstraction. Character is about understanding responsibility and about being responsible. Character is about decency. Character is about the golden rule. Character is about not being a bum. But it is an indication of the moral squalor of our times that *bum* used to mean a shiftless, lazy, or irresponsible person. Contemporary dictionaries define the word now in a different way: a bum is an "enthusiast of a recreational pastime" (such as a *ski bum*). The late Mr. Beckwith would never understand.

But this is all so "unacademic." Aren't the arguments here—especially the attempts at defining character at the close of nearly every paragraph above—becoming more of a bumper sticker than an academic thesis? In our headlong rush as academics to know more and more about less and less, to publish our abstruse and arcane findings about matters of little practical consequence to anyone else, we too often neglect what education is really all about: the development of ladies and gentlemen of character. The idea seems so medieval, so impossibly anachronistic, or perhaps so sanctimonious, that we abandon it as too "political." The well-known scholar Robert Coles had this brought home to him in a powerful way recently. A bright young woman, working her way through Harvard by cleaning the rooms of some of her fellow students, approached Professor Coles to tell him about the conduct of so many of her fellow students. They were patronizing, condescending, rude, and crude. They were *crude* in the sense of openly propositioning her. In fact, one student who propositioned her a number of times had even taken two courses in moral reasoning with her. She asked Coles this question: "I've been taking all these philosophy courses, and we talk about what's true, what's important, what's *good*. Well, how do you teach people how to be good?" And she added: "What's the point of *knowing* good, if you don't keep trying to *become* a good person?"[9] Character is the ability and the desire to treat others as we ourselves wish to be treated.[10]

There is, I think, an answer to that critical question. We must hire, promote, and tenure teachers who are competent, compassionate models of character. In the multiversity, in huge academic bureaucracies, in publicly supported state universities, is it really possible anymore to hire men and women of "character"? What if "character" is a subterfuge for hiring only people of a given political persuasion, McCarthyites or

Jacobins, right- or left-wing extremists who are bent upon teaching one or another ideology? Even many Catholic institutions, which used to be clear about their primary purpose, actively pursue "academic excellence" occasionally at the price, one might argue, of literally losing their identity.[11] I think it is a sign of our times that public and many private universities have, for the most part, thrown up their hands in resignation, saying that they *cannot* use "character" as a consideration in the hiring or tenuring process. Character is about knowing who the real heroes are.

Is there not something manifestly wrong, even corrupt, about education that cannot educate for character because it no longer understands character and the cardinal virtues? Think of professors for a moment not as researchers and writers but as *leaders*. Josiah Bunting makes the point well:

> Those we wish to hold up as examples to be emulated cannot be men and women who themselves fall far short of the ideals they propound.
>
> We want to retain therefore honorable men and women who have answered an unignorable vocation to teach and serve the young: both by what they know and believe, and by how they live their lives. We want persons passionately devoted to the pursuit and propagation of truth wherever it leads them, and who are loyal to our students and the mission of the College.[12]

VIRTUE ETHICS

Largely unexamined throughout the book to this point has been the importance—and moral vitality—of what philosophers call virtue ethics.[13] Deontological (or rule-based) ethics is concerned with establishing principles to govern what we decide and do. Teleological (or outcome-oriented) ethics is concerned with which actions we take. Virtue ethics, however, is concerned not so much with *doing things* as with *becoming someone;* the emphasis here is on being rather than doing.

There is great confusion in various texts about these concepts, which in fact are not enigmatic, provided the terms are explained. The term *deontology* sometimes refers to any theory that holds that there are moral absolutes or exceptionless moral norms (see chapter 6). Most natural law theories (see chapter 4) are deontological in this sense. Theories that deny that there are moral absolutes are teleological, for they dwell on outcomes, results, or consequences. (Utilitarianism is a teleological theory.)

It begins to get a little more complicated at this point. In chapter 5 we discussed human goods, which tell us what human beings can and should become. But teleological ethics can also be concerned with actions that are in harmony man's natural destiny and ultimate end, which, for religious believers, is the supreme good, God Himself.[14] In this respect, teleological ethics may be understood as absolute. Deontological (or duty-based) ethics has another meaning as well. When deontological ethics is derived (as Immanuel Kant would have had it) from mere intuition of duty or from the idea of universalizability,[15] it of itself is an inadequate guide to moral conduct. Deontology can become dry legalism. As Patrick Lee puts it, deontology in this sense "reduces human action to the passing of an arbitrary test."[16] Father Pinckaers makes this point: "Clearly we are dealing with two different types of moral teaching: on the one hand, a morality of virtues, whose task is to educate to the practice of virtue, notably prudence and concrete discernment; on the other hand a morality of cases of conscience, scrutinized in their relation to legal obligations."[17]

An example suggested by Michael Stocker will help. Suppose your friend is in the hospital. Day after day, you fight the traffic and take time off from work to visit him. Your friend is very grateful for your kindness and cordially thanks you for your friendship. "Oh, no," you insist, "I visit you only out of a sense of duty; there is really no friendship to it!"[18] Somehow, the visits mean something less to your friend now. One of the many advantages of virtue ethics is that it allows and encourages us to consider motivation (such as friendship)[19] in the course of ethical decision making. Also very important in the idea of virtue ethics is the concept of habitus (see chapter 7), or a stable moral disposition. Recall that habits can be automated actions, whereas the term *habitus* means a pattern of reflection, reasoning, and decision—a state of character.

To be sure, this is not intended to denigrate the idea of duty, once described by Robert E. Lee as "the sublimest word in our language." It is to suggest, however, that obligations can conflict—can amount to dueling duties—and that when the focus is moved to the actor or the one deciding and to the context of the action, we may improve our reasoning process. There are three classic focus points for morality: the outcome (teleological ethics: a good result), the act (deontological ethics: a dutiful deed), and the agent (an actor of good character).[20] These are roughly equivalent to end, means, and the circumstances surrounding the actor. In much the same sense, the sources of morality, says the *Catechism of the Catholic Church,* are the intention, end, or goal of action; the object chosen (a somewhat confusing term for the means to the end); and the circumstances encompassing the action (where the action is done, with whom, when, and so on). If one steals a car in order to have flashy transportation, the end or goal is possession of an ostentatious automobile; the object of the act—or the means—is theft; the circumstances may involve where the car was stolen, violence used in the robbery, from whom, and when (for example, was the car stolen from a woman about to take her ailing mother to the hospital for emergency surgery?). For an act to be morally good, defects are impermissible in any of the three elements.[21]

"One may not do evil so that good may result from it." The *Catechism* continues: "It is therefore an error to judge the morality of human acts by considering only the intention that inspires them or the circumstances (environment, social pressure, duress or emergency, etc.) which supply their context. There are acts which, in and of themselves, independently of circumstances and intentions, are always gravely illicit by reason of their object[—]such as blasphemy and perjury, murder and adultery."[22]

We can now see why virtue ethics is indispensable to the profession of arms.[23] Armies exist to win battles and wars.[24] Military ethics is thus teleological (in the one sense of the term), for it is necessarily utilitarian and consequentialist. But military ethics is also deontological, for soldiers can and must be taught principles and learn duties. The very nature of the profession of arms—which entails killing or preparing to kill, destruction or preparation for wreaking destruction—involves soldiers in the ethical anguish of what I have called dueling duties. Decision "logic trees," moral checklists, ethical flow charts—none of these things can help soldiers resolve some of the most pressing problems they confront (often without benefit of much time for reflection and analysis).

Understandably, philosophers spend a good deal of time explaining and separating deontological, teleological, and virtue-based ethics systems. There are advantages and disadvantages to each.[25] According to philosopher Louis Pojman, pure aretaic ethics insists that moral principles derive from duties.[26] The standard deontic view is that virtues are derived from principles.[27] Pojman describes a third system, "Complementarity Ethics," or *pluralistic ethics,* according to which principles and virtues complement each other.[28] I do not plan here to enter this somewhat abstruse debate. In the field of military ethics, we might agree with William Frankena, who is probably right in saying, "I am inclined to think that principles without traits are impotent and traits without principles are blind."[29]

Over the years, the military services have taught leadership by reference both to enduring principles and character traits. This is, I think, all to the good. But there is no question that what matters beyond all else is the development of good character. Here is the reason. The essence of military professionalism is responsible choice. Military choices are sometimes made under terrible pressure. Moreover, such exigent choices may be between, or among, competing "absolutes" (see chapter 6 for a discussion of universalism). We know that we cannot do evil that good may come of it. What, then, would the naval officer do in these circumstances? The commander of an American submarine sees an enemy merchant vessel, which is a legitimate military target. Through his intelligence services, the officer knows that there are several innocent children on board who will be killed as a result of a submarine attack. Is the torpedo attack morally permissible?

According to Father John A. Hardon, the attack is permissible. The officer intends to lessen enemy power, not to kill innocent children, although their deaths are foreseen. The action of torpedoing the ship is not evil in itself. The evil effect—the death of the children—is not the cause of the good effect (the lessening of enemy power). There is a proportionately grave reason for permitting the evil effect, which is the sinking of the vessel.[30] This, of course, is the principle of double effect, a rather labyrinthine effort to deal with evil and with moral obligation.

"DIRTY HARRY"

In chapter 6 we discussed the idea that military ethics is teleological (in the sense of outcome-based utilitarian thinking), something that I regard as ethically acceptable up to a point. All humans—but especially people in the profession of arms, which is, after all, charged with delivering violence on the battlefield—must think through the idea that there must come times and circumstances that will *not* permit them to follow certain nefarious orders, to destroy, or to kill. This was, and is, particularly true of air force officers in underground bunkers, who are prepared even now to release nuclear missiles upon American national enemies. Can they ethically participate in a decision that could kill tens of thousands of human beings? Can bomber pilots drop their ordnance on targets where the innocent will die? How much collateral damage is permissible? Suppose the merchant vessel upon which we just fired our torpedo had not a few or several children, but dozens, scores, hundreds? What is our decision point? Where do we cross the line? Must we agree with Sidney Axinn that "if we lose the prohibition against killing the innocent, there is no line between legitimate acts of war and simple murder"?[31]

Axinn, perhaps better than anyone else, has made clear the terrible problems confronted by soldiers by drawing upon a now-thirty-year-old film, *Dirty Harry*. In the film, Harry, a policeman, tortures a psychopathic killer to find out where a child is who has been kidnapped and buried (with only a few hours' air supply) by that criminal.[32] Can we ever use immoral means to reach a necessary goal? Remember the testimony of Pope John Paul II and the biblical injunction (Rom. 3:8) against precisely that.[33] About twenty years ago, I sat in a classroom at the University of Massachusetts during a National Endowment for the Humanities summer session and heard Michael Walzer say, with evident intellectual pain, that a "supreme emergency" may well require statesmen and soldiers to use others to do evil: "A nation fighting a just war, when it is desperate and survival itself is at risk, must use unscrupulous or morally ignorant soldiers; and as soon as their usefulness is past, it must disown them." Carefully note what Walzer is saying. He expands his theme this way: "I would rather say something else: that decent men and women, hard-pressed in war, must sometimes do terrible things, and then they themselves have to look for some way to reaffirm the values they have overthrown. But the first statement is probably the more realistic one."[34]

In chapter 7 I argued that English does not have words to explain some things (such as what we call the "bravery" of the bad man). Now I contend that neither moral philosophy nor military science has a word to explain the anguish that besets soldiers in ultimate conflict situations. Can we really use "unscrupulous soldiers" to do our dirty work, disowning them after they have done their deed? Is torture always wrong? (What if your father, mother, son, or daughter was being held by the killer tortured by Dirty Harry?) Is the killing of the innocent always wrong?

(Consider all the truly innocent Germans killed in World War II—even, perhaps, seventeen-year-old children drafted into the German army and thus, technically, "combatants." But how many production workers or young soldiers fought the Allies, preventing them, for many months, from reaching the death camps where millions were being killed?) I know of no concept or even word that adequately conveys the moral anxiety that besets decent soldiers and airmen as they think about bombing and shooting other people.

Many of the problems that appear in these pages as lifeless, abstract, academic exercises have been encountered, in real life, in situations of great stress, by a number of the men and women whom I have had the honor of teaching at the Air War College. Their training ground has not been library carrels or private studies (as has my own); rather, their experiences have occurred in the skies over Vietnam, Iraq, Bosnia, Kosovo, and elsewhere. Sometimes they ask me questions that, in a few cases that I am aware of, derive from great personal and professional anguish. For most undergraduates the questions, however serious, rarely derive from troubled personal experience, but a number of the officers I teach ask me for answers to problems that, in all candor, I am grateful never to have faced myself.

There is a general principle that may be of some help. It appears in Axinn's book. He explains that Kant contrasted a political moralist to a moral politician. The first shapes morality to fit political ends; the second makes political activities fit within moral limits. By extension, Axinn argues that "We must contrast a *military moralist,* who would restrict morality to military bounds, to a *moral militarist,* who would restrict military activity to moral limits. The former subordinates principles to ends, the latter ends to principles."[35] That helps—but, frankly, not much. The cases I hear of are about specifics; and the application of principle, however important it is both in the classroom and on the battlefield, is a parlous and perplexing enterprise. "Damn it! Don't talk to me about principles; tell me whether what I did was right or wrong!" I labor. I search. If I ask, as some pious people counsel us, "What would Jesus do?" I have, I fear, no ready answers. If, like Socrates, I employ maieutics, I fail again. I have neither the wit nor the wisdom to answer the intractable questions too frequently put to me by airmen whose consciences require a remedy beyond my poor means to prescribe. I look to duty, and no simple answers come forth, for I know about dueling duties, and so, much more realistically, do the airmen asking my counsel. I look to consequences (Dirty Harry, by the way, was too late; the child was dead, and the killer was let go because of Harry's illegal means of "information retrieval"), and I see no simple answers. There are cases, however, in which the claim of "national security" cannot and does not excuse abominable actions.

"I Am Not Especially Proud of It"

During the 1950s, thousands of American soldiers were subjected to nuclear testing, as Thomas Saffer describes in his book *Countdown Zero.* American families living near Fernald, Ohio, and Hanford, Washington, were exposed to very high levels of radiation. Eugene Halton tells us that the American government, though claiming there was no danger to troops or towns, "did know the dangers." Public health officials, Halton claims, allowed uranium miners to breathe polluted air, "rationalizing that the increased lung-cancer deaths from lack of breathing masks were the cost of keeping the mining secret from the Russians." In a letter to Halton, Dr. Victor E. Archer, who was the principal investigator for the mining study from 1956 until 1979, said, "Although I recognize that what I did was the only real way to achieve control of the hazard, I am not especially proud of it, since many lives were sacrificed. But that has frequently been the way of human progress—some must be sacrificed for the *greater good of all.* This has been true in war and peace. Modern ethics and morality may soften this path to progress, but only at the cost of slowing the process."[36] Is that what we want to be done in our name? Is that what we are all about? Is that what national defense means? Is that the way of "human progress"? Whenever anything is justified in the name of "the greater good of all," be careful: there may be no "good" to it at all. Whenever one is admonished to "get on the team," be careful: it may not be a team of which you want any part at all.

There are times, I hope, when we *can* make clear ethical judgments. There are times when we know, in head and in heart, that something is wrong and intolerable. Who can read from the letter of Dr. Archer without wanting to scream, "NO! What you have done, what you have said, what you have implied is all morally evil. How dare you indict *me* in your monstrous experiments by claiming that they were done *for me* ('the greater good of *all*')! How dare you even mention *ethics* in a description of your experiments? And when someone walks over your grave, what word will come to mind—*patriot? scientist? utilitarian?* Or another, shorter, but more appropriate description that Mr. Beckwith would have understood?" There are lines we cannot ethically cross—and no one of decency places at risk the lives of thousands of people in order to get better data.

ADVICE ABOUT ETHICS TO MILITARY OFFICERS

There are times when, although we cannot speak from the head, we can speak from the heart. In ten years of listening to exigent questions about critical circumstance, I have come to understand the great value of both the earnest question *and the noble questioner.* What little wisdom I have about dueling duties or about deontology/teleology/value ethics is contained in this: after a soldier or airman makes an anguished decision about killing, about destroying, about doing things that, at other times and in other places, would bring him only shame and mortification, he must find solace in four facts about himself and about the profession and the people he serves:

- The very fact of his anguish is testimony to the decency of his heart and the nobility of his soul (note that Dr. Archer was hardly anguished); and this is precisely the kind of man, the kind of woman, I want in the public service or in the uniform of our country.
- Without exception, the cases I am aware of have already been aired and "adjudicated" through legal, professional, or fraternal[37] means. Sidney Axinn is thus entirely correct: if a weighty moral matter cannot be made public, he says, "it can't be right."[38] This does not mean that every military problem finds its way onto page one of the *New York Times.* It does mean, however, that others, either formally or informally, know about the problem, consider it, review it, and offer counsel to the reflecting person (or take official actions, if required).
- Again—without exception—the difficult problems I know about have involved decent, even noble, men in making decisions that led them to the point where they *took a stand,* either by refusing to do certain things or by doing them. They may subsequently question whether "the point" they made was, in that case, either too restrictive or too

permissive. And they may question whether that one "point" was in keeping with the other ethical points of their careers or lives, all of which comprise the "line" they will not cross. But all of them have had such lines that they would not violate (see chapter 6). Not one has ever said "Anything goes," for such men have no decency—let alone nobility—about them, and an anguished ethical moment is beyond their ken. Mr. Beckwith knew their kind.

- If I can offer good men precious little by way of erudite answers to pressing combat problems, I can tell them what I deeply believe: "A whole life of morally good choices putting to work all of a person's elements—talents and skills, psychological dispositions [habitus], ways of self-expression, feelings, and all the rest—makes one an integrally good person; of such an individual we say that he or she is a person of good character. The different aspects of good character are the virtues."[39]

In positions of authority and power, in any organization, I want leaders who can and will be decisive, because abulia (the inability to make decisions) will destroy the organization led by one so afflicted. But I want leaders blessed, at the same time, by the habitus of constructive self-examination (and here, emphatically, I do not mean self-pitying, unremitting rationalization). The power of virtue ethics is that it shows all of us that there are heroes to be emulated; that we must listen and learn and read in order to lead; that praiseworthy principles and honorable traits must be internalized and annealed into habitus; that the habitus of prudence and justice and courage and temperance become sound character.[40] A man or a woman of sound and substantial character is no perfect insurance of impeccable virtue in this troubled world. But upon such rocks as these are built churches and countries, universities and armies. There is an old saying about the price of things: if circumstances compel you to ask the question, you do not have enough money. There might be a saying, too, one day about the value of things and about people of character who, troubled by the world and their part in it, plaintively wonder whether they have done the right thing in choosing the paths they have. And to them I want to say: if you have to ask the question, your character is not in doubt. Such people wonder and worry, but they lead. Such people question authority and examine themselves, but they act. Such people know that duties can conflict and that their profession requires of them occasional imperfect choices in an imperfect world, but they accept the responsibility of their station.[41] It is such people that induce us to say that although character is hard to define, it is easy to identify. And I see it in him, and in her, and in him, and in her, and in him. . . . We feel privileged to be in their company, and we know that if such as these lead, we ourselves can follow.

"And so, Colonel Jones, I do not have a specific answer to your question. But I know that by thinking about it and by asking about it, you have, in some ineffable way, already answered it; you have informed your mind and, some would say, your conscience by the process that led you to this discussion; fortified by such examination, you are increasingly prepared for the adversities of leadership. For you have learned by leading (and I, by listening) that the foremost leaders are truly the most conscientious; that character means doing the best you can with the means and knowledge you have; and that the unexamined life is not worth living. I cannot (always) be sure what your duty was in the case you discussed. I cannot (always) be sure (any more than you can always be sure) of the outcome of what you did. But I can be sure of your commitment to doing what is right as you best discern it and, more important, I can be sure of you. Your organization did well assigning you the responsibilities you undertook so conscientiously."

Virtue ethics is truly eclectic in that it wishes people to attempt to bring about the best possible outcome by fulfilling, reasonably and well, the duties they have. It is a point worth making that the word *virtue* comes from the Latin *virtus,* meaning "moral strength" or "manliness." In turn, one who is manly, the dictionary says, is "strong, frank, brave, noble, independent, and honorable"—qualities as much descriptive, of course, of virtuous women as of virtuous men. In a society in which morals are under the gun—and in the profession of arms, in which morals are always amid the guns of war—virtue ethics holds out the promise that if we concern ourselves with *being* the kind of people we should be, then *doing* what we should do will surely follow.

CHARACTER AND THE MILITARY SERVICE

Over the past several years, a number of scholars have suggested that American civil-military relations have become disordered. Three reasons are invariably cited for the decline in civil-military relations: (1)

there are fewer civilians in power who have spent time in uniform—a matter of fact, (2) there is an increasing number of professional soldiers who identify themselves as conservatives or Republicans—again a matter of fact,[42] and (3) there is a growing estrangement in military ranks from the values of mainstream America. There is great concern in some quarters about the second and third reasons for the tension in civil-military relations. The argument that the American military is "too Republican" is bizarre. The empirical data are no doubt correct, and one does not quarrel with them. The simple truth is that Republicans are by and large more conservative than Democrats; consequently, more military professionals are drawn to the Republican Party. There is hardly anything new about this fundamental fact of political sociology. Forty years ago, after all, Samuel Huntington characterized the military ethic as "realistic and conservative."[43] But it is the fallacy of composition to say that what is true of individuals is necessarily true of the group. That most military officers may be Republican does not necessarily mean that the institution itself has been mortgaged to the GOP.[44]

In the early 1970s, as I was leaving active army service, the military forces were in moral chaos. How did the military effect repairs and essentially reconstitute itself? For thirty years it has drawn upon those truths that are at the heart of any good organization; they are, indeed, at the heart of any good human being. The values and virtues esteemed by the military *at its best* are exactly those needed in our society at large.

"Is it possible to deny that the military values—loyalty, duty, restraint, dedication—are the ones America most needs today? That the disciplined order of West Point has more to offer than the garish individualism of Main Street? Historically, the virtues of West Point have been America's vices, and the vices of the military, America's virtues. Yet today America can learn more from West Point than West Point from America." That sentiment is as germane now as it was when it was written by Samuel Huntington more than forty years ago. Is it not striking that no one calls Charles Moskos and John Sibley Butler militarists when they write in *All That We Can Be* that the American military can teach the rest of society valuable lessons about racial integration "the Army Way"?[45] Can it be that the military's emphasis on such ideas as patriotism, valor, fidelity, and abilities (the words found on officers' commissions) are worthy of emulation or cultivation by civilians?

Of course, soldiers must continually be taught the essentials of our democratic system and of the Constitution they are sworn to "support and defend"; civilian leaders must continuously exercise wise and firm control of the constitutional powers they are elected to exercise—as well as set a model of decency, especially in the White House. There *is* a widening gap between the military and society. But if that gap is the result of recruits who learn respect and discipline and fairness and a sense of honor where before there were gangs and drugs and lawlessness and violence, it is all to the good. If a graduate of basic training or boot camp repudiates "civilian society" and the society thus shunned is one of drug dealing and crime, credit, I think, and not blame, accrues to the military training regimen.

On 18 November 1997 the 1998 Defense Authorization Act was signed by President Clinton. By law, officers must be good examples of "virtue, honor, patriotism, *and subordination*" (my emphasis). They must be "vigilant" in monitoring the conduct of subordinates. They must "suppress all dissolute and immoral practices" and make certain that laws and regulations are obeyed. Moreover, they are responsible for the morale, well-being, safety, and general welfare of the people under their command. Some will think this law unnecessary, for the vast majority of officers were acting in an exemplary fashion—in character—before the law was passed. Others will think the entire notion bizarre and akin to the vaporous Eighteenth Amendment, for how are *dissolute* and *immoral* to be defined? Numerous legal challenges have been mounted without success to the idea of "conduct unbecoming an officer and gentleman" (article 133 of the *Uniform Code of Military Justice*). If officers do not have a prima facie idea of what being a lady or a gentleman means, as outlined in chapter 8, they are likely to become faltering officers. The idea that officers should be virtuous seems curious, quaint, and medieval; but it is also a functional imperative of the profession. As Lord Moran wrote in *The Anatomy of Courage:* "A free people is only ready to resist aggression when the Christian virtues flourish, for a man of character in peace is a man of courage in war." If officers do not act with prudence, justice, fortitude, and temperance—that is, if they have failed characters—they will be failed officers.[46]

Consciously, deliberately, and intentionally to instruct civilians about the cardinal virtues—this is emphatically *not* the province or duty of active duty military professionals. At the same time, however, armed services professionals are never relieved of their responsibility to set a good moral example. To expect anything less, particularly of our officer corps, than that they set a high moral example is to undermine the most noble element of the military ethic. An air force officer, for example, recently and erroneously wrote that military officers cannot reasonably be asked to be "saints" and that human beings can form "extremely complicated, situation-sensitive dispositions."[47] In other words, soldiers might have to be honest or courageous "on duty," but they are not necessarily expected to display such noble actions "off duty." In trying to make his point, the writer uses an SS example. Were not Himmler's troops expected to be "honest, decent, loyal, and comradely to members of [their] own blood"? But this is rather like arguing that Hitler was a "good" leader, albeit a "bad" man. It is an absurdity to think that Himmler's vile forces could be composed of men of courage (see chapter 7) and character. One cannot be a good person if one contributes knowingly and willingly to a diseased moral order. Nor can one turn character on and off, as though it were a spigot.

In Anton Myrer's novel *Once an Eagle*, the hero—a military officer named Sam Damon—instructs his son in "virtue ethics": "If it comes to a choice between being a good soldier and a good human being, try to be a good human being." To draw a dichotomy between good soldiers and good human beings is logically defective and morally dangerous. In 1969, dissenting in the case of *O'Callahan v. Parker*, which concerned the jurisdiction of military law over off-duty acts of soldiers, Justice John Marshall Harlan made this indispensable point: "The soldier who acts the part of Mr. Hyde while on leave is, at best, a precarious Dr. Jekyll when back on duty."[48]

Military professionals, then, are expected—now legally required by statute—to be "exemplary." For "there are certain moral attributes common to the ideal officer and the perfect gentleman [or lady], a lack of which is indicated by acts of dishonesty, unfair dealing, indecency, indecorum, lawlessness, injustice, or cruelty." That language, extracted from article 133 of the *UCMJ*, contends that power, pace Acton, must *not* be allowed to have the tendency to corrupt. The article continues: "Not everyone can be expected to meet unrealistically high moral standards, but there is a limit of tolerance based on customs of the service and military necessity below which the personal standards of an officer . . . cannot fall without seriously compromising the person's standing as an officer . . . or the person's character as a gentleman."

The scholars who complain, and not without reason, about declining civil-military relations point out that military affairs generally are too infrequently discussed on college campuses. When so few college faculty members have service experience; when ROTC units are expelled, however foolishly, from campuses; when "military" virtues are dismissed as the property of cranks or antediluvians—how can we expect serious discussion of military problems?

To some it seems repugnant to suggest that the values and virtues of a hierarchical, authoritarian, conservative military can serve hortatory purposes for an egalitarian, democratic, liberal society. The fundamental purpose of the military—to wage and win war—is unpleasant to a society that prefers to avert its gaze from the things and thoughts of war.

None of this is about expecting officers to deliver homilies to a populace sitting in the pews of the nation, awaiting the revealed word. The military task, most assuredly, is not to counsel our society about wisdom, justice, courage, and temperance. But ethics is caught as well as taught. Those who suggest that there are no moral exemplars today— or that we do not need them—are manifestly mistaken. Heroes—genuine heroes (that is, men and woman of character)—are always needed and always present to us, if we will but look around us. What I argue, then, boils down to this: just as there are failed officers who murder at My Lai, or who molest women in the corridors of hotels, or who, as bums, otherwise stain and sully the national uniform they wear, so there are heroes who have served their God, their country, and their profession at the price of limb and life and spirit. The standard of the lady or the gentleman—the standard of the cardinal virtues—sits in condign judgment on the failures and in humble thanksgiving for the successes.

And all of us, if the harsh truth be told, occasionally snicker about that and lampoon it and dismiss the creed and disparage the standard as fatuous anachronisms in modern times. But to the members of the profession of arms, the ideas of chivalry, of the cardinal virtues, and of character are not mere gasconade or parade-ground prattle. These things—and hard-nosed, well-drilled competence in military skills— are their stock in trade; for without them, they are but armed thugs, mercenaries without morals. If we say that they have nothing to teach us about virtue, the tragedy is rather that we implicitly say that we have nothing to learn. The nihilists will say that nothing is worth dying for when, in fact, what they mean is that nothing beyond their own skins is worth living for.

One cannot be both an egotist and a military professional, because in the end the soldier must be prepared to risk not only his life but also his very soul for his country. Such commitment and dedication may strike us today as a strange atavism, but it is the emotional heart of the profession of arms. If we can learn no lesson from that, then our country is spiritually spent and morally impoverished beyond repair.

Epilogue

Posterity may know we have not loosely through silence
permitted things to pass away as in a dream.

—*Richard Hooker*

It ha[s] always been strange that the mass of people who will
believe in anything should be at the mercy of the few who believe
in nothing.

—*Lord Moran*

What can the armed services do to improve the characters and consciences
of those joining the military, either in the grade of E-1 (private) or O-1
(second lieutenant)?[1] Certainly this has been a major topic for the profession of arms in the past decade; it appears to be even more pressing
today. Before concluding with a few suggestions, I should frankly say
that in the end there is no ultimate solution to this problem. There is no
one book, there is no one school, there is no one teacher, there is no one
training regimen that can ensure that our armed services will recruit or
train only morally and mentally sound people—people who truly possess "ordinary sense and understanding." But the fact that this is not a
task that can be completed does not relieve the profession of arms from
its paramount responsibility to promote—to put it squarely—the proper
formation of conscience among its troops.

SOME RECOMMENDATIONS

How can that be done? First, build a culture of high ethical expectation,
in line with this advice from Dee Hock to the corporate world: "Hire

and promote first on the basis of integrity; second, motivation; third, capacity; fourth, understanding; fifth, knowledge; and last and least, experience. Without integrity, motivation is dangerous; without motivation, capacity is impotent; without capacity, understanding is limited; without understanding, knowledge is meaningless; without knowledge, experience is blind. Experience is easy to provide and quickly put to use by people with all the other qualities."[2]

If the unscrupulous and immoral are routinely appointed, or elected, to positions of power—if character truly does not matter—then we must fear for the service, corporation, or country that speaks thus of itself. The quotation from Title 10 of the U.S. Code bears repetition: "All commanding officers and others in authority in the [military services] are required to show in themselves a good example of virtue, honor, patriotism, and subordination; to be vigilant in inspecting the conduct of all persons who are placed under their command; to guard against and suppress all dissolute and immoral practices"[3] (secs. 3583, 5947, and 8583). The creation of a climate of high ethical expectation is thus not only a moral imperative; it is a legal requirement as well."[4]

Second, excellent drill instructors, drill sergeants, and technical instructors must be recognized and rewarded. Part of their "training to train" must involve knowledge of the cardinal virtues. This is not an attempt to make drill sergeants into philosophers; it is an effort to impress upon those who develop soldiers, sailors, airmen, and marines that the ideas of wisdom or prudence, justice or truthfulness, courage (moral and physical), and temperance are part and parcel of the uniformed services: "that is the way we do business here." If drill sergeants are rightly expected to be physically fit, how much more important is it that they be ethically fit?[5]

Third, recognize and reward the officers who teach, lead, and inspire the noncommissioned officers and cadets, midshipmen, candidates, and trainees under their command—the lieutenant colonels, colonels, commanders, and captains who administer ROTC, Officer Candidate School, and the federal academies. Once this becomes a "dead-end" job (as "corridor talk" has had it for years), the "best and brightest" officers understandably will seek to avoid this kind of duty.

Fourth, drop the various "core values" of the services and develop a serious, substantial, phased program of instruction in the cardinal virtues.[6] What does it suggest when the services have different "core" values—or when they have six and then three, or eight or seven or four (depending upon which list one uses)? If the core values are merely words—and not introductions to moral reasoning—they may as well be regarded as simple shibboleths or bumper-sticker slogans, useful perhaps for decorative hall posters but not as an aid to serious thought. Not for nothing have the cardinal virtues endured for two thousand years.[7]

Fifth, develop a list of books and films that every service member is expected to read or view. Although good education will not solve all the world's problems, surely providing service members with the opportunity for moral development is a sound investment. The services led the way for our country in helping to provide an improved racial climate.[8] Is it too much to expect that the same kind of effort might wisely be invested in a program of moral development?[9] If the services can develop programs to help prevent sexual harassment, can it be that much more difficult to expand the curriculum to teach members always to act wisely and well?[10] The goal is nothing less than to help members of the armed forces to reason morally, thus being able to reach a higher "Kohlberg stage"[11] than would be practicable without such education.[12]

Sixth, rediscover the leadership principles and traits of leaders that used to be employed in leadership development courses.[13] Such principles as "Take responsibility for your actions," "Set the example," "Look out for the welfare of your [people]" are timeless. Improvisational management techniques have their place, but not at the expense of the military ethic. The entrepreneurial spirit, too, has its place, but the U.S. military is not a business with "customers"; it is a fighting force whose first Code of Conduct article tells its members that they are fighters—warriors.[14] The development of a sound ethics is not in the least a depreciation of the warrior spirit; rather, the development and inculcation of a sound moral code adds to that spirit and renders it dignified (in the full sense of that term) and defensible.

Seventh, employ the heritage of the installation to promote examples of moral worth. Do the troops at, say, Fort Benning know who Benning was? Do the troops at Maxwell Air Force Base know who Maxwell was? Ranges, buildings, streets, and so on are frequently named after fallen warriors. Who tells their stories? Do the troops understand the meaning of taps? The connection between current troops and the "long gray line" must be made again and again by articulate speakers.

Eighth, adopt the air force approach to teaching. Although I have some reservations about the "core values" chosen, the air force technique of encouraging commanders and leaders to speak about ethics and ethical situations (and the cascading effect from that strong, positive influence) is wise and may well work when speakers talk from the heart. The goal of interjecting "ethics situations" and the core values at appropriate moments across the curriculum is exactly the right approach. The idea is to keep the concepts of wise and virtuous conduct "on the radar screen."

I have used the phrase "morals under the gun" in two ways. It can refer simply to military ethics. I have argued that the military ethics, rightly understood and nobly lived, can serve as an ethical exemplar for all of us, for few other professions deal, as the profession of arms must, with wisdom, justice, courage, and temperance. Without the character resulting from these classical virtues, military officers will fail professionally because they will fail, first and foremost, as people. If, however, the cardinal virtues are the military core values, civilians need have no fear about "morals under the gun" or military ethics.

On Mystic Chords of Memory

Paul Johnson tells of attending a conference on medical ethics where a speaker used the phrase "the sanctity of human life." Another, described by Johnson as "a dauntingly clever philosopher," responded that human life may be sacred to us but that he did not know that as a fact. He wanted it proved to him. Why should human life be sacred? Johnson writes:

> I found this a chilling moment, and many of those to whom
> I have described the incident found it chilling too. I had
> always thought that the sanctity of life was one of those
> "truths" which sensible men and women "hold to be self-
> evident." It did not need to be proved. It just was. Proving
> it is not easy. I doubt if I could prove it. But then I do not
> need to prove it because I know it to be true just as surely
> as I know that I am a human being. I think most of us feel
> that way. There are a number of beliefs to do with
> behaviour and morality and civilisation which are so self-
> evident that the request to prove them creates uneasiness.[15]

If we do not know that life is sacred, if that must be "proved," then of what can we be sure? There may be no more important question than the epistemological query "What do we know?" This book has been based on a number of assumptions, both stated and unstated. Its thesis is that there is a bridge between moral theology-philosophy and the profession of arms. Moreover, I have contended that the cardinal virtues of wisdom or prudence; justice or truthfulness; bravery, courage, or fortitude; and temperance or moderation are at the heart of the military ethic. Each of the armed services has its own "core values." These should be scrapped because the true values at the core—at the heart—of the profession of arms are the hinge virtues—the classical virtues, the cardinal virtues— of wisdom, justice, courage, and temperance. In fact, I am not sure that I have proved my case, although, like Paul Johnson, I *know* that the four cardinal virtues are really just different facets of morally sound character.

To the extent that the men and women, the ladies and gentlemen, of the profession of arms model these virtues for the rest of us, they can and should serve as moral exemplars. Their creed, their *profession,* learned well and lived nobly, can and should be a source of moral inspiration for a society too often beset by moral bewilderment. Moral exemplification is not the premier purpose of the military. But military services bereft of the cardinal virtues are no more than groups of armed thugs. The cardinal virtues therefore are essential to the profession of arms in much the same way they are fundamental to other professions (such as the ministry, law, medicine, and teaching).

Venality, corruption, and rampant careerism have been found over the centuries in all trades and professions. But if this book is correct, a major peril facing American Society is that too many professional people think of moral depravity and ethical degradation only as the "intolerant" judgment of an antiquated philosophy.

Nonetheless, some standards are timeless and immutable, in much the same way that human nature itself is timeless and immutable. As long as human beings roam God's earth, there will be conflict between the moral virtues and their opposites, the deadly sins. The task of preserving virtue, both personal and professional, is never finally accomplished. We must debate and decide every day what to do, how to act, what kind of man or woman to be. Each major decision is a moral point, and the sequence of points that we make becomes a line. Life is a series of "connect the dots," for by that process, day in and day out, we determine our habitus, our character, and our destiny. With Reinhold Niebuhr we learn that "nothing that is worth doing can be achieved in our lifetime; therefore we must be saved by hope. Nothing which is true or beautiful or good makes complete sense in any immediate context of history; therefore we must be saved by faith. Nothing we do, however virtuous, can be accomplished alone; therefore we are saved by love. No virtuous act is quite as virtuous from the standpoint of our friend or foe as it is from our standpoint. Therefore we must be saved by the final form of love which is forgiveness."[16]

We are not alone.[17] In learning and doing what we should, we have good moral examples to follow. We have from our parents, grandparents, teachers, priests and ministers, and fellow countrymen examples of what it means to have character—what a gift we have received! We incur, thereby, an obligation and a responsibility both to those who have gone before and to those who will come after. We are part of a family, and of a nation, and of a human community. All of these people might say to us, as the dying captain in the movie *Saving Private Ryan* says to the young soldier spared by the heroism of an army squad, "Earn this!"— earn the life, the opportunity, the gift we have given you. If and when we visit the graves and see the family photos, do we, if only for a moment, reflect on what our heritage and our history are all about? Edmund Burke said that such ties, though insubstantial to our senses, bind one to his country with "ties which though light as air, are as strong as links of iron." "That," Walter Lippmann said, "is why young men die in battle for their country's sake and why old men plant trees they will never sit under."[18] We must always remember, as James Stockinger has written, what we owe to others' hands:

> Each of us lives in and through an immense movement of
> the hands of other people. The hands of other people lift us
> from the womb. The hands of other people grow the food
> we eat, weave the clothes we wear and build the shelters
> we inhabit. The hands of other people give pleasure to our
> bodies in moments of passion and aid and comfort in times
> of affliction and distress. It is in and through the hands of
> other people that the commonwealth of nature is appropri-
> ated to the needs and pleasures of our separate, individual
> lives, and, at the end, it is the hands of other people that
> lower us into the earth.[19]

"Morals under the gun" has referred, in addition to military ethics, to the erosion of virtue in the American republic. As Lincoln said in his first inaugural address, "The mystic chords of memory, stretching from every battlefield and patriot grave to every living heart and hearthstone, will yet swell the chorus of [our country] when again touched, as surely they will be, by the better angels of our nature." In that day, when we remember those to whom we owe so much and when we commit ourselves to making the cardinal virtues a reality in our personal and professional lives, our country's morals will no longer be under the gun.

Notes

1. Prov. 29:18 (NAB).
2. See Wis. 8:7.
3. Lewis, *Abolition of Man.* See his appendix, "The Law of General Beneficence."
4. See, for example, Kernan, *In Plato's Cave.*
5. We owe even those who did not provide us enough moral nourishment (such as the ancestors referred to in the excerpt from Lamentations), for they gave us life, even if not a sufficient example for good living.
6. As this book goes to press, I am reminded of the last words in a fine old book about the children of Naples: "If it [that book] dies unread, so be it. But let it die from lack of talent in the writer, not from lack of love in the human family, nor from want of belief in the fatherhood of God and the brotherhood of Man." West, *Children of the Sun.*

1. The Necessary Immorality of the Military Profession

The material in this chapter was originally prepared as a paper for the Joint Services' Conference on Professional Military Ethics, Washington, D.C., 1994.

1. According to the *Baltimore Sun,* the U.S. Army Rangers sent into Somalia were "supposed to grease Aidid [the warlord chief]. Push his button. Punch his ticket. Ice the guy." But what of the U.S. executive order against assassinations? "If you send in one guy carrying a sniper-scoped rifle to cancel Aidid's contract, that's assassination. But if you send in 400 troops trained in 'counterterrorism' and they happen just to stumble upon Aidid one day and slit his throat, well that's the fortunes of war" (29 Aug. 1993, 2).
2. *Time,* 16 Aug. 1993, 48.
3. Murray Kempton, "Ribbons and Bibbons," *New Republic,* 30 Nov. 1963, 14. Cited by Malham M. Wakin in "The Ethics of Leadership I," in Wakin, *War, Morality, and the Military Profession,* 198 n. 21.
4. Quoted in Anthony Hartle, "The Ethical Odyssey of Oliver North," *Parameters* 23 (summer 1993): 29.
5. 1 John 5:17. See also Matt. 23:24, 12:36; 1 Cor. 6:9–10. See also Geisler, *Christian Ethics,* 116–17.
6. E.M. Forster, *Two Cheers for Democracy* (New York: Harcourt, Brace, 1951), 68.
7. "Sailing through Troubled Seas," *Newsweek,* 27 Sept. 1993, 44.
8. Ibid.
9. At the Naval Academy, for example, students use old tests (known as "gouge") to prepare for exams. During the recent scandal, some midshipmen may have thought that pilfered tests were merely gouge. The distinction between stolen exams and gouge may not be as clear as some might cavalierly contend.

10. Anger, envy, gluttony, greed, lust, pride, and sloth.

11. The same may be true of codes of conduct. See Elliott Gruner, "What Code? Or, No Great Escapes: The Code of Conduct and Other Dreams of Resistance," *Armed Forces and Society* 19 (summer 1993): 599–610.

12. Hartle, "Oliver North," 33.

13. 18 Aug. 1993, 1. See also the editorial in the next day's issue of the newspaper. Actually, there is a great deal of debate about this imbroglio. See the editorial "Congress Is Scuppering Missile Defense" in the *Wall Street Journal,* 23 Aug. 1993, A11, and the exchange of letters in the *Times* on 3 Sept. 1993, A10. Army officials vigorously denied rigging the SDI test. See *Aviation Week and Space Technology,* 30 Aug. 1993, 25.

14. *Prince,* chap. 18.

15. Ibid.

16. The series was entitled "Ethics in America," and it was produced, I believe, by PBS. The particular exchange I refer to occurred in 1987 and was part of a program on military ethics.

17. *The Catechism of the Catholic Church* (Liguori, Mo.: Liguori, 1994), nos. 2488, 2489, emphasis in the original.

18. *U.S. News and World Report,* 13 Sept. 1993, 22.

19. See Jeff Stein, *A Murder in Warfare* (New York: St. Martin's, 1992).

20. *Prince,* chap. 18.

21. The Israeli military, too, has begun to employ TQM. See "Israeli Military Tries Total Quality Management to Make the Most of a Small Army and Budget," *Wall Street Journal,* 24 Aug. 1993, 6.

22. *U.S. News and World Report,* 13 Sept. 1993, 52.

23. *Wall Street Journal,* 8 Sept. 1987, 1.

24. Ibid., 23 Apr. 1987, 1. Cf. Ronald E. Berenheim, "The Corporate Ethics Test," *Business and Society Review* 81 (spring 1992): 77–80; John W. Hill, Michael B. Metzger, and Dan R. Dalton, "How Ethical Is Your Company?" *Management Accounting,* July 1992, 59–61; and A. Thomas Young, "Ethics in Business," *Vital Speeches of the Day* 58 (15 Sept. 1992): 725–30.

25. By Gil Dorland and John Dorland (New York: Holt, 1992).

26. "Lies, Lies, Lies," *Time,* 5 Oct. 1992, 32.

2. A New Beginning

1. See Bernstein, "Wilson's Theory." "[Wilson] genuinely feels that once we know enough about physics, chemistry, and biology, there will be nothing on earth we cannot explain" (64).

2. For a superb piece on natural law, see Budziszewski, "Revenge of Conscience"; also very good is Harbour, "Basic Moral Values." See also Rushworth Kidder, *Shared Values for a Troubled World* (San Francisco: Jossey-Bass, 1994); Outka and Reeder, *Prospects for a Common Morality;* and Rommen, *Natural Law.* See also note 36 of this chapter and note 21 of chapter 4.

3. The story I relate about what I was told at the Ranger School at Fort Benning, however, is true. It is also wrong. Soldiers exist to protect the weak and defenseless— not to murder them, even on the field of battle. "Double-tapping" *is not* taught as approved practice by the Ranger School.

4. How about the case of a public affairs officer (PAO) misleading journalists about an imminent American military strike? Insofar as it is possible to avoid being in such a situation (by establishing certain ground rules, by using a "no comment" strategy, and

the like), I believe that a PAO may deceive journalists given serious and substantial military necessity for such deceit. After the military necessity is resolved (presumably after the military strike is accomplished), the PAO would have the responsibility for explaining the circumstances surrounding his deceit. At this point, the PAO is subjecting himself to the "sunshine test," explaining the dilemma in which he found himself and allowing journalists to question his judgment about ends, means, and circumstances. Such procedures would educate journalists about the necessarily secretive nature of many military operations without relieving the PAO or the services of the responsibility to tell the truth. It is, let us suppose, 15 May 1944. Major Jones appears before the press. "Major," asks a reporter, "we have heard that within a few weeks there will be a massive assault on the beaches at Normandy. Is that true?" Says Major Jones, who wants to tell the truth: "Yes, it is. We plan to hit the beaches at Normandy on or about 5 June." Acceptable? Of course not; the Nazis could read. Says Jones, "There are no such plans currently under consideration." After D-Day, Jones appears, truthfully confesses the deception, apologizes, and explains as much as he can of the circumstances obliging his deceit. Will the reporters (and people in "Peoria") understand and agree with Jones? I think so.

5. Told in Bennett, *Death of Outrage,* 129.

6. Quoted in Morris, *If Aristotle Ran General Motors,* 168.

7. Cf. Mark 8:38 and Luke 9:26.

8. Marsden, *Christian Scholarship,* 35; see also 20, 24.

9. Ibid., 57, 55; the emphasis is mine. Cf. Acts 5:29.

10. For a succinct explanation of why Christian perspectives need not undermine the scholarly standards of the mainstream academy, see Marsden, *Christian Scholarship,* esp. chaps. 3 and 4.

11. See, e.g., Tob. 4:15 or Prov. 3:27.

12. See, e.g., Matt. 7:12.

13. Sagan, "Rules to Live By," 12. See also Marsden, *Christian Scholarship,* 74.

14. Samuel P. Huntington, *The Soldier and the State* (New York: Random House, 1957), 155.

15. See, for example, MacIntyre, *After Virtue.* I presented these arguments at greater length in my book *The Sword and the Cross.*

16. *Chronicle of Higher Education,* 10 Nov. 1993, B63.

17. *Montgomery (Ala.) Advertiser,* 15 Dec. 1993, 6A, my emphasis.

18. Kreeft, *Back to Virtue,* 30.

19. George Roche, *A World without Heroes* (Hillsdale, Mich.: Hillsdale College Press, 1987), 89.

20. Quoted in Robert K. Carlson, *Truth on Trial: Liberal Education Be Hanged* (Crisis Books, 1995), 69.

21. Romantic, yes, but not to the extent of forgetting the hard lessons of theology, philosophy, and history about the realistic need for balance of power and separation of powers.

22. Sir John W. Hackett, "The Military in the Service of the State," in Wakin, *War, Morality, and the Military Profession,* 119.

23. Joel Rosenthal, "Today's Officer Corps: A Repository of Virtue in an Anarchic World?" *Naval War College Review* 50, no. 4 (autumn 1997): 111, quoted in my book *True Faith and Allegiance,* 20.

24. Fogleman continued: "The American people expect this [high standard] of us, and rightly so. In the end, our behavior must merit their trust, respect and support." *Air Force Times,* 13 May 1996, 33.

25. Matthews, "Officer as Gentleman."

26. Ibid, 28. The original quotation from the pamphlet may be found on 3–4.

27. Matthews, "Officer as Gentleman," 29.

28. Ibid.

29. Ibid., 30.

30. Hartle, "Better Warriors?" 23.

31. Matthews, "Officer as Gentleman," 31. See also Matthews, "American Military Ideals."

32. See *Uniform Code of Military Justice,* art. 133.

33. *UCMJ,* art. 134.

34. L. Jesse Lemisch, ed., *Benjamin Franklin: The Autobiography and Other Writings* (New York: Signet, 1961), 94–96.

35. Sir Harold Nicolson, *Diplomacy,* 3d ed. (New York: Oxford Univ. Press, 1970), 67.

36. For background, see Lewis, *Abolition of Man;* Budziszewski, *Written on the Heart;* and Rice, *Fifty Questions.* See also note 2 of this chapter.

37. See 1 Cor. 13:13.

38. James F. Childress and John Macquarrie, eds., *The Westminster Dictionary of Christian Ethics* (Philadelphia: Westminster Press, 1986), 77.

39. Peter Kreeft, ed., *Summa of the Summa* (San Francisco: Ignatius, 1990), 404 n.

40. There are, of course, other lists that are very important, chief among them being the Ten Commandments (found in Exodus 20) and the eight Beatitudes (found in Matthew 5): happy are those who need God, have self-control, are sorry for their sin, hunger for holiness, are merciful, are pure in heart, are peacemakers, and suffer for doing what is right. See Pinckaers, *Pursuit of Happiness.* The corporal works of mercy are to feed the hungry, to give drink to the thirsty, to clothe the naked, to visit the imprisoned, to shelter the homeless, to visit the sick, and to bury the dead. The spiritual works of mercy are to admonish the sinner, to instruct the ignorant, to counsel the doubtful, to comfort the sorrowful, to bear wrongs patiently, to forgive all injuries, and to pray for the living and the dead.

41. Elizabeth Austin, "In Search of Virtue," *Notre Dame Magazine* 27, no. 3 (autumn 1998): 28–29.

42. Ibid., 28. Father Keenan is quoted in Austin. In his book *Virtues for Ordinary Christians,* Keenan nonetheless proposes a new set of cardinal virtues: justice, fidelity, self-care, and prudence.

43. I like Austin's idea that prayer is about asking God "What do you want me to do?" Virtue, she suggests, is the nature and quality of our response to God's answer to that prayer: "What would you do if I [God] told you?"

44. Pinckaers, *Sources of Christian Ethics,* 225. Father Pinckaers distinguishes habitus from habits, which he defines as "psychological mechanisms that diminish the moral commitment to an action."

3. MORALS UNDER THE GUN

1. See 2 Pet. 2:1–3.

2. Sommers, "Ethics without Virtue," 386.

3. Quoted in Adler, *Six Great Ideas,* 97.

4. Kreeft, *Back to Virtue,* 63.

5. Sommers, "Hazards of Repudiating Tradition."

6. Moynihan, "Defining Deviancy Down."

7. Twitchell, *For Shame,* x, 11, 15.

8. Nicolaus Mills, *The Triumph of Meanness: America's War against Its Better Self* (Boston: Houghton Mifflin, 1997). He also alludes to shame (38–39).

9. In Michigan recently, a man named Boomer fell from a canoe, leading to a three-minute obscene tirade (said a deputy sheriff). In accordance with an 1897 law prohibiting cursing in front of women and children, Boomer was cited for disorderly conduct and obscene language—in part because nearby children were subjected to his profanity. One mother literally covered her daughter's ears with her hands. The American Civil Liberties Union is taking up Boomer's case as a First Amendment cause. The idea that, if Boomer cursed for three minutes *anywhere,* he should be ashamed of himself does not come under consideration in the news piece. *Montgomery (Ala.) Advertiser,* 25 Jan. 1999, 2A.

10. "What I find most satisfying," says Kevorkian, is the prospect of making possible the performance of invaluable experiments. No aim could be too remote, too silly, too simple, too absurd; and no experiment too outlandish." Quoted in *Our Sunday Visitor,* 17 Jan. 1999, 3. The world saw this once before—in other death camps.

11. The technique involves partly delivering a baby, puncturing the skull, vacuuming out the brain to kill the child, then crushing the skull and completing delivery.

12. In researching his book *How Good People Make Tough Choices,* Rushworth Kidder came across the work of Walter T. Stace, who offers this ringing indictment of relativism: "If we believe that any one moral standard is as good as any other, we are likely to be more tolerant. We shall tolerate widow-burning, human sacrifice, cannibalism, slavery, the infliction of physical torture, or any other of the thousand and one abominations which are, or have been, from time to time approved by one moral code or another. But this is not the kind of toleration we want" (96). Kidder told me at a conference about Stace's 1937 book *The Concept of Morals,* in which Stace mounts a strong attack on ethical relativism. Kidder has publicly recommended the book.

13. It is in the false name of mercy (which is actually murder) that we look with indifference on the deaths of the elderly in euthanasia. It is in the false name of choice (which is also murder) that our laws permit the deaths of unborn children. George Orwell once said that political dissolution is masked by rhetorical euphemism. See Weaver, *Ethics of Rhetoric,* 228–30. The U.S military is also a master of the art of euphemism.

14. Bennett, *Death of Outrage,* 122. See also McDowell and Hostetler, *New Tolerance.*

15. Fukuyama, "Great Disruption," 56.

16. Moynihan, "Defining Deviancy Down," 19.

17. John Stuart Mill quoted in Nash, *Answering the "Virtuecrats,"* 155. Nash also makes this point effectively on 181, where he tells his students, "Show respect for each other by *initially* finding the truth in what you oppose and the error in what you espouse, *before* declaring the truth in what you espouse and the error in what you oppose." This is a sensible and defensible approach to "moral conversation," as Nash terms it. It assumes, however, that there is truth in other viewpoints (those of the Nazis?) and it downplays Truth at the expense of truths (see 168).

18. John Paul II, *The Gospel of Life* (Boston: Pauline Books and Media, 1995), nos. 70, 71.

19. Quoted in Nash, *Answering the "Virtuecrats,"* 1.

20. Wilson, *Moral Sense,* 4. Wilson, in turn, is critiqued, I think very effectively, in Budziszewski, *Written on the Heart,* 212–19. Also see Nash, *Answering the "Virtuecrats,"* 170–74, 182.

21. Hans J. Morgenthau, *The Purpose of American Politics* (New York: Vintage, 1960), 357.

22. Wilson, *Moral Sense,* 250.

23. Bok, *Common Values,* 16–17, 55; and Walzer, *Thick and Thin.* See also Kidder, *Shared Values,* esp. 18–19, and see the discussion of natural law in chap. 2 of this volume.

24. Reo M. Christenson, *Heresies Right and Left* (New York: Harper and Row, 1973), 1–15.

25. Lewis, *Abolition of Man.*

26. John Paul II, *The Splendor of Truth* (Boston: St. Paul Books and Media, 1993), no. 97.

27. Krauthammer, "Coffee, Tea, or He?" 92.

28. John Paul II, *Splendor of Truth,* no. 102; Budziszewski, *Written on the Heart,* 69.

29. Wilson, "Biological Basis," 54.

30. Wilson, "Back from Chaos," 49; see also the *Wilson Quarterly* 22, no. 1 (winter 1998), for articles by Wilson, Richard Rorty, and Paul Gross.

31. As a Catholic, I would strongly quarrel with Wilson on this point. But I imagine that he does not know the devotional prayer "The Way of the Cross," which, in fourteen stations, speaks of Christ's agony and death on Golgotha.

32. Wilson, "Biological Basis," 68.

33. Wolfe, *One Nation, after All,* 298. Cf. Rev. 3:16.

34. Richard John Neuhaus, *The Naked Public Square* (Grand Rapids, Mich.: Eerdmans, 1986); Nash, *Answering the "Virtuecrats,"* 83–84; Carter, *Culture of Disbelief,* 51.

35. Although Rorty does have the grace—perhaps the wrong word here—to say, "Most of us philosophy professors now look back on logical positivism with some embarrassment." "Against Unity," 32.

36. For example, William Bennett, Allan Bloom, Marva Collins, James Kilpatrick, Edward A. Wynne, Kevin Ryan, and Thomas Lickona. It may tell more about Nash than he understands when he upbraids Lickona (author of *Educating for Character*) for the dedication of Lickona's book: "For God." To Nash, that hints at Lickona's "authoritarianism."

37. Nash, *Answering the "Virtuecrats,"* 39.

38. Garcia is quoted in ibid., 15.

39. About 48 percent of workers recently admitted to taking unethical or illegal actions during a previous year. See *U.S.A. Today,* 4–6 Apr. 1997, 1. An example of rampant consumerism may well come from your telephone and the hucksters ("telemarketers") who call you multiple times during the day and evening.

40. McDowell and Hostetler, *Right from Wrong,* 6. I have rounded the figures.

41. Figures based on *Our Sunday Visitor,* 17 Jan. 1999, 3. The rate of abortion in the United States—about twenty abortions a year for every thousand women ages fifteen to forty-four—is the highest in the Western world.

42. David Carlin, "It Was Never Meant to Be a 'Pro-Choice' Alibi," *Our Sunday Visitor,* 2 Aug. 1998, 19.

43. Krauthammer, "Of Headless Mice," 76.

44. Catholic Bishops' Statement, "Living the Gospel of Life: A Challenge to American Catholics," *Our Sunday Visitor,* 13 Dec. 1998, nos. 3, 4, their emphasis.

45. Schlosser, "Prison-Industrial Complex." Unfortunately, prison inmates may be getting an "education" in crime that we can scarcely imagine. About 2005, New York is going to see approximately thirty thousand inmates a year released, many of whom may be more violent and antisocial than they were when they were first incarcerated. See Abramsky, "When They Get Out."

46. Walinsky, "Crisis of Public Order," 53.

47. Michael Medved, *Hollywood vs. America* (New York: HarperCollins, 1992), 11, 19, 70, 95, 122, 138, 161, 176, 195, 216. The quotation is on 267. Also see his article "As Bad As It Gets."

48. Quoted in Medved, *Hollywood vs. America,* 194. Cf. Gal. 5:16–26.

49. Quoted in Mills, *Triumph of Meanness,* 22.

50. Dwight D. Murphey, "America Faces a Civilizational Crisis," in *Is America in Decline?* (pamphlet containing chap. 3 of Dwight D. Murphey, *American Values: Opposing Viewpoints* [San Diego: Greenhaven Press, 1995), 127. More than half of the million babies born out of wedlock are born to white mothers.

51. Ashe, *Days of Grace,* 144.

52. Neil Postman, *The End of Education* (New York: Knopf, 1995), 196; William Bennett, *The Index of Leading Cultural Indicators* (New York: Simon and Schuster, 1994), 104.

53. *Montgomery (Ala.) Advertiser,* 13 Apr. 1998, 4A. Perhaps, only perhaps, we are, by halting half-steps, struggling back toward the light of truth and away from the darkness of relativism. In 1997 the nation's violent crime rate declined nearly 7 percent; the robbery rate during the same period declined 17 percent; the U.S. abortion rate held steady in 1996 at its lowest level in two decades (although states reported 1,221,585 abortions in 1996); 64 percent of voters in November 1998 said they believed the country was going in the proper direction, the highest positive percentage in a quarter-century; from 1994 to 1998, the welfare caseload dropped 40 percent; real educational reform is said to be progressing; homicides in New York City for 1997 were fewer than in 1964; the number of births to teenagers is down by 12 percent since 1991; since the late 1970s the percentage of Americans saying that religion is "very important" in their lives increased from 52 percent to 61 percent; between 1977 and 1995, there has been a doubling of the number of people volunteering for charities. *Montgomery (Ala.) Advertiser,* 28 Dec. 1998, 1A; 4 Dec. 1998, 7A; Michael Barone, "Our Vast Contentment," *U.S. News and World Report,* 21 Dec. 1998, 33; 11 Jan. 1999, 25; George Will, syndicated column in the *Montgomery (Ala.) Advertiser,* 4 Jan. 1999, 8A. Nonetheless, Schlosser reports that "the level of violent crime in the United States, despite recent declines, still dwarfs that in Western Europe." "Prison-Industrial Complex," 52.

54. Can anyone improve on Ashe's comment: "I can't define myself finally as an African American, or as an American. My humanity comes first"? *Days of Grace,* 138.

55. Brzezinski, *Out of Control,* 102–7.

56. I have heard former secretary of the navy Jim Webb say that he deeply resents that analogy. In 1969, during Woodstock, he was leading a marine rifle platoon in Vietnam. Thousands of others served their country during this period. Webb's point is very well taken.

57. Bergen Evans, in the *Dictionary of Quotations* (New York: Delacorte Press, 1968), 219.

58. Mark Shea, "The Year of the Father," *Our Sunday Visitor,* 3 Jan. 1999, 10.

59. Nelson DeMille, *Plum Island* (New York: Warner, 1997), 567.

60. Wilson, *Moral Sense,* 251.

61. Gergen, "Keeping Faith in Our Kids," 80.

4. MORAL REASONING AND THE CARDINAL VIRTUES

This chapter was originally prepared as a paper for the Joint Services' Conference on Professional Ethics.

1. A common definition of *conscience* is this one: "a knowledge or sense of right and wrong, with a compulsion to do right; moral judgment that opposes the violation of

a previously recognized ethical principle and that leads to feelings of guilt if one violates such a principle." *Webster's New World Dictionary,* second college edition, David B. Guralink, ed. (New York: Simon and Schuster, 1980). One finds this definition of *conscience* in the *Catechism of the Catholic Church:* "a judgment of reason whereby the human person recognizes the moral quality of a concrete act that he is going to perform, is in the process of performing, or has already completed" (no. 1778).

2. We are told, for example, to pay taxes, respect, and honor to those who deserve such (Rom. 13:7); see also Acts 5:29.

3. Christopher, *Ethics of War and Peace,* 145.

4. Thomas Merton, the Trappist monk, put it this way: "You must know when, how, and to whom you must say 'no.' This involves considerable difficulty at times. You must not hurt people, or want to hurt them, yet you must not placate them at the price of infidelity to higher and more essential values." *Conjectures of a Guilty Bystander,* 97.

5. There is another aspect of this, which I cannot consider at length here. What happens when a court-martial holds someone guilty of committing war crimes? Can it be that the jury itself comes to face opprobrium? That seems to have happened after the Calley trial. See Capt. Aubrey Daniel's letter to the president in the *New York Times,* 7 Apr. 1971, 12. See also *Facts on File* (1971): vol. 31, 224, 247.

6. Anthony E. Hartle, *Moral Issues in Military Decision Making* (Lawrence: Univ. Press of Kansas, 1989), 84.

7. Myers, "Core Values," 40, 51.

8. Aside from agent, act, and outcome, there are the traditional constitutive elements of object, intention, and circumstances. See *Catechism of the Catholic Church,* no. 1750.

9. Plato, *Laws,* 1.631C.

10. To the list one should add the theological virtues of faith, hope, and charity (or love). See 1 Cor. 13:13.

11. This discussion is based on *Catechism of the Catholic Church,* nos. 1833–38.

12. Those interested in moral theology and this point may consult Germain Grisez et al., *The Way of the Lord Jesus,* vol. 1, *Christian Moral Principles* (Chicago: Franciscan Herald, 1983), chap. 3.

13. See, for example, James B. Stockdale, "In War, in Prison, in Antiquity," in Lloyd J. Matthews and Dale E. Brown, eds., *The Parameters of Military Ethics* (Washington, D.C.: Pergamon-Brassey's), 1989. John Stoessinger quotes Aeschylus: "Even in our sleep / Pain that we cannot forget / Falls drop by drop upon the heart / Until in our despair / Against our will / Comes wisdom / Through the awful grace of God." *Why Nations Go to War,* 5th ed. (New York: St. Martin's, 1990), epigraph.

14. Hartle, *Moral Issues,* 128.

15. *The Cambridge Dictionary of Philosophy,* gen. ed. Robert Audi (New York: Cambridge Univ. Press, 1995), 784. In this sense, synderesis cannot err, but conscience (especially poorly formed conscience) can.

16. *Encyclopedia of Catholicism,* gen. ed. Richard McBrien (New York: HarperCollins, 1995), 1234.

17. "The natural law prescribes those acts which are morally good for man, i.e., in accord with his natural inclinations: namely, in common with all living things, to maintain his life; . . . to pursue truth, exercise freedom, and cultivate virtue. These are the basic natural inclinations of all men, at all times, everywhere. However, man's understanding of them increases with experience and with intellectual development." Aristotle insisted that there must be a starting point for our thought; synderesis, then, was "the natural or innate habit of the mind [except when defective, demented, or damaged] to

know the first principles of the practical or moral order without recourse to a process of discursive reasoning." *New Catholic Encyclopedia* (New York: McGraw-Hill, 1967), vol. 13, s.v. "Synderesis."

18. See, for example, Rom. 2:15.

19. Quoted in *The Essential Catholic Handbook* (Liguori, Mo.: Liguori, 1997), 217. See also Ralph McInerny, "The Case for Natural Law," *Modern Age* 26, no. 2 (spring 1982): 168–74; and Christenson, *Heresies Right and Left,* esp. 1–15.

20. Why, then, do societies have apparently different legal codes, customs, manners, and so on? One explanation is that natural law has one intrinsic meaning but varied instrumentalities; that it has a primary purpose but secondary expressions; that it has both "thin and thick" realities. See Walzer, *Thick and Thin;* see also Larry Arnhart, *Political Questions* (New York: Macmillan, 1987), esp. 105–31.

21. Peter J. Stanlis, *Edmund Burke and the Natural Law* (Ann Arbor: Univ. of Michigan Press, 1965), 7. See also chap. 2 of this book, notes 2 and 36.

22. R.L. Bledsoe and B.A. Boczek, *The International Law Dictionary* (Santa Barbara, Calif.: ABC-Clio, 1987), 17. Natural law is the *jus naturale* dating to the Stoics and involving such thinkers as Francisco de Vitoria (1480–1546), Francisco Suarez (1548–1617), Alberico Gentili (1552–1608), and Hugo Grotius (1583–1645).

23. John Paul II, *Splendor of Truth, 77.* Conscience, the encyclical contends, is not the agent merely of acting "authentically" or "sincerely"; its function, rather, is "to apply the universal knowledge of the good in a specific situation and thus to express a judgment about the right conduct to be chosen here and now" (48).

24. Based on Arnhart, *Political Questions, 43–44.* There are numerous problems with Kohlberg's theories. See, for example, Sommers, "Ethics without Virtue."

25. Christopher Lasch, *The Revolt of the Elites* (New York: W. W. Norton, 1995), 180; see also Mills, *Triumph of Meanness,* esp. chap. 2, "The New Savagery." Both conservatives and liberals will find much in Mills's book to dispute, but they would probably agree with his argument that "there is a meanness in our public and private lives that [although not new, he says] has changed the way we see ourselves and the future" (15).

26. Quoted in John Paul II, *Splendor of Truth,* 116.

27. For the figure of speech, I am indebted to Leo Strauss, "An Epilogue," in Herbert J. Storing, ed., *Essays on the Scientific Study of Politics* (New York: Holt, Rinehart and Winston, 1962), 327.

28. See Matt. 15:8–9, 16:23; Mark 8:33, 7:6–8, John 8:15, 12:43, 14:27, 16:33.

29. Cf. Sir. 7:36.

5. Prudence and the Profession of Arms

1. Quoted in Cessario, *Moral Virtues,* 78.

2. Aristotle, *Nicomachean Ethics,* 172.

3. Based on McBrien, *Encyclopedia of Catholicism,* 1065.

4. Pieper, *Four Cardinal Virtues,* 3, 5.

5. Michael Gerson, "A Pontiff in Winter."

6. Nash, *"Answering the Virtuecrats,"* 33.

7. Are good manners merely conditioned social reflexes, means by which the powerful oppress the powerless? Or are civility and courtesy simple manifestations of our concern for others? On a university campus some years ago, I held open a large door for a female student who was struggling with her books as she entered the library. She passed me with the single, serious comment "Chauvinist!" Holding a door open for

someone seems to me not to be a function of male dominance but of (what used to be) common courtesy. (I would have expected her to hold the door open for me had she been at the door first and seen me struggling with my books.)

8. Grisez and Shaw, *Fulfillment in Christ*, 28. "And for mature *Christian* consciences: What is the wise and holy thing to do?" (28)

9. Patrick Lee, "Human Goods," in Shaw, *Sunday Visitor's Encyclopedia*, 302.

10. Based on ibid., 302–3; Budziszewski, *Written on the Heart*, 196–97; Grisez and Shaw, *Fulfillment in Christ*, 54–55. Budziszewski limits the list to seven, excluding marriage, not because he has any reservations at all about marriage (I suspect), but because some people choose, for personal or religious reasons, not to marry. The first four goods are existential or reflexive, based on free choice; the next three are substantive and can be understood apart from the idea of free choice. Marriage and family are both substantive and reflexive in their different aspects.

11. Grisez and Shaw, *Fulfillment in Christ*, 56.

12. John Paul II, *Splendor of Truth*, 66.

13. Pinckaers, *Pursuit of Happiness*, 37, 35.

14. Rom. 2:1–16; Heb. 8:10. See also J. Budziszewski's letter in *First Things*, Nov. 1998, 3.

15. Henry Fairlie, *The Seven Deadly Sins Today* (Notre Dame, Ind.: Univ. of Notre Dame Press, 1995), 64.

16. My discussion is based on the writings of Pinckaers, *Sources of Christian Ethics.*

17. "Do not conform yourself to this age but be transformed by the renewal of your mind, that you may discern what is the will of God, what is good and pleasing and perfect" (Rom. 12:2).

18. Austin, "That Perilous Gift," 43.

19. The discussion that follows is based upon Grisez and Shaw, *Fulfillment in Christ*, chaps. 8, 26; Budziszewski, *Written on the Heart*, chap. 15; Shaw, *Sunday Visitor's Encyclopedia*, 450–51; Pinckaers, *Pursuit of Happiness*, passim; Fairlie, *Seven Deadly Sins Today*, passim; and Kreeft, *Back to Virtue*, chap. 6.

20. One is not obligated, however, to say "So help me God" after the "oath."

21. I am willing to let a friend borrow my car, but I would be reluctant to let a nonfriend borrow it. When I recommend one of two people for a promotion, however, I make the reference on the basis of performance, not personal partiality borne of friendship for one but perhaps not the other.

22. Cf. Rom. 3:8. Budziszewski again: "Not every evil is a moral evil; for instance the pain of being spanked or grounded is an evil but not a moral one. If we were never to inflict *any* evil that good may result, we could not even discipline our children" (*Written on the Heart*, 198). There may be times when we must choose between apparent evils. For example, a surgeon inflicts pain upon a patient when he removes an inflamed appendix. There may also be times when we cannot commit evil even though good might result. Deliberately bombing civilian population centers to weaken the will of an enemy is one such example. (But suppose, in a just war, a country's air force is bombing a legitimate military target with the concomitant danger of collateral damage. Is everything reasonably possible being done to prevent the deaths of innocent people? If so, the bombing is probably morally justifiable. This is the principle of double effect. An action that produces an evil effect is permissible if the action also has a good effect; one does not seek the bad effect either as end or means; one does not produce the good effect through the bad effect; and the good effect outweighs the bad effect. The principle "is a guide to prudence rather than a substitute for it." See *Cambridge Dictionary of Philosophy*, 645.

23. Cessario, *Moral Virtues,* 23, 78, 84. On the difference between intellectual and moral virtues, see Thomas Aquinas, *Summa Theologica,* 1–2.Q58, art. 2: "Accordingly for a man to do a good deed, it is requisite not only that his reason be well disposed by means of a habit [habitus] of intellectual virtue, but also that his appetite be well disposed by means of a habit [habitus] of moral virtue. And so moral differs from intellectual virtue even as the appetite differs from the reason."

24. The classical Greeks knew that virtue is a matter of practice, of "conditioning," of "fitness." On the idea of "ethical fitness," see Kidder, *How Good People Make Tough Choices,* chap. 3.

25. John P. Martin, "The Insanity Defense: A Closer Look," *Washington Post,* 27 Feb. 1998; Schaefer, "Wisdom and Morality," 221–22. The psychiatrist referred to is Karl Menninger; Schaefer draws from Menninger's book *The Punishment of Crime* (New York: Viking, 1968).

26. Schaefer, "Wisdom and Morality," 222. To pursue this point, consult *Black's Law Dictionary.*

27. "The root of modern totalitarianism is to be found in the denial of the transcendent dignity of the human person who, as the visible image of the invisible God, is therefore by his very nature the subject of rights which no one may violate—no individual, group, class, nation or state. Not even the majority of a social body may violate these rights, by going against the minority, by isolating, oppressing, or exploiting it, or by attempting to annihilate it." Pope John Paul II, *Veritatis Splendor,* no. 99.

28. Eric Voegelin, *The New Science of Politics* (Chicago: Univ. of Chicago Press, 1952), 69.

29. See, however, Martin, *With God on Our Side;* and Anne C. Loveland, *American Evangelicals and the U.S. Military, 1942–1993* (Baton Rouge: Louisiana State Univ. Press, 1996).

30. Robert Bork, *Slouching towards Gomorrah* (New York: Regan, 1996), 275. He continues: "Since secular habituation is grounded only in tradition, that moral capital will be used up eventually, having nothing to replenish it, and we will see a culture such as the one we are entering." Mark Schwehn has made a similar argument—something that "infuriated several of [Robert Nash's] students. They found it to be both denigrating and inaccurate." Nash argues that virtues, to be "worthwhile" must be "valid in their own right." Few of his students "know, or care about, the religious foundations of these dispositions. In fact, in the view of many, religion has been responsible for the *degradation* [his emphasis] of these virtues in American life, and, *whether the stereotype is true or not, no amount of counterevidence convinces these students otherwise,*" my emphasis. That is a sad, and I fear, entirely accurate characterization. (Christians will be reminded of Rom. 1:18–21.) It is as if the students Nash describes were saying "I don't know, and I don't care, and don't bother me with the facts." Nash, by the way, is a professor of *education.* He says he does want to teach students the religious origin of the virtues but to "decouple" the virtues and secularize them. He contends, undoubtedly correctly, that religious discussion of the virtues can easily become "too triumphalistic and foundationalist for most students in my classes." Nash, *Answering the "Virtuecrats,"* 166. One wonders what Nash says about Martin Luther King's moving "Letter from Birmingham Jail."

31. *Summa Theologica,* 1–2.Q58, art. 5.

32. This case study is based solely upon *public* sources.

33. The fourth and sixth modes of responsibility, in my view, should have led Pellerin to ground Holland. Prudence is not timidity; it is, as I have pointed out in this chapter, the ability to make connections between the general demands of morality and

specific cases. The excessively lenient decision of Pellerin to let Holland continue flying was imprudent and derelict. Imprudence—in the classical sense explained here—and dereliction are often complementary. See, for example, McMaster, *Dereliction of Duty.*

34. Based upon Michael Ruane, "Echoes of Air Force Crash," *Philadelphia Inquirer,* 1 May 1995, 1, 4; Mark Thompson, "Way, Way Off in the Wild Blue Yonder," *Time,* 29 May 1995, 32–33; Julie Byrd, "Shaken Base Begins Recovery Process," *Air Force Times,* 11 July 1994, 4, 6; and Kitfield, "Crisis of Conscience," 14–24.

6. JUSTICE AND THE PROFESSION OF ARMS

1. John Paul II, *Veritatis Splendor,* 17. Emphasis in original.

2. Based on *Cambridge Dictionary of Philosophy,* 697.

3. Cf. John 8:32, 14:6.

4. Cf. Prov. 19:5; Acts 5:1–11.

5. Act deontologists "see each act as a unique ethical occasion." Ethicist Louis Pojman divides act deontologists into two camps: intuitionists (such as W.D. Ross) and decisionists (such as Jean Paul Sartre), better known as existentialists. Rule deontologists contend that "in making moral judgments we are appealing to principles or rules." Pojman, *Ethics,* 134–37. Ethicist William Frankena (in his book *Ethics,* 16–17) suggests consulting the work of E.F. Carrit and, in places, H.A. Prichard, Joseph Butler, and Aristotle to see examples of act deontology. Writers whose work shows rule deontology include Samuel Clarke, Richard Price, Thomas Reid, Immanuel Kant, and, of course, W.D. Ross.

6. But natural-law ethics is also teleological insofar as it prescribes a determination of right from wrong as based on a reasoned choice of human goods, in which the agent chooses action on the basis of ultimate benefit or ultimate responsibility (which is to God) (see chap. 9). Deontological ethics, by contrast, can smack of legalism, in creating "tests" that must be "passed" before the agent chooses a course of action. "Catholic moral theology objects to deontological ethics because it does not give an adequate place to prudence and to the necessity of fulfilling our moral obligations in such a way that true goods are actually brought into existence through our actions." Peter Stravinskas, *Catholic Encyclopedia,* rev. ed. (Huntington, Ind.: Our Sunday Visitor, 1998), 320.

7. I believe that we must always love God and neighbor. *How* we discharge our duties in those respects, however, can be difficult to determine. If we must love our neighbors absolutely and unconditionally, we must become pacifists. Or is it possible to love our neighbors (e.g., the World War II Germans) while shooting and bombing them? I think it is. In pursuing the good (victory in World War II), men of conscience did not will the deaths of the Germans or the Japanese they were fighting—and indeed regretted inflicting death. (This would be true until and unless these soldiers were overcome by hatred, fear, anger, and so on.) War obliged the soldiers to make terrible choices, and, as combatants, they prosecuted a just war. Had they all chosen not to, a swastika would be flying still, no doubt, at least over Europe.

8. There is an exception to every rule except that one, to which there is no exception!

9. Although Malham M. Wakin does not use the noun *universalism* in his writings, I infer the term from him. See "The Ethics of Leadership I," in Wakin, *War, Morality, and the Military Profession,* 195. General Wakin discusses universal moral obligations, which he properly says can conflict. See note 11 of this chapter.

10. One is reminded of Jacques Maritain: "Man is by no means for the state. The State is for man." *Man and the State,* 13.

11. Wakin illustrates this effectively. Suppose you promise to meet your boss at noon for lunch. On the way there, you see an accident, and you have the chance to help the victims—but it will make you late. Do you violate your promise to your boss? You have the duty of keeping your word. You have the duty of helping the victims. Clearly, you should help the victims. Circumstances, Wakin tells us, certainly do matter in making decisions—but that is not the same as situation ethics (which rarely admits of overarching principles). We break our word in this case because reason tells us we have a higher obligation. That emphatically does not mean that henceforth we treat promise-keeping cavalierly; we still recognize it as a solemn obligation. Thus, universal ethical obligations are neither absolute nor relative. Compare note 12 below.

12. Some Christian writers would take great exception to Wakin's formulation. Although I find Wakin's position to be logically unassailable, Norman L. Geisler and Helmut Thielicke, for example, would argue that absolutism, despite equally competing claims, still exists. General Wakin and I both believe in God and share the same religious tradition; we are both absolutists in that respect. But, as Wakin rightly says, there are few unchallengeable absolutes. When an "absolute" such as not stealing rightly permits exceptions, it can no longer claim to be absolute. That hardly means, however, that it has lost its moral authority or that it does not apply in the vast majority of cases. Thielicke tries to escape the word dilemma by using the term "conflicting absolutism"; Geisler relies on "graded absolutism." Both terms are oxymorons. Both writers seem to fear that if we find limited usefulness for the term *absolute*, we run the immediate risk of falling into the diabolical clutches of relativism. See Geisler, "Any Absolutes? Absolutely!" *Christian Research Journal*, summer 1995, 10–27. A careful reading of this article and a comparison to Wakin's position suggests that they may be closer than one might first think. See note 11 of this chapter. To pursue Geisler's thought, see his book *Christian Ethics*, chaps. 5–7.

13. Malham M. Wakin, "The Ethics of Leadership, I," in M.M. Wakin, ed. *War, Morality, and the Military Profession*, 2d.ed. (Boulder, Colo.: Westview Press, 1986), 195.

14. *Catechism of the Catholic Church*, nos. 2488, 2489.

15. Ibid., no. 2408.

16. The example is based on a story by Bernard Williams as cited in Miller, *Questions That Matter*, 395.

17. *Catechism of the Catholic Church*, no. 1756.

18. In Rushworth Kidder's book *Good People Make Tough Choices*, the trooper sprays the trapped driver with foam from a fire extinguisher, causing the injured man to pass out (57–58, 164–67). Shortly thereafter the cab explodes in flames, and the man (still unconscious) is burned to death. Is there another, third option—such as knocking the man unconscious with the butt of the weapon? Perhaps. But in the absence of such options, I still could not kill him. The eighth mode of responsibility ("Do what is right, but do not try to get the best results at *any* price") counsels me here. At a certain point in some ethical dilemmas, Christians must trust in God's providence. There are things Christians cannot do (e.g., euthanasia) because they are immoral wolves in sheep's clothing (euthanasia is invariably presented as an act of "mercy"). See Grisez and Shaw, *Fulfillment in Christ*, 93, 340–43. They write that "fidelity requires both refusing to do evil for the sake of good results and avoiding the supposedly 'prudent' rationalizations which deter people from doing their duty because they anticipate painful consequences" (365).

19. See, for example, Department of the Army Field Manual 27-10, The Law of Land Warfare: "A commander may not put his prisoners to death because their presence

retards his movements or diminishes his power of resistance by necessitating a large guard, or by reason of their consuming supplies, or because it appears certain that they will regain their liberty through the impending success of their forces. It is likewise unlawful for a commander to kill his prisoners on grounds of self-preservation, even in the case of commando or airborne operations" (par. 85). See also Hartle, *Moral Issues*, 75.

20. Army Field Manual 27-10, art. 271. As Air Force Pamphlet 110-31 *(International Law—The Conduct of Armed Conflict and Air Operations)* puts it: "Physical or mental torture or any other form of coercion to secure information of any kind whatever is prohibited" (art. 13-3). For a different view, see Richard Marcinko, *Rogue Warrior* (New York: Pocket Books, 1992), 117–18. One reviewer (David Murray) says that Marcinko "comes across as less the genuine warrior than a comic-book superhero." *New York Times Book Review*, 19 Apr. 1992, 12. See also Frederick Downs, *The Killing Zone* (New York: W.W. Norton, 1978). One of my favorite books is David Donovan [Terry Turner], *Once a Warrior King* (New York: McGraw-Hill, 1985). Downs and Donovan provide two first-person accounts of Vietnam War combat and ethical crises.

See chapter 9 for the "Dirty Harry" problem of torturing a criminal to get information from him about where he has buried a child who will soon run out of air. Why a "qualified" no? Torture is wrong. Can it ever be justified? Is there such a thing as "Supreme Emergency" (Michael Walzer's term, defined in chap. 9) in nonpolitical situations, such as a police crisis? With trepidation about my words (Matt. 12:36–37), I have to answer that I think there may be. At the same time, I know that hard cases make bad law. In the vast majority of cases, the right ethical decision will not be difficult to make. In fact, the cause of ethics education is ill served by those of us who trot out almost impossible cases to make points, giving students the impression that ethics is only an exercise in brain-teasing *(mea culpa!)*. For example, military ethicists like to raise questions about taking hills in impossible combat situations, whereas most problems in military ethics concern lying, fraud, waste, abuse, and sexual harassment.

21. See note 22 of chapter 5.

22. So does that mean World War III would ensue, killing even more millions of American and Soviet citizens? First, that outcome, although admittedly likely, was not certain, whereas the death of the New Yorkers was certain. Second, we cannot deliberately kill people to bring about good results—remember the American asked to shoot one hostage? (All we have done here is to enlarge the numbers.) Third, I think there are times when we must trust in God's providence and mercy. And fourth, again, hard cases make bad law.

23. Pope John Paul II, *Veritatis Splendor*, 10.

24. As Pinckaers says: "Egoism also has the power to vitiate and twist the answers to all the questions we have been examining. 'I love' becomes, beneath the surface, 'I love myself' or 'I love to be loved' by God or neighbor. 'I seek happiness' is transformed into 'I seek my happiness' or 'I seek happiness for myself.' 'I look for truth' becomes 'I look for my truth, the truth that suits me' or indeed 'I make my own truth.' 'I want justice' means 'I want my justice, my rights,' or 'I do justice to myself.' The distinctions are very subtle, because egoism uses the terms of love so as to give the appearance of it." *Sources of Christian Ethics*, 43. See also 29.

25. Tradition is critically important. But it is not enough. Tradition, for example, upheld slavery. To reduce ethics to tradition is to imprison it in cultural relativism. There must be something beyond custom: "If the object of the concrete action is not in harmony with the true good of the person, the choice of that action makes our will and ourselves morally evil, thus putting us in conflict with our ultimate end, the supreme

good, God himself." John Paul II, *Veritatis Splendor,* 72. When human acts are ordered toward God, in keeping with the Commandments, the Beatitudes, and the modes of responsibility, we have a means of judging the wisdom and the justice of those acts.

26. Kekes, *Moral Wisdom and Good Lives,* 208.

27. Shattuck, "When Evil Is 'Cool,'" 76.

28. Quoted in Miller, "Banality of Evil," 55.

29. Ibid., 59.

30. Quoted in Morris D. Forkosch, "Justice," in *Dictionary of the History of Ideas,* ed. Philip P. Wiener (New York: Scribner's, 1973), 2:655. For a trenchant criticism of John Rawls, see Adler, *Six Great Ideas,* chap. 24. Justice is more than fairness.

31. Pieper, *Four Cardinal Virtues,* 73–74. See also *Catechism of the Catholic Church,* no. 2411.

32. We could also examine formal justice, which is the impartial application of principles (whether or not they are themselves just), substantive justice (concerned with rights and closely related to commutative and distributive justice), retributive justice (punishment), corrective justice (claims in matters of civil damages), and social justice (increasing emphasis on need over equality and merit). The latter is explained well by Ralph Barton Perry, whose discussion of liberty is concise and cogent. "If you dismiss your son from your door without food, money, or education and tell him that the whole wide world is now open to him, you have not given him 'effective personal freedom.'" *Puritanism and Democracy* (New York: Harper and Row, 1964), 526. That sentiment is found in James 2:14–17. Perry's discussion of the three types of liberty—under government (legal), against government (civil), and for government (political)—I have always found helpful (521).

33. See chap. 19 of Adler's *Six Great Ideas.*

34. Ibid., 147. See also Pinckaers, *Sources of Christian Ethics,* chap. 19, "Freedom for Excellence." On Adler, see the revealing discussion about Adler and Robert Maynard Hutchins as opposed to Sidney Hook and John Dewey in Marsden's fine book *Soul of the American University,* 375–84.

35. MacIntyre, *After Virtue,* 220.

36. Neither do I mean to suggest that advanced study leads to wise action. It should. But it may not. From Plato's *Meno* to the present, there has been a debate about teaching virtue. Plato did not understand the importance of grace. However important knowledge is, grace is required for us to act as we ought.

37. Morris, *If Aristotle Ran General Motors,* 165, 164.

38. To use the language of moral theology instead of just my metaphor: "Among the interior principles are located the *habitus,* which received St. Thomas's special attention. These are stable dispositions that develop the power of our faculties and render us capable of performing actions of high quality. They are not to be confused with our ordinary understanding of habits—psychological mechanisms that diminish the moral commitment to an action. The *habitus* as St. Thomas intended it is a principle of progress and resourcefulness through full commitment. It is through these *habitus* or stable dispositions that we acquire mastery over our actions and become entirely free." Pinckaers, *Sources of Christian Ethics,* 225.

39. *Oxford Dictionary of Quotations,* 3d.ed. (New York: Oxford Univ. Press, 1979), 314.

40. George C. Wilson, "Washington: The Lavelle Case," *Atlantic,* Dec. 1972, 6.

41. Senate Committee on Armed Services, 92-2, Nomination of John D. Lavelle, Gen. Creighton W. Abrams, and Adm. John S. McCain, 11 Sept. 1972, 3.

42. Wilson, "Washington, The Lavelle Case," 10.

43. *Time,* 25 Sept. 1972, 20.

44. Senate Committee on Armed Services, 19 Sept. 1972, 310, my emphasis. Of course Lavelle *had questioned orders* and broken them in the name of protecting his troops. In chapter 4 we discussed the need to disobey "illegal" orders, conscience, and "ordinary sense and understanding." If we criticize Slay because he did not challenge Lavelle's orders to him, should we congratulate Lavelle because he did challenge the orders (ROE) given to him? In an exchange with Slay, Sen. Barry Goldwater said that certain members of the press, concerned with Slay's reluctance to question his orders, would "see some moral wrong in what you did—I can't—[because] it is a case of doing what you have been trained to do" (312). It apparently did not dawn on Goldwater that Slay's training *and education* were, evidently, deficient.

45. *Facts on File* 32, no. 1664 (17–23 Sept. 1972): 745. Franks said that more than two hundred pilots and officers of the Seventh Air Force were involved in falsifying the reports after the raids.

46. The Senate Armed Services Committee voted on 6 October 1972 to strip Lavelle of another star and to retire him at the rank of major general (two-star general). *Facts on File* 32, no. 1667 (8–14 Oct. 1972): 807.

47. Quoted in Wakin, *War, Morality, and the Military Profession,* 180.

48. There are numerous implications of this short case study. Some writers contended that the next chief of staff of the army, Gen. Creighton Abrams, must have known about the falsifications and that he should therefore not have been appointed to be head of the army. Some saw a danger to American civil-military relations. Some saw Lavelle's strikes as impeding the peace process in Vietnam. See *Time,* 26 June 1972, 14; *Nation,* 2 Oct. 1972, 259–60; *Time,* 4 Sept. 1972, 21.

INTERLUDE: OBITER DICTA

I am indebted to Prof. J. Budziszewski of the University of Texas for the idea of presenting obiter dicta in this way. See his book *Written on the Heart,* 169–75.

1. A partial list of the colleges I know from personal study there or from having spoken or visited there (for sufficient time to have a reaction to the institution): University of Notre Dame, College of William and Mary, St. Anselm College (N.H.), University of New Hampshire, University of Vermont, University of Massachusetts, Norwich University (Vt.), Marlboro College (Vt.), University of Saint Thomas (Minn.) American International College, Western New England College, Springfield College (Mass.), Auburn University (Ala.), Auburn University at Montgomery, University of Alabama, Texas A&M University, University of San Diego, Air War College (Ala.), Naval War College (R.I.), U.S. Coast Guard Academy (Conn.), and U.S. Air Force Academy (Colo.). A partial list of the high schools where I have taught or coached: Manchester Memorial High School (N.H.), Monson High School (Mass.), Riley High School (South Bend, Ind.), John Adams High School (South Bend, Ind.), North Liberty High School (Ind.), Northfield High School (Vt.), U-32 High School (Vt.), and Montgomery Catholic High School (Ala.).

2. See, for example, Martin Anderson, *Impostors in the Temple* (New York: Simon and Schuster, 1992); Donald Barr, *Who Pushed Humpty Dumpty?* (New York: Atheneum, 1971); Steven M. Cahn, *The Eclipse of Excellence* (Washington, D.C.: Public Affairs Press, 1973); Steven M. Cahn, *Saints and Scamps: Ethics in Academia* (Totowa, N.J.: Rowman and Littlefield, 1986); Robert K. Carlson, *Truth on Trial* (South Bend, Ind.: Crisis Books, 1995), which concerns hostility directed toward (and finally the death of) the Integrated Humanities Program at the University of Kansas; Dinesh

D'Souza, *Illiberal Education* (New York: Random House, 1992); Kernan, *In Plato's Cave;* Roger Kimball, *Tenured Radicals* (New York: Harper and Row, 1990); Russell Kirk, *Decadence and Renewal in the Higher Learning* (South Bend, Ind.: Gateway, 1978); Postman, *End of Education;* Thomas Sowell, *Inside American Education* (New York: Free Press, 1993); Charles J. Sykes, *ProfScam: Professors and the Demise of Higher Education* (New York: St. Martin's, 1989).

3. See, for example, Sidney Simon, Leland Howe, and Howard Kirschenbaum, *Values Clarification* (New York: Hart, 1972). One of the better denunciations of this kind of nonsense comes from Sommers. See her article "Teaching the Virtues." See also Thomas Lickona, *Educating for Character* (New York: Bantam, 1991), chap. 1.

4. Lasch, *Revolt of the Elites,* 177.

5. Russell Shaw, "Washington," *Columbia,* Feb. 1999, 5. Hanson and Heath point out in *Who Killed Homer?* that "When one truly rejects the West, corpses mount" (77). "It is not reductionist or fantastic to ask why it is that even the most vociferous academic critic of the West would prefer to fly Swissair, check into the Mayo Clinic, scream obscenities in Times Square, run a red light in Omaha, swim with his girlfriend on Santa Cruz beach, or live next to a U.S. Army [post] in Texas—rather than board a Congolese airliner, leave his appendix in Managua General, use Allah's name in vain in downtown Jeddah, jump the curb in Singapore, wear a bikini and Speedos in Iran, or vacation near the home of the Korean National Guard" (57).

6. *United States Air Force Core Values* ("Little Blue Book," 1 Jan. 1997), 3:1.

7. Marsden, *Soul of the American University,* 383.

8. Bennett, *Death of Outrage,* 9.

9. Quoted in Toner, *True Faith and Allegiance,* 135.

10. Hanson and Heath, *Who Killed Homer?* 154–55. As Charles Sykes put it: Faculty at the "best" universities today "have tenure, sabbaticals, and summers off. They drive Volvos, invest in mutual funds, live in attractive Tudors, drink California wines, and insist they feel oppressed whenever anyone uses words like *classic* to describe a work of literature. They have transformed the intellectual landscape of academia." *A Nation of Victims* (New York: St. Martin's Press, 1992), 5.

11. Hanson and Heath in *Who Killed Homer?* make the point that too many professors travel to too many conferences to give too many papers about too many arcane topics to too many bored colleagues at too great an expense. The object of any publication requirement is this: to help teachers keep reading, thinking, discussing, and writing. "Publication," in my view, can take the form of organized presentations beyond, but complementary to, the teacher's normal classroom duties. (These presentations can be to fellow faculty members, to students, to civic and church groups, and so on. Have we forgotten that professors are "missionaries" for their field of learning?) Preparation of conference papers may well be unnecessary. See also Steven Cahn, *Education and the Democratic Ideal* (Chicago: Nelson-Hall, 1979), chap. 12. Cahn is the editor of *Morality, Responsibility, and the University: Studies in Academic Ethics* (Philadelphia: Temple Univ. Press, 1990).

12. See John W. Meaney, *O'Malley of Notre Dame* (Notre Dame, Ind.: Univ. of Notre Dame Press, 1991).

13. Lest this be understood as the product of anti–Notre Dame bias, I should say that I am an alumnus of Notre Dame and have great respect for the university. But it is in danger of forgetting its roots, its premier purpose, and the person after whom it is named. See also below, note 19.

14. Josiah Bunting III, *An Education for Our Time* (Washington, D.C.: Regnery, 1998), chap. 6. See George Will's column about that book in *Newsweek,* 17 Aug. 1998, 70.

15. Bunting, *Education for Our Time*, 10.

16. See, for example, John Leo's column "Repackaging the Perps," *U.S. News and World Report*, 17 May 1999, in which the commitment and purpose of Georgetown University are questioned (14).

17. *First Things*, Mar. 1999, 71. See also Ralph M. McInerny, *What Went Wrong With Vatican II* (Manchester, N.H.: Sophia Institute Press, 1998), 140–42.

18. See, for example, Richard John Neuhaus, "The Public Square: The Dying of the Academic Light," *First Things*, Apr. 1999, 71–72. On this general theme, see Burtchaell, *Dying of the Light*.

19. There is much to this debate that cannot be explored here. For two balanced secular viewpoints, see Kernan, *In Plato's Cave*. Kernan says little about his World War II service as a sailor (beyond commenting about his friendship with Richard Boone, who was to play Paladin) and Fussell's *Doing Battle*. I recommend Fussell because of his views about education, but his acid views on his World War II army service make the book important, if occasionally irksome, to all military readers. Marsden's two fine books reveal how a believer can produce superb scholarship—*Soul of the American University* and *Christian Scholarship*. Two short articles from *First Things* can be recommended in this connection: Marsden's "Defining Academic Freedom" is in the December 1998 issue, and Schwehn's "A Christian University" is in the May 1999 issue.

20. In the Gospel of Matthew alone, for example, see 4:19, 8:19, 8:22, 9:9, 16:24, and 19:21.

21. Henry Adams, *The Education of Henry Adams*, ed. Jean Gooder (New York: Penguin, 1995), 287. Adams was right about teachers but dead wrong about parents when he said, "A parent gives life, but as a parent, gives no more" (287). Giving life is the easy part; giving meaningful life requires the commitment of a lifetime.

22. See also chap. 8, note 39.

7. Courage and the Profession of Arms

1. Cf. the response of Pope John Paul II. Modern philosophy, he says, "*is purely rationalist.*" Its history begins "with Descartes, who split thought from existence and identified existence with reason itself: *'Cogito, ergo sum'* ('I think, therefore I am'). How different from the approach of Saint Thomas, for whom it is not *thought which determines existence, but existence,* 'esse,' *which determines thought!* I think the way I think because I am that which I am—a creature—and because He is He who is, *the absolute uncreated Mystery.* If He were not Mystery, there would be no need for Revelation, or, more precisely, there would be no need for *God to reveal Himself.*" *Crossing the Threshold of Hope*, 38. Emphasis in original.

2. It is rather like asking, as philosophers since Plato have, whether things are good (or just) because God loves them or whether God loves things because they are good (or just).

3. I would make the theological argument that our character, our eternal destiny, is not settled even at death. I believe that the prayers of our family and friends, the intercessions of the Communion of Saints, and the timeless benedictions of the church militant can have spiritual impact upon our continued formation.

4. See Jim and Sybil Stockdale, *In Love and War* (New York: Bantam, 1985); and Stockdale, *Philosophical Fighter Pilot*.

5. I have always found consolation in reading about Peter's denials of Christ (John 18) and Peter's own resurrection in John 21:15–19. Peter's courage was lacking at one point, but he found the ultimate courage of a consecrated life and a martyred death.

6. Aristotle, *Nicomachean Ethics,* trans. Martin Oswold (Indianapolis, Ind.: Bobbs-Merrill, 1962), 70, 70–71 (3.7).

7. *Great Dialogues of Plato,* ed. Eric H. Warmington and Philip G. Rouse, trans. W.H.D. Rouse (New York: Mentor, 1956) 444, 446.

8. *Nicomachean Ethics,* III (7) (p, 1115b (25). Pojman, in *Ethics,* contends that "courage itself is not a moral virtue." He tells us to think of the "courageous murderer" (175). Precisely because courage is, indeed, a moral virtue, we *cannot* think of a courageous murderer.

9. This line of reasoning leads us in directions we may not like. Can we, by extension, suggest that the heroism of Confederate soldiers in the Civil War was improper because, had they been victorious, slavery would have endured longer than it did? Yes. Thousands of southern soldiers served well in a bad cause. We lack an adjective in English to describe selfless and valiant conduct in a bad cause. It is wrong, surely, to dismiss honored and heroic Confederate soldiers as "lacking bravery." But if bravery means wise discrimination about the ultimate ends served by bravery, we must find a different adjective to honor the gallantry of the Southerners. (The close reader will wonder, as I do, whether I can, in the sense I outline, fairly use the words *valiant* and *gallant.*) In the text, I attempt to resolve this dilemma by suggesting that soldiers invincibly ignorant of the evil ends of their state may, indeed, perform brave acts. But soldiers who *knowingly* serve evil ends, however resolutely or boldly, cannot be correctly described as "brave" any more than a criminal is "brave." *Nicomachean Ethics,* 71.

10. In *Mask of Command,* Keegan describes Hitler as a "false heroic."

11. Quoted in Pieper, *Four Cardinal Virtues,* 115.

12. For their legal responsibility, see the *Uniform Code of Military Justice,* art. 92; for their religious responsibility, see Titus 3:1 and Rom. 13:1–7; for the matter of obedience that disobeys the moral law, see Army Field Manual 27-10, par. 509; and Acts 5:29.

13. John A. Hardon, *Pocket Catholic Dictionary* (New York: Doubelday, 1985), 200.

14. The German resistance had been trying since 1938 to kill Hitler. On 20 July 1944, Hitler narrowly escaped death from the blast of a bomb that had been placed in his briefing room by a German officer (Claus von Stauffenberg). Resistance to Hitler was *brave.*

15. Pieper, *Four Cardinal Virtues,* 123.

16. Ibid., 125.

17. See Gordon Zahn, *In Solitary Witness: The Life and Death of Franz Jägerstätter* (Boston: Beacon Press, 1964). Zahn, a pacifist, understandably admires Jägerstätter, who refused induction into Hitler's army, protesting that the German war was unjust and that his Catholic conscience would not permit him to serve: "I cannot and may not take an oath in favor of a government that is fighting an unjust war" (107). He was beheaded on 9 August 1943. I admire Jägerstätter, too, as I told Zahn in a debate we had a number of years ago. But I stop short of universalizing him because I contend that soldiers can be moral. I asked Zahn if he thought the Allied victory in World War II had saved millions of lives and had prevented the martyrdom of more good men like Jägerstätter and the Lutheran pastor Dietrich Bonhoeffer, also executed by the Nazis for his resistance to their infamous cause. Zahn replied that Hitler should never have come to power. I agreed, but the fact was that Hitler did have power. Loving one's neighbor can mean protecting him, by violence if need be. I have argued this in my book *The Sword and the Cross.* But if every German soldier had had the courage of Franz Jägerstätter, no German army would have served Hitler's evil designs.

18. Grisez and Shaw, *Fulfillment in Christ,* 113.

19. In *The Man in the Mirror: A Life of Benedict Arnold* (New York: Random House, 1994), author Clare Brandt has suggested that Arnold was a man of high physical courage but low moral courage and that although he adhered closely to a rigid code of personal honor, he had little integrity. It is entirely possible to find even senior leaders who have proved their physical valor but may still be lacking in moral courage. Arnold, apparently, was one such officer.

20. Merton, *Conjectures of a Guilty Bystander,* 98.

21. Matthew B. Ridgway, *The Korean War* (Garden City, N.Y.: Doubleday, 1967), 189. Jeffrey Barnett, an air force officer, suggests in the *Los Angeles Times* of 6 June 1994 that war's worst risk is to the soul (11).

22. Stephen L. Carter, "The Insufficiency of Honesty," *Atlantic Monthly,* Feb. 1996, 74. See also his book *Integrity.*

23. See, e.g., Ex, 4:21; Deut. 15:7; 1 Sam. 6:6; Ps. 95:8; Heb. 3:8, 4:7.

24. Merton, *Conjectures of a Guilty Bystander,* 97.

25. McMaster, *Dereliction of Duty,* 330. The chief problem with McMaster's account is that he rather largely ignores the will and wiles of the North Vietnamese army and of the Viet Cong.

26. Timberg, *Nightingale's Song,* 415, 416, 417.

27. McCormick, *Downsized Warrior,* 145, 144.

28. See Caputo, "Black Badge of Courage," which concerns the tragic deaths in ranger training of four soldiers in 1994.

29. Lippmann, *Public Philosophy,* 28.

30. Fulton J. Sheen, *The Life of Christ* (New York: McGraw-Hill, 1958), 375.

31. One of the scenes in the play that has always bothered me is one in which More's family comes to him to plead for him merely to sign a paper, which, after his signature, will effect his release. Has he the right to go to the gallows, leaving his wife and family behind? Can he so "indulge" himself? There is a striking parallel in the Gospels. Jesus tells his disciples of his impending death, leading Peter to question him. "Get thee behind me, Satan," Jesus rebukes Peter. "You are thinking not as God does, but as human beings do" (Mark 8:33). According to Christianity, Jesus was prepared to die, and Peter was acting as a deterrent. Had More complied with the wishes of his family, he would have returned to them physically alive—but morally dead. In a few years, he would have been physically dead in any case; as it is, he remains morally alive. He also might have said to his wife, "Get thee behind me, Satan." Nonetheless, the scene painted by Bolt is moving.

32. Pinckaers, *Sources of Christian Ethics,* 225.

33. Cessario, *Moral Virtues,* 37, 40.

34. Pinckaers, *Sources of Christian Ethics,* 364.

35. Moran, *Anatomy of Courage,* 159–60.

36. For background, consult Seymour Hersh, *My Lai 4* (New York: Random House, 1970).

37. Vistica, "Quiet War over the Past," 41. See also William R. Peers, *The My Lai Inquiry* (New York: W.W. Norton, 1979), 74, where Lieutenant General Peers, who headed up the inquiry, verifies Thompson's order to Colburn.

38. Lawrence Rockwood, "A Contemptible Day, Now Remembered," *Army Times,* 16 Mar. 1998. Rockwood, by the way, was the U.S. Army officer court-martialed in May 1995 for his actions in September 1994 as an army counterintelligence officer when he went without authority to get an accountability for the political prisoners held by the Haitian government. See *Newsweek,* 22 May 1995, 38; *Washington Post,* 15 May 1995, 10; *New York Times,* 12 May 1995, 1; *USA Today,* 15 May 1995, 2A. Vistica says

in the *Newsweek* article that Thompson refused the award. Other sources say he accepted it. Seymour Hersh says that Thompson accepted it—"in the Army, one just doesn't refuse such honors"—but that Thompson felt guilty about it. Hersh verifies Thompson's story. Hersh, *Cover Up* (New York: Random House, 1972), 211–14, quotation on 213. Hersh confirms Thompson's gallantry (103–4, 109, 114–18, 130, 134–39, 149–54, 211–13).

39. *Army Times*, 16 Mar. 1998, 14, 62. For details, consult Peers, *My Lai Inquiry*, chap. 8.

40. When I say "bravery," I use the term precisely as I have defined it in this chapter, meaning that I believe that despite the savagery and evil of My Lai (and indeed, of many other aspects of that violent, prolonged conflict), the war in Vietnam was fought in the main by honorable soldiers for politically legitimate ends. As Guenter Lewy once put it, "the commitment to aid Vietnam was made by intelligent and reasonable men who tackled an intractable problem in the face of great uncertainties, including the future performance of an ally, and the actions and reactions of an enemy. The fact that some of their judgments . . . can be showed to [be] flawed and that the outcome [was] a fiasco does not make them villains or fools. . . . Policy-makers always have to act on uncertain assumptions and inadequate information, and some of the noblest decisions in history have involved great risks. As long as there exists a reasonable expectation of success, the statesman who fails can perhaps be pitied, but he should not be condemned." *America in Vietnam* (New York: Oxford Univ. Press, 1978), 440–41. Certainly, there were numerous instances of "dereliction of duty" on the part of soldiers and, particularly, on the part of high-ranking civilian leaders. But I remember very well that a number of my college contemporaries glibly compared Lyndon Johnson to Hitler, which was utter nonsense. When Thompson and Colburn were finally honored by the army, Thompson, "his voice quavering with emotion," remarked, "I proudly and humbly accept it not only for myself but for the men who served their country with honor on the battlefield in Southeast Asia." *New York Times*, 7 Mar. 1998, A9.

41. Vistica, "Quiet War over the Past," 41.

42. *Army Times*, 16 Mar. 1998, 14.

43. *New York Times*, 7 Mar. 1998, A9.

8. TEMPERANCE AND THE PROFESSION OF ARMS

This chapter was originally prepared as a paper for a Joint Services' Conference on Professional Ethics, Springfield, Va., 1998.

1. *Catechism of the Catholic Church*, no. 1809.

2. Webster's *Third New International Dictionary.*

3. *Newsweek*, 28 Sept. 1998, 42.

4. Lewis Carroll, *Alice's Adventures in Wonderland and Through the Looking Glass*, ed. Hugh Haughton (New York: Penguin, 1998), 186.

5. Alasdair MacIntyre, *A Short History of Ethics* (New York: Touchstone, 1966), 77, 96.

6. *Facts on File* 54, no. 2787 (28 Apr. 1994): 301.

7. Based on *Facts on File* 56, no. 2926 (31 Dec. 1996): 977; 57, no. 2936 (13 Mar. 1997): 163; 57, no. 2943 (1 May 1997): 301. On 20 March 1997, army captain Derrick Robertson was sentenced to four months in prison after pleading guilty to having consensual sex with a private; the most serious charges against him (rape and indecent assault) had been dropped as part of an agreement. *Facts on File* 57, no. 2938 (27 Mar. 1997): 213.

8. Such as the case of Sgt. Maj. of the Army Gene McKiney, who, on 13 March 1998, was *acquitted* of eighteen charges, ranging from adultery to indecent assault, but convicted of obstruction of justice. "Many legal experts said that McKinney's March 13 acquittal on sexual misconduct charges illustrated the particularly difficult burden of proof faced by prosecutors in a court-martial. Under military law, sexual misconduct was a criminal rather than a civil offense, requiring proof beyond a reasonable doubt. However, experts said, such cases rarely produced the type of physical evidence necessary to fully demonstrate that misconduct had occurred. Many observers noted that the McKinney trial had come down to one person's word against another." *Facts on File* 58, no. 2989 (19 Mar. 1998): 169–70.

9. *Facts on File* 57, no. 2949 (12 June 1997): 410.

10. *Facts on File* 56, no. 2926 (31 Dec. 1996): 977.

11. See Rodney Barker, *Dancing with the Devil—Sex, Espionage, and the U.S. Marines: The Clayton Lonetree Story* (New York: Simon and Schuster, 1996).

12. *Facts on File* 56, no. 2926 (31 Dec. 1996): 978.

13. *Time,* 4 May 1998; *Facts on File* 57, no. 2949 (12 June 1997): 409–10.

14. *Time,* 4 May 1998, 32. This article, "Sex, the Army and a Double Standard," tells the nefarious tale of Army Major General David Hale, who was permitted to retire from active duty despite charges of improper conduct involving the wives of subordinate officers.

15. Steven Butler, "Outrage on Okinawa," *U.S. News and World Report,* 26 Oct. 1998, 42.

16. *United States Air Force Core Values,* 1 Jan. 1997, I(2).

17. Fairlie, *Seven Deadly Sins Today,* 155.

18. Ibid.

19. Will Herberg, "What Is the Moral Crisis of Our Time?" *Intercollegiate Review* 22, no. 1 (fall 1986).

20. Kreeft, *Back to Virtue,* 25.

21. *Catechism of the Catholic Church,* nos. 2290, 2291. Emphasis in original.

22. Twitchell, *For Shame,* 14–15.

23. Fyodor Dostoyevsky, *The Brothers Karamazov,* trans. Constance Garnett (New York: The Modern Library, [1937]), 69.

24. Sykes, *Nation of Victims,* 9.

25. Ibid., 39–40.

26. Feed the hungry, give drink to the thirsty, clothe the naked, shelter the homeless, comfort the sick, visit those in prison, bury the dead.

27. William Kilpatrick, *Why Johnny Can't Tell Right from Wrong* (New York: Touchstone, 1992), 118–19.

28. Wolfe, *One Nation after All,* 298, 300.

29. Schumacher, *Guide for the Perplexed,* 132.

30. Twitchell, *For Shame,* 30.

31. Bloom, *Closing of the American Mind,* 25.

32. Helen F. North, "Temperance," in *Dictionary of the History of Ideas,* 4:367.

33. Ibid., 4:368–70. The quotation is on 371.

34. Miller, *Questions That Matter,* 12.

35. Budziszewski, *Written on the Heart,* 11.

36. See, for example, ibid., 31–33.

37. Horn, "Shifting Lines of Privacy," 57, 58.

38. Morris, *If Aristotle Ran General Motors,* 120.

39. Hans J. Morgenthau, "Epistle to the Columbians on the Meaning of Morality," *New Republic,* 21 Dec. 1959, 9.

40. Bennett, *Death of Outrage,* 9, 121.

41. A word is in order here about the command not to judge lest we be judged (Matt. 7:1; Luke 6:37). Utterly to condemn someone, with no spirit of charity, is clearly contrary to the counsels of Christianity. But forgiveness of the person does not mean that we accept or condone vile or sinful practices. The idea that "forgiveness should render a person incapable of moral criticism collapses under the sheer weight of biblical evidence," writes Bennett. "The attempt to use God's forgiveness as a pretext to excuse moral wrong is a dangerous (and old) heresy known as antinomianism—literally 'against the law.' Essentially it rejects the moral law as a relevant part of Christian experience. The thought that God's grace, given to us through Christ's death at Golgotha, would justify licentiousness has long been considered contemptible by saints and scholars through the ages." Bennett, *Death of Outrage,* 116–18.

42. J. Budziszewski, *True Tolerance* (New Brunswick, N.J.: Transaction, 1992), 7. This is a fascinating, if inchoate and incondite, work. The same may be true of the evangelical work by McDowell and Hostetler, *New Tolerance.* While oversimplifying issues and overlooking even sources that would buttress their own argument, they offer evidence that "the Bible makes it clear that all values, beliefs, lifestyles, and truth claims are *not* equal" (20), that truth and morality are not mere cultural creations (63), and that there are ways to resist the "new tolerance" (which they see as multiculturalism, political correctness, and postmodernism [208, 38]). A far better and much more scholarly argument can be found in *Splendor of Truth,* Pope John Paul's encyclical: "In the end, only a morality which acknowledges certain norms as valid, always and for everyone, with no exception, can guarantee the ethical foundation of social coexistence, both on the national and international levels" (119). For a criticism of that encyclical, see Peter Hebblethwaite's column in the *National Catholic Reporter,* 7 Oct. 1994, 18. The encyclical *Faith and Reason,* appearing in October 1998, continues the arguments advanced by the Pope in his earlier communications and should be of interest to philosophers, theologians, and political scientists (and to those, such as McDowell and Hostetler, who decry—correctly, in my view—an absence of absolutes in education and in modern life).

43. As it is clear, as well, for Christians: "From the Christian point of view, all cultures . . . in our fallen world are . . . imperfect and . . . subject to moral criticism. The repeated imperative of the New Testament is to conform oneself to Christ, not to the world as it is. Christianity does not believe one can find moral truth by looking to and living by the norms of any existing human culture. Rather, Christian standards and norms point toward one ideal . . . human community: the kingdom of God." Grisez and Shaw, *Fulfillment in Christ,* 43.

44. *Air Force Times,* 8 Dec. 1997, 7. This is explained in more detail in chapter 2. See Title 10 of the *U.S. Code,* secs. 3583, 5947, 8583.

45. Kitfield, "Crisis of Conscience," 16.

46. He continues: "Unlike prudence and justice, temperance is not an attribute of God; it cannot even be ascribed to the holy angels, for it can belong only to animals with bodily needs and appetites." Geach, *Virtues,* 131. I am grateful to my son, Christopher H. Toner, for calling this book to my attention.

47. Cessario, *Moral Virtues,* 78. Cessario quotes Saint Augustine.

48. *Newsweek,* 24 Nov. 1997, 60. In her book *Proud to Be,* Ms. Flinn says that Zigo had moved in with her before her commanding officer ordered her to stop seeing him. It was an order, said Flinn, that was "impossible to obey"; Flinn thought that "it was a setup" (192). She signed a statement saying that she understood the order. She contends that she "didn't understand how I was to obey it" because Zigo, a married man, was already living with her and now she was enjoined from communicating with him. Yet she refused to talk with her commander without an attorney present. Apparently, Flinn

could think of no manner, either through the law or through the police, of evicting Zigo, who (by Flinn's own admission) had been already been cruel to her in various ways.

49. This account is based on *Facts on File* 57, no. 2947 (29 May 1997): 374–75; Kelly Flinn, "Sex, Lies, and Me," *Newsweek,* 24 Nov. 1997; Flinn, *Proud to Be,* chap. 8; and the *Washington Post,* 29 Apr. 1997, D1.

50. Flinn did say that her problems derived "in large measure, [from] a failure of my education." Although the air force had taught her much, she said she "had no knowledge of the workings of the human heart. I had never read a manual that could tell me how to love and be loved." *Washington Post,* 20 Nov. 1997, 25. See also *Proud to Be,* xiii–xiv. "The Air Force succeeds beautifully in teaching its members how to operate complex machinery, but is utterly incapable of imbuing them with a sense of how to be human beings in the modern world" (62). Flinn could have started with the *Manual for Courts-Martial,* art. 90 ("willfully disobeying superior commissioned officer"), art. 107 ("false official statements"), art. 133 ("conduct unbecoming an officer"), and art. 134 ("adultery"). If Flinn had never "read a manual that could tell [her] how to love and be loved," she had not listened very well when she attended church. There, at every mass, a book is read that contains the very advice she so much needed.

51. Frank Thilly, rev. by Ledger Wood, *A History of Philosophy,* 3d ed. (New York: Holt, Rinehart and Winston, 1957), 86.

52. Quoted in Frederick Copleston, *A History of Philosophy,* vol. 1, *Greece and Rome* (New York: Doubleday Image, 1993), 210.

53. Ibid.

54. Did Kelly Flinn deserve the punishment she received? Could she have been militarily "rehabilitated"? I think I owe the reader my views, which are based only upon readings and conversations with people who know both Flinn and people in her chain of command. The differences between, say, Ralston and Flinn are so obvious, I think, as not to require comment. (The notion that Ralston, a general, was "let off the hook" whereas Flinn, a junior officer, was "persecuted" is absurd.) Flinn's conduct indicated a pattern: meaningless sex with a friend, sexual fraternization with an enlisted man, followed by an adulterous relationship with a man married to an air force enlisted woman. Flinn refused a direct order; Flinn lied; Flinn's subsequent actions and statements indicate, at least in my judgment, an immature person confused about the very values and virtues she was supposed to model as an air force officer. I believe the air force treated Flinn fairly and justly. Whether she might be allowed, after the passage of a few years, to join the Air Force Reserve and thus once again fly the planes she knew in the service that she says she loves is a matter well beyond my legal knowledge. Such, however, may be a possibility, for she was not an evil person, a traitor, or a coward. Although ready, apparently, to serve well as a pilot, she simply was not ready for the responsibilities of service as an officer. The nation "expects a living portrayal of the highest standards of moral and ethical behavior. The expectation is neither fair nor unfair; it is a simple fact of the profession. The future of the services and the well-being of its people depend on the public perception and fact of the honor, virtue and trustworthiness of the officer corps." *The Armed Forces Officer* (DoD GEN-36A) (American Forces Information Service, 1988), 3.

9. Character and the Profession of Arms

1. Hartle, *Moral Issues,* 84.

2. Kupperman, *Character,* 13.

3. Wilson, *On Character,* 108.

4. I do not mean to suggest that our moral bearings must always be taken from family, friends, and associates. Religious believers would and should place their conception of God and of his Commandments, the Beatitudes, the modes of responsibility, and the human goods above the opinion of others. Nevertheless, friends—as Aristotle points out in book 9 of the *Nicomachean Ethics*—are very important, and much of what we do is done in and for community. The good opinion of good people is to be desired.

5. One of the disputes that should arise from any difference of opinion about whether there has been moral erosion would be the abortion question. I regard abortion as moral evil, the unjust taking of innocent human life. Others view abortion as a civil right, neglecting, it seems to me, the right to life of the unborn child. But is abortion a step "forward" in the march of freedom? Is partial-birth abortion a "civil right"? Abortions have "always" happened, we are told. But on this scale? Families have "always" been challenged, we are told. But to this extent? Euthanasia has "always" been supported by some, but to the point of legal acceptance? Of course, if one regards abortion and euthanasia as good, or if one thinks of marriage as basically outdated, we are making "progress."

6. See, for example, Rosenblatt, "Teaching Johnny to be Good," 36ff.

7. At the same time, we are bound to see the dark side. The 1930s and the 1940s were, in some respects, halcyon if you were male, white, middle- or upper-class, lived in the right city in the right state, and were Protestant. It was a different story for women, African Americans, the poor, those living in many rural areas, and many Jews and Catholics. We are also obliged to compare the life, say, of poor, rural, African Americans in Alabama in the 1930s (as difficult as their circumstances were) with that of most of the people at that time in Africa, Asia, or South America. Few Alabamians, black or white, would have wanted to trade places with people in other countries on other continents. My own family came to America from Ireland during the Potato Famine. As poor Irish Catholics, they encountered a number of prejudices, but none of them left America to return to Ireland.

8. *U.S. News and World Report,* 1 Mar. 1999, 14. There is danger of a fallacy here, however. A number of lower-ranking, one-tour enlisted members intensely disliked the military services. Their election to Congress would not necessarily mean a Congress "friendlier" to the military services.

9. Coles, "Disparity between Intellect and Character," A68.

10. An absolute? Almost. There is a problem even here, however. Suppose the one treating others as he wishes to be treated is masochistic or otherwise psychopathic?

11. One happy exception to that is Father David O'Connell, current president of the Catholic University of America. Another is Father Michael Scanlan, TOR, current president of the Franciscan University of Steubenville.

12. Bunting, *Education for Our Time,* 201–2.

13. I am referring in particular to the philosophers Alasdair MacIntyre and Philippa Foot. See also Kotva, *Christian Case for Virtue Ethics.* Virtue ethics is also known as aretaic ethics (from the Greek *arete,* meaning "excellence" or "virtue"). I am indebted for many of the ideas in this section to Pojman, *Ethics,* and to Frankena, *Ethics.*

14. As Pope John Paul II says in *Veritatis Splendor:* "If the object of the concrete action is not in harmony with the true good of the person, the choice of that action makes our will and ourselves morally evil, thus putting us in conflict with our ultimate end, the supreme good, God himself." The moral life, consequently, "has an essential 'teleological' character, since it consists in the deliberate ordering of human acts to God, the supreme good and ultimate end (*telos*) of man. (92–93). See 93–96 for a dis-

cussion of teleological ethics (in the sense of consequentialism or proportionalism). We also discussed this in chapter 6.

15. This is the idea that one should act in such a way that he would be prepared to see *everyone* act in a similar manner.

16. Patrick Lee, "Deontology," in Shaw, *Sunday Visitor's Encyclopedia,* 163.

17. Pinckaers, *Sources of Christian Ethics,* 233.

18. Cited by Kotva, *Christian Case for Virtue Ethics,* 10–11.

19. See, for example, David Konstan, *Friendship in the Classical World* (Cambridge: Cambridge Univ. Press, 1997); and Paul J. Wadell, *Friendship and the Moral Life* (Notre Dame, Ind.: Univ. of Notre Dame Press, 1989).

20. Suzy Platt, ed. *Respectfully Quoted* (Washington, D.C.: Library of Congress, 1989), 93; see Myers, "Core Values."

21. *Catechism of the Catholic Church,* nos. 1750–56.

22. Ibid., no. 1756; see also Rom. 3:8.

23. Space does not permit lengthy discussion here of virtue ethics, but those interested in the field should consult the writings of such scholars as Alasdair MacIntyre, Martha Nussbaum, and Nancy Sherman. A number of Christian moral theologians, both Catholic and Protestant, are rebuilding Christian ethics within the virtue ethics tradition. See, for example, Stanley Hauerwas, L. Gregory Jones, James F. Keenan, Joseph Kotva, Gilbert Meilaender, Jean Porter, and Paul Wadell.

24. Of course deterrence of war is also an important function of the profession of arms. Ralph Peters's understanding of ethics is vulnerable to criticism, but his article "A Revolution in Military Ethics?" *Parameters* 26, no. 2 (summer 1996): 102–8, is worth reading.

25. J.L.A. Garcia, "Virtue Ethics," *Cambridge Dictionary of Philosophy,* for example, suggests that virtue ethics can be antiquarian, circular, arbitrary and irrelevant to modern society, of no practical use, egoistic, and fatalistic, although, Garcia then admits, "there may be versions of virtue ethics that escape the force of all or most of the objections" (842). It relies on conceptions of human nature "whose teleology renders them obsolete" (841), he says. (Thus does he cavalierly dismiss human nature—a profound mistake, in my view.) Right action, he says, is defined in terms of virtue, whereas virtue is defined in terms of right actions. But virtuous action is taken for its own sake, Kotva would reply. (*Christian Case for Virtue Ethics,* 25). Virtue ethics is irrelevant, Garcia says, because "there is today no accepted standard . . . of what constitutes human flourishing" ("Virtue Ethics," 841). Garcia's point is valid (as chapter 3 points out), but it is also regrettable. Just because there is no *accepted* standard hardly means there is *no* standard. Garcia might start his search with *Veritatis Splendor.* Virtue ethics, Garcia contends, "offers no guidance when virtues seem to conflict" (841). Is that to say that a good character is of no use? Virtue ethics he regards as egoistic because one's attention is directed to himself; but here he confuses virtue ethics with solipsism. Virtue ethics depends upon synderesis, informed conscience. He contends also that it is fatalistic because it depends upon "luck." He has a good point, finally. See Kotva, *Christian Case for Virtue Ethics,* 29–30; and Kekes, *Moral Wisdom and Good Lives,* 207. On "luck," we might profitably consult Stockdale, *Philosophical Fighter Pilot.*

26. Pojman says Aristotle, Philippa Foot, Alasdair MacIntyre, and Richard Taylor represent this approach.

27. Scholars such as William Frankena, Bernard Gert, Alan Gewirth, John Rawls, and Geoffrey Warnock represent this school, contends Pojman.

28. Pojman says that Robert Louden, Walter Schaller, and Gregory Trianosky are in this school. See Pojman, *Ethics,* 170–71.

29. Frankena, *Ethics,* 65.

30. Hardon, *Pocket Catholic Dictionary,* 119–20. On double effect, see chap. 5, note 22.

31. Sidney Axinn, *A Moral Military* (Philadelphia: Temple Univ. Press, 1989), 73.

32. Ibid., 139.

33. In *The Gospel of Life,* Pope John Paul II says that elected officials might in good conscience vote for bills that, with abortion already legal, replace more permissive legislation with more restrictive legislation. "This does not in fact represent an illicit cooperation with an unjust law, but rather a legitimate and proper attempt to limit its evil aspects" (120–21).

34. Walzer, *Just and Unjust Wars,* 325. Walzer points out that Machiavelli, in the *Discourses,* wrote that it is very rare "that a good man should be found willing to employ wicked means," even when such means are morally required.

35. Axinn, *A Moral Military,* 144–45.

36. Halton, "That Quiet Decade," 44–45. The emphasis is mine.

37. I do not mean the college kind of "fraternity." I mean by this term, rather, that soldiers seek the counsel of others who have known similar circumstances. (See Gal. 6.) Combat soldiers frequently contend that only those who have been in combat can judge them. I cannot agree with that—for many reasons—but I understand the sentiment. And I understand also how important it is to combat soldiers to have the benediction of others who have "been there and done that." This does not imply that such soldiers think "anything goes." I have never talked with even one combat-tested soldier who approves of what Calley did at My Lai in Vietnam in 1968.

38. Axinn, *A Moral Military,* 145.

39. Grisez and Shaw, *Fulfillment in Christ,* 304.

40. On this subject, consult Sherman, *Fabric of Character,* esp. chap. 5, "The Habituation of Character."

41. In my book *The Sword and the Cross,* I tried to deal with this problem at greater length.

42. See, for example, *Armed Forces and Society* 24, no. 3 (spring 1998): 375–462, for a symposium on civil-military relations; in the same journal's summer 1998 issue (24, no. 4), there are follow-up articles (589–602); *Orbis* similarly devotes much of its winter 1999 issue (43, no. 1) to articles on "The Future of American Military Culture"; Andrew J. Bacevich, "He Won't Ask, They Won't Tell," *Washington Post,* 3 Jan. 1999; Bacevich and Kohn, "Grand Army of the Republicans," 22, 24–25; Peter D. Feaver, "The Civil-Military Problematique," *Armed Forces and Society* 23, no. 2 (winter 1996): 149–78; Ficarrotta, "Military Professionals"; Kitfield, "Standing Apart"; Richard Kohn, "Out of Control: The Crisis in Civil-Military Relations," *National Interest* 35 (spring 1994); John P. Lovell and David E. Albright, eds. *To Sheathe the Sword: Civil-Military Relations in the Quest for Democracy* (Westport, Conn.: Greenwood, 1997); Thomas Ricks, "Internal Dissent," a review of *To End a War,* by Richard Holbrooke, *Washington Monthly,* Oct. 1998, 48–49; Ricks, "Widening Gap"; Ricks, *Making the Corps,* esp. chap. 9; Rosenthal, "Today's Officer Corps."

43. Huntington, *Soldier and the State,* 79.

44. See for example, Adam Clymer, "Sharp Divergence Found in Views of Military and Civilians," *New York Times,* 9 Sept 1999, A15.

45. Samuel P. Huntington, *The Soldier and the State* (New York: Vintage, 1957), 465–66; Moskos and Butler, *All That We Can Be.* Certainly, this is not to say that the military has not been severely troubled by racism and institutional cowardice. For one such example, see Galloway, "A Soldier's Story."

46. See Title 10 of the U.S. Code, sections 3583, 5947, and 8583; Moran, *Anatomy of Courage,* xviii.

47. Ficarrotta, "Military Professionals," 73, 65. In fact, we are instructed by Truth Himself to become "perfect" (Matt. 5:48). Soldiers are not released from this admonition, this calling to holiness. I concede that we are unwise if we expect that soldiers (or any other people, for that matter) *are* saints; but we must expect that they, and we, are trying to *become* saints.

48. *O'Callahan v. Parker,* 395 U.S. 258, 281 (1969).

EPILOGUE

1. As we saw in chapter 9, this can become dangerous business. It is received almost as a truism in the corridors of some service schools and on some bases and posts that "we" (members of the military) have and must maintain an ethical order higher than that of the civilian populace whom "we" serve. How far—and where—will this self-congratulatory rhetoric take us? For one thing, I am not persuaded that it is wholly true; for another, I think this ultimately becomes a serious matter for civil–military relations seminars. If every profession reasoned, however mistakenly, that its standards were far superior to those of the poor benighted souls presumably served by that profession, we might well call into question what it is that the profession ostensibly professes.

2. Dee Hock, quoted in Morris, *If Aristotle Ran General Motors,* 211. The U.S. military too often seems to be given to a culture of fads, whether it be the Tofflers, TQM, or Stephen Covey seminars. For background, see "Now They Want Your Kids," *Time,* 29 Sept. 1997, 64–65.

3. See Paul Roush, "A Tangled Web," *U. S. Naval Institute Proceedings* 123 (August 1997): 45.

4. During the Lt. Kelly Flinn imbroglio, however, a number of people seemed to say that it was only her lies and fraternization that brought her integrity—and military competence—into question. The question of adultery? Well, "don't ask; don't tell," some seemed to say. But adultery, aside from being flat-out wrong, is a violation of the *UCMJ* (art. 134), and commanders legally cannot "look the other way." For a discussion of adultery in the context of synderesis, see the *New Catholic Encyclopedia,* 13:883.

5. On this topic see Kidder, *Good People Make Tough Choices,* chap. 3; see also Roger H. Nye, *The Challenge of Command* (Wayne, N.J.: Avery, 1986), chap. 6; and Kenneth Blanchard and Norman V. Peale, *The Power of Ethical Management* (New York: Fawcett Crest, 1988).

6. The air force program sensibly suggests that core values instruction is not done the same way at basic training and at war college. Clearly, a phased, gradual program is required.

7. See, for example, Pieper, *Four Cardinal Virtues.*

8. See Moskos and Butler, *All That We Can Be.*

9. I believe the military services can and must teach moral development—at one time called "character guidance"—in a "secular" manner (i.e., without favoring the doctrines or dogmas of a particular creed). That it can be done requires no more than a reading of, say, Lewis, *Abolition of Man,* in which he shows how the world's religions are in substantial agreement on numerous fundamental moral issues; one can argue that there is a cross-cultural "canon" of values, virtues, and verities that infuse the "secular" and "profane" as well as the religious and sacred.

Robert Bork has said that highly ethical persons without religious conviction "are living on the moral capital of prior religious generations." *Slouching towards Gomorrah,* 275. See also Loveland, *American Evangelicals and U.S. Military.*

10. See, for example, Kilpatrick, *Why Johnny Can't Tell Right from Wrong,* chap. 15, where he provides a reading list of excellent books. Every bookstore now has such books as William Bennett, *The Book of Virtues* (New York: Simon and Schuster, 1993). The federal academies have English departments that routinely offer courses in "Military Literature," some of the suggested readings from which might be worthwhile even at the basic training level.

11. For more information on Kohlberg, consult *Moral Development,* vol. 5, *New Research in Moral Development,* ed. Bill Puka (New York: Garland, 1994), esp. 126–88.

12. See, for example, Stockdale, *Philosophical Fighter Pilot,* and Grossman, *On Killing.*

13. See *Essentials of Military Training* (Harrisburg, Pa.: Stackpole, 1962), 165.

14. As some wag said about TQM, "It's both good and original. But what's good about it is not original, and what's original about it is not good." Precisely so.

15. Paul Johnson, *The Quest for God* (New York: HarperCollins, 1996), 117.

16. Niebuhr, *Irony of American History,* 63.

17. Christians can consult Matt. 28:20.

18. Burke, quoted in Lippmann, *Public Philosophy,* 35; Lippmann, *Public Philosophy,* 35.

19. Quoted in Toner, *True Faith and Allegiance,* 131–32. Original in Robert N. Bellah et. al., *The Good Society* (New York: Knopf, 1991), 104.

Select Bibliography

ARTICLES

Abramsky, Sasha. "When They Get Out." *Atlantic Monthly,* June 1999, 30–36.

Austin, Elizabeth. "That Perilous Gift." *Notre Dame Magazine* 25, no. 3 (autumn 1996): 40–43.

Bacevich, Andrew J. "Who Will Serve?" *Wilson Quarterly* 22, no. 3 (summer 1998): 80–91.

Bacevich, Andrew J., and Richard H. Kohn. "Grand Army of the Republicans." *New Republic,* 8 Dec. 1997, 22–25.

Barnett, Jeffrey. "War's Worst Risk Is to the Soul." *Los Angeles Times,* 6 June 1994, 11.

Barone, Michael. "Our Vast Contentment." *U.S. News and World Report,* 21 Dec. 1998, 33.

Bennett, William J. "The Lure of Learning." *U.S. News and World Report,* 25 Nov. 1985, 54–55.

Bernstein, Carl. "The Idiot Culture." *New Republic,* 8 June 1992, 22–28.

Bernstein, Jeremy. "E. O. Wilson's Theory of Everything." *Commentary,* June 1998, 62–65.

Bole, William. "Survival of the Faithful?" *Our Sunday Visitor,* 12 July 1998, 10–11.

Budziszewski, J. "The Revenge of Conscience." *First Things,* June–July 1998, 21–27.

Caputo, Philip. "The Black Badge of Courage." *Esquire,* Sept. 1995, 99–116.

Carroll, James. "An American Requiem." *Atlantic Monthly,* Apr. 1996, 76–88.

Coles, Robert. "The Disparity between Intellect and Character." *Chronicle of Higher Education,* 22 Sept. 1995, A68.

Colson, Charles W. "Can We Be Good without God?" *Imprimis* 22, no. 4 (Apr. 1993).

———. "A Question of Ethics." *Airpower Journal* 10, no. 2 (summer 1996): 4–12.

Dilulio, John J., Jr. "Moral Poverty." *Chicago Tribune,* 15 Dec. 1995, sec. 1, p. 31.

Ficarrotta, J. Carl. "Are Military Professionals Bound by a Higher Moral Standard?" *Armed Forces and Society* 24, no. 1 (fall 1997): 59–75.

Fogleman, Ronald. "A Question of Trust, Not Sex." *Newsweek,* 24 Nov. 1997, 60.

————. "What the Air Force Expects of You." *Air Force Times,* 13 May 1996, 33.

Fukuyama, Francis. "The Great Disruption." *Atlantic Monthly,* May 1999, 55–80.

Galloway, Joseph L. "A Soldier's Story." *U.S. News and World Report,* 31 May 1999, 42–53.

Gergen, David. "Keeping Faith in Our Kids." *U.S. News and World Report,* 31 May 1999, 80.

Gerson, Michael J. "A Pontiff in Winter." *U. S. News and World Report,* 25 Jan. 1999, 32–33.

Halton, Eugene. "The Truth about That Quiet Decade." *Notre Dame Magazine* 28, no. 1 (spring 1999): 43–48.

Hammer, Dean C. "Meaning and Tradition." *Polity* 24, no. 4 (summer 1992): 551–67.

Harbour, Frances V. "Basic Moral Values: A Shared Core." *Ethics and International Affairs* 9 (1995): 155–70.

Hartle, Anthony E. "Do Good People Make Better Warriors?" *Army,* Aug. 1992, 20–23.

Himmelfarb, Gertrude. "Private Lives, Public Morality." *New York Times,* 9 Feb. 1998, A19.

Holsti, Ole R. "A Widening Gap between the U.S. Military and Civilian Society? Some Evidence, 1976–96." *International Security* 23, no. 3 (winter 1998–99): 5–42.

Horn, Miriam. "Shifting Lines of Privacy." *U.S. News and World Report,* 26 Oct. 1998, 57–58.

Houk, Andrea L. "The Honor Principle." *Newsweek,* 12 Jan. 1998, 14.

Keenan, James F. "On Giving Moral Advice." *America,* 2 Mar. 1996, 12–16.

Kitfield, James. "Crisis of Conscience." *Government Executive* 27, no. 10 (Oct. 1995): 14–25.

————. "Standing Apart." *National Journal,* 13 June 1998, 1350–58.

Krauthammer, Charles. "Of Headless Mice . . . and Men." *Time,* 19 Jan. 1998, 76.

————. "Will It Be Coffee, Tea, or He?" *Time,* 15 June 1998, 92.

Langan, John. "The Catholic Vision of World Affairs." *Orbis* 42, no. 2 (spring 1998): 241–61.

Lemann, Nicholas. "Kicking in Groups." *Atlantic Monthly,* Apr. 1996, 22–26.

Leo, John. "Empty College Syndrome." *U.S. News and World Report,* 19 Apr. 1999, 19.

————. "Repackaging the Perps." *U.S. News and World Report,* 17 May 1999, 14.

Matthews, Lloyd J. "The Army Officer and the First Amendment." *Army,* Jan. 1998, 25–34.

———. "The Evolution of American Military Ideals." *Military Review* 78, no. 1 (Jan.–Feb. 1998): 51–61.

———. "Is the Military Profession Legitimate?" *Army,* Jan. 1994, 15–23.

———. "The Need for an Officers' Code of Professional Ethics." *Army,* Mar. 1994, 21–29.

———. "The Officer as Gentleman: A Waning Ideal?" *Army,* Mar. 1997, 27–31.

———. "The Speech Rights of Air Professionals." *Airpower Journal* 12, no. 3 (fall 1998): 19–30.

Medved, Michael. "As Bad As It Gets." *American Legion Magazine,* Aug. 1998, 18–22.

Miller, Stephen. "A Note on the Banality of Evil." *Wilson Quarterly* 22, no. 4 (autumn 1998): 54–59.

Moynihan, Daniel Patrick. "Defining Deviancy Down." *American Scholar* 62 (winter 1993): 17–30.

Murphy, Cullen. "Broken Covenant?" *Atlantic Monthly,* Nov. 1996, 22, 24.

Murray, A.J.H. "The Moral Politics of Hans Morgenthau." *Review of Politics* 58, no. 1 (winter 1996): 81–107.

Myers, Charles R. "The Core Values: Framing and Resolving Ethical Issues for the Air Force." *Airpower Journal* 11, no. 1 (spring 1997): 38–52.

Newman, Richard J. "A General Salutes by Quitting." *U.S. News and World Report,* 11 Aug. 1997, 5.

Oakes, Edward T. "Nature as Law and Gift," review of *Natural Law in Judaism,* by David Novak. *First Things* 93 (May 1999): 44–51.

Peters, Ralph. "The New Warrior Class." *Parameters* 24, no. 2 (summer 1994): 16–26.

Pinker, Steven. "Why They Kill Their Newborns." *New York Times Magazine,* 2 Nov. 1997, 52–54.

Priest, Robert F., and Johnston Beach. "Value Changes in Four Cohorts at the U.S. Military Academy." *Armed Forces and Society* 25, no. 1 (fall 1998): 81–102.

Rayner, Richard. "The Warrior Besieged." *New York Times Magazine,* 22 June 1997, 24–29.

Rehberg, Carl D. "Is Character Still an Issue?" *Airpower Journal* 12, no. 1 (spring 1998): 79–86.

Ricks, Thomas. "The Widening Gap between the Military and Society." *Atlantic Monthly,* July 1997, 66–78.

Rorty, Richard. "Against Unity." *Wilson Quarterly* 22, no. 1 (winter 1998): 28–38.

Rosenblatt, Roger. "Teaching Johnny to Be Good." *New York Times Magazine,* 30 Apr. 1995, 36.

Sagan, Carl. "A New Way to Think about Rules to Live By." *Parade,* 28 Nov. 1993, 12–14.

Schaefer, David L. "Wisdom and Morality: Aristotle's Account of *Akrasia.*" *Polity* 21, no. 2 (winter 1988): 221–51.

Schlosser, Eric. "The Prison-Industrial Complex." *Atlantic Monthly,* Dec. 1998, 51–77.

Schwehn, Mark R. "A Christian University: Defining the Difference." *First Things* 93 (May 1999): 25–31.

Shattuck, Roger. "When Evil Is 'Cool.'" *Atlantic Monthly,* Jan. 1999, 73–78.

Snider, Don M. "An Uninformed Debate on Military Culture." *Orbis* 43, no. 1 (winter 1999): 11–26.

Sommers, Christina Hoff. "Ethics without Virtue: Moral Education in America." *American Scholar* 53 (summer 1984): 381–89.

———. "The Hazards of Repudiating Tradition." The Alice McDermott Memorial Lecture in Applied Ethics, United States Air Force Academy, Colorado, 6 Apr. 1994.

———. "Teaching the Virtues." *Public Interest* 111 (spring 1993): 3–13.

Stengel, Richard. "Bowling Together." *Time,* 22 July 1996, 35–36.

Thompson, Mark. "Sex, the Army and a Double Standard." *Time,* 4 May 1998, 30–32.

Toner, James H. "Gallant Atavism: The Military Ethic in an Age of Nihilism." *Airpower Journal* 10, no. 2 (summer 1996): 13–22.

———. "Leadership, Community, and Virtue." *Joint Force Quarterly* 11 (spring 1996): 98–103.

———. "Mistakes in Teaching Ethics." *Airpower Journal* 12, no. 2 (summer 1998): 45–51.

———. "Readings in Military Ethics." *Military Review* 76, no. 1 (Jan.–Feb. 1996): 35–42.

Vistica, Gregory L. "A Quiet War over the Past." *Newsweek,* 24 Nov. 1997, 41.

Walinsky, Adam. "The Crisis of Public Order." *Atlantic Monthly,* July 1995, 39–54.

Wilson, Edward O. "Back from Chaos." *Atlantic Monthly,* Mar. 1998, 41–62.

———. "The Biological Basis of Morality," *Atlantic Monthly,* Apr. 1998, 53–70.

———. "Resuming the Enlightenment Quest." *Wilson Quarterly* 22, no. 1 (winter 1998): 16–27.

Woodward, Kenneth L. "What Is Virtue?" *Newsweek,* 13 June 1994, 38–39.

Books

Adler, Mortimer J. *Six Great Ideas.* New York: Collier, 1981.

———. *Ten Philosophical Mistakes.* New York: Macmillan, 1985.

Albom, Mitch. *Tuesdays with Morrie.* New York: Doubleday, 1997.

Aristotle. *Nicomachean Ethics.* Trans. Martin Oswald. Indianapolis: Bobbs-Merrill, 1962.

————. *The Politics.* Ed. and trans. Ernest Barker. New York: Oxford Univ. Press, 1972.

Ashe, Arthur, with Arthur Rampersad. *Days of Grace.* New York: Knopf, 1993.

Banfield, Edward C. *The Moral Basis of a Backward Society.* New York: Free Press, 1958.

Barry, James A. *The Sword of Justice.* Westport, Conn.: Praeger, 1998.

Bauman, Zygmunt. *Postmodern Ethics.* Malden, Mass.: Blackwell, 1993.

Bennett, William J. *The Death of Outrage.* New York: Free Press, 1998.

Bloom, Allan. *The Closing of the American Mind.* New York: Simon and Schuster, 1987.

Bochenski, Joseph M. *The Road to Understanding.* North Andover, Mass.: Genesis, 1996.

Bok, Sissela. *Common Values.* Columbia: Univ. of Missouri Press, 1995.

————. *Lying.* New York: Vintage, 1989.

Brennan, Joseph G. *Foundations of Moral Obligation.* Newport, R.I.: Naval War College Press, 1992.

Brzezinski, Zbigniew. *The Grand Chessboard.* New York: Basic Books, 1997.

————. *Out of Control.* New York: Scribner's, 1993.

Budziszewski, J. *Written on the Heart.* Downers Grove, Ill.: InterVarsity Press, 1997.

Burtchaell, James Tunstead. *The Dying of the Light: The Disengagement of Colleges and Universities from their Christian Churches.* Grand Rapids, Mich.: Eerdmans, 1998.

Cahill, Thomas. *How the Irish Saved Civilization.* New York: Anchor, 1995.

Carter, Stephen L. *The Culture of Disbelief.* New York: Basic Books, 1993.

————. *Integrity.* New York: Basic Books, 1996.

Cessario, Romanus. *The Moral Virtues and Theological Ethics.* Notre Dame, Ind.: Univ. of Notre Dame Press, 1991.

Christopher, Paul. *The Ethics of War and Peace.* Englewood Cliffs, N.J.: Prentice-Hall, 1994.

Cromartie, Michael, ed. *A Preserving Grace.* Washington, D.C.: Ethics and Public Policy Center, 1997.

DeMarco, Donald. *The Heart of Virtue.* San Francisco: Ignatius, 1996.

Denby, David. *Great Books.* New York: Simon and Schuster, 1996.

Derber, Charles. *The Wilding of America.* New York: St. Martin's, 1996.

Donagan, Alan. *The Theory of Morality.* Chicago: Univ. of Chicago Press, 1977.

Eliot, T.S. *Christianity and Culture.* New York: Harcourt Brace, 1976.

Fletcher, Joseph. *Situation Ethics.* Philadelphia: Westminster Press, 1966.

Flinn, Kelly. *Proud to Be.* New York: Random House, 1997.

Frankena, William. *Ethics.* 2d ed. Englewood Cliffs, N.J.: Prentice-Hall, 1973.

Frankl, Viktor E. *Man's Search for Meaning.* 4th ed. Part 1 trans. Ilse Lasch. Boston: Beacon Press, 1992.

Friedrich, Carl. J. *Tradition and Authority.* New York: Praeger, 1972.

Fussell, Paul. *Doing Battle.* Boston: Little, Brown, 1996.

Garner, Richard. *Beyond Morality.* Philadelphia: Temple Univ. Press, 1994.

Geach, Peter. *The Virtues.* Cambridge: Cambridge Univ. Press, 1977.

Geisler, Norman L. *Christian Ethics.* Grand Rapids, Mich.: Baker Book House, 1989.

Gewirth, Alan. *Reason and Morality.* Chicago: Univ. of Chicago Press, 1978.

Grisez, Germain, and Russell Shaw. *Fulfillment in Christ.* Notre Dame, Ind.: Univ. of Notre Dame Press, 1991.

Grossman, Dave. *On Killing.* Boston: Little, Brown, 1995.

Hanson, Victor Davis, and John Heath. *Who Killed Homer?* New York: Free Press, 1998.

Harris, C.E., Jr. *Applying Moral Theories.* 3d ed. Belmont, Calif.: Wadsworth, 1997.

Hart, H.L.A. *Law, Liberty, and Morality.* New York: Vintage, 1963.

Himmelfarb, Gertrude. *The De-Moralization of Society.* New York: Knopf, 1995.

Hinman, Lawrence M. *Contemporary Moral Issues.* Upper Saddle River, N.J.: Prentice-Hall, 1996.

———. *Ethics: A Pluralistic Approach to Moral Theory.* 2d ed. Fort Worth, Tex.: Harcourt Brace, 1998.

Hirschman, Albert O. *Exit, Voice, and Loyalty.* Cambridge, Mass.: Harvard Univ. Press, 1970.

Huntington, Samuel P. *The Clash of Civilizations and the Remaking of World Order.* New York: Simon and Schuster, 1996.

Ignatieff, Michael. *The Warrior's Honor.* New York: Holt, 1997.

John Paul II. *Crossing the Threshold of Hope.* Ed. Vittorio Messori. New York: Knopf, 1995.

———. *The Gospel of Life.* Boston: Pauline, 1995.

———. *Redemptor Hominis.* Washington, D.C.: Office for Publishing and Promotion Services, U.S. Catholic Conference, 1979.

———. *The Splendor of Truth.* Boston: St. Paul, 1993.

Jones, E. Michael. *Degenerate Moderns.* San Francisco: Ignatius, 1993.

Keegan, John. *The Mask of Command.* New York: Viking, 1987.

Keenan, James F. *Virtues for Ordinary Christians.* Kansas City, Mo.: Sheed and Ward, 1996.

Kekes, John. *Moral Wisdom and Good Lives.* Ithaca, N.Y.: Cornell Univ. Press, 1995.

Kernan, Alvin. *In Plato's Cave.* New Haven, Conn.: Yale Univ. Press, 1999.

Kidder, Rushworth. *How Good People Make Tough Choices.* New York: Fireside, 1995.

Kitfield, James. *Prodigal Soldiers.* New York: Simon and Schuster, 1995.

Kotva, Joseph J., Jr. *The Christian Case for Virtue Ethics.* Washington, D.C.: Georgetown Univ. Press, 1996.

Kreeft, Peter. *Back to Virtue.* San Francisco: Ignatius, 1992.

Kupperman, Joel. *Character.* New York: Oxford Univ. Press, 1991.

Lewis, C.S. *The Abolition of Man.* New York: Simon and Schuster, 1996. Originally published in 1944.

Lickona, Thomas. *Educating for Character.* New York: Bantam, 1991.

Lippmann, Walter. *The Public Philosophy.* New York: Mentor, 1955.

Machiavelli. *The Prince.* Trans. Luigi Ricci. New York: Mentor, 1952.

MacIntyre, Alasdair. *After Virtue.* 2d ed. Notre Dame, Ind.: Univ. of Notre Dame Press, 1984.

———. *A Short History of Ethics.* New York: Simon and Schuster, 1966.

Margolis, Jon. *The Last Innocent Year.* New York: Morrow, 1999.

Maritain, Jacques. *Man and the State.* Chicago: Univ. of Chicago Press, 1951.

Marsden, George. *The Outrageous Idea of Christian Scholarship.* New York: Oxford Univ. Press, 1997.

———. *The Soul of the American University.* New York: Oxford Univ. Press, 1994.

Martin, William. *With God on our Side: The Rise of the Religious Right in America.* New York: Broadway, 1996.

McCormick, David. *The Downsized Warrior.* New York: New York Univ. Press, 1998.

McDowell, Josh, and Bob Hostetler. *The New Tolerance.* Wheaton, Ill.: Tyndale House, 1998.

———. *Right from Wrong.* Dallas: Word, 1994.

McMaster, H.R. *Dereliction of Duty.* New York: HarperCollins, 1997.

Merton, Thomas. *Conjectures of a Guilty Bystander.* New York: Doubleday, 1989.

Miller, Ed. L. *Questions That Matter:* An Invitation to Philosophy. 2d shorter ed. Boston: McGraw-Hill, 1998.

Moran, Lord. *The Anatomy of Courage.* Garden City Park, N.Y.: Avery, 1987.

Morris, Tom. *If Aristotle Ran General Motors.* New York: Holt, 1997.

———. *Making Sense of It All.* Grand Rapids, Mich.: Eerdmans, 1992.

Moskos, Charles C., and John Sibley Butler. *All That We Can Be.* New York: Basic Books, 1996.

Nash, Robert J. *Answering the "Virtuecrats."* New York: Teachers College Press, 1997.

Niebuhr, Reinhold. *An Interpretation of Christian Ethics.* New York: Meridian, 1960.

———. *The Irony of American History.* New York: Scribner's, 1962.

———. *Moral Man and Immoral Society.* New York: Scribner's, 1960.

Nozick, Robert. *The Examined Life*. New York: Simon and Schuster, 1989.

Nussbaum, Martha C. *Cultivating Humanity*. Cambridge, Mass.: Harvard Univ. Press, 1997.

———. *The Fragility of Goodness*. Cambridge: Cambridge Univ. Press, 1986.

O'Connor, Flannery. *The Habit of Being*. Ed. Sally Fitzgerald. New York: Farrar, Straus, and Giroux, 1979.

Olasky, Marvin. *The American Leadership Tradition*. New York: Free Press, 1999.

Outka, Gene, and John P. Reeder Jr., eds. *Prospects for a Common Morality*. Princeton, N.J.: Princeton Univ. Press, 1993.

Pelikan, Jaroslav. *The Vindication of Tradition*. New Haven, Conn.: Yale Univ. Press, 1984.

Perry, Michael. *Morality, Politics, and Law*. New York: Oxford Univ. Press, 1998.

Pieper, Josef. *A Brief Reader on the Virtues of the Human Heart*. Trans. P.C. Duggan. San Francisco: Ignatius, 1991.

———. *In Defense of Philosophy*. Trans. Lothar Krauth. San Francisco: Ignatius, 1992.

———. *The Four Cardinal Virtues*. Trans. by Richard and Clara Winston, Lawrence E. Lynch, and Daniel F. Coogan. Notre Dame, Ind.: Univ. of Notre Dame Press, 1966.

———. *Hope and History*. Trans. David Kipp. San Francisco: Ignatius, 1994.

———. *Leisure: The Basis of Culture*. Trans. Alexander Dru. New York: Random House, 1963.

———. *On Hope*. Trans. Mary Frances McCarthy. San Francisco: Ignatius, 1986.

Pinckaers, Servais. *The Pursuit of Happiness—God's Way: Living the Beatitudes*. Trans. Mary Thomas Noble. New York: Alba House, 1998.

———. *The Sources of Christian Ethics*. 3d ed. Trans. Mary Thomas Noble. Washington, D.C.: Catholic Univ. of America Press, 1995.

Plamenatz, J.P. *Consent, Freedom and Political Obligation*. New York: Oxford Univ. Press, 1968.

Plato. *Great Dialogues*. Trans. W.H.D. Rouse. New York: Mentor, 1956.

Pojman, Louis P. *Ethics: Discovering Right and Wrong*. Belmont, Calif.: Wadsworth, 1995.

Readings, Bill. *The University in Ruins*. Cambridge, Mass.: Harvard Univ. Press, 1996.

Regan, Richard J. *The Moral Dimensions of Politics*. New York: Oxford Univ. Press, 1986.

Rice, Charles. *Fifty Questions on the Natural Law*. San Francisco: Ignatius, 1995.

Richardson, Elliot. *Reflections of a Radical Moderate*. New York: Pantheon, 1996.

Ricks, Thomas E. *Making the Corps.* New York: Scribner's, 1997.

Rommen, Heinrich A. *The Natural Law.* Trans. Thomas R. Hanley. Indianapolis: Liberty Fund, 1998.

Royce, Josiah. *The Philosophy of Loyalty.* New York: Macmillan, 1908.

Sandel, Michael J. *Democracy's Discontents.* Cambridge, Mass.: Belknap Press of Harvard Univ. Press, 1996.

Scheffler, Samuel. *Human Morality.* New York: Oxford Univ. Press, 1992.

Schumacher, E.F. *A Guide for the Perplexed.* New York: Harper and Row, 1977.

Seabury, Paul, and Angelo Codevilla. *War: Ends and Means.* New York: Basic Books, 1989.

Shaw, Russell, ed. *Our Sunday Visitor's Encyclopedia of Catholic Doctrine.* Huntington, Ind.: Our Sunday Visitor, 1997.

Sherman, Nancy. *The Fabric of Character: Aristotle's Theory of Virtue.* Oxford: Clarendon Press, 1989.

———. *Making a Necessity of Virtue.* Cambridge: Cambridge Univ. Press, 1997.

Simon, Yves. *A General Theory of Authority.* Notre Dame, Ind.: Univ. of Notre Dame Press, 1980.

Sommers, Christina, and Fred Sommers. *Vice and Virtue in Everyday Life.* 3d ed. New York: Harcourt Brace, 1993.

Sorley, Lewis. *Honorable Warrior.* Lawrence: Univ. Press of Kansas, 1998.

Stace, W.T. *The Concept of Morals.* Gloucester, Mass.: Peter Smith, 1975.

Sterling, Diane, Georgia Archibald, Linda McKay, and Shelley Berg. *Character Education Connections.* Saint Louis: Cooperating School Districts, 1998.

Stockdale, Jim. *Thoughts of a Philosophical Fighter Pilot.* Stanford, Calif.: Hoover Institution Press, 1995.

Tillich, Paul. *The Courage to Be.* New Haven, Conn.: Yale Univ. Press, 1952.

Timberg, Robert. *The Nightingale's Song.* New York: Simon and Schuster, 1995.

Toner, James H. *The Sword and the Cross.* New York: Praeger, 1992.

———. *True Faith and Allegiance.* Lexington: Univ. Press of Kentucky, 1995.

Twitchell, James B. *For Shame: The Loss of Common Decency in American Culture.* New York: St. Martin's, 1997.

Voegelin, Eric. *History of Political Ideas.* Ed. James L. Wiser. Vol. 23 of *The Collected Works.* Columbia, Mo.: Univ. of Missouri Press, 1998.

———. *Religion and the Rise of Modernity.* Ed. James L. Wiser. Vol. 5 of *The Collected Works.* Columbia, Mo.: Univ. of Missouri Press, 1998.

Wakin, Malham M. *War, Morality, and the Military Profession.* 2d ed. Boulder: Westview Press, 1986.

Walsh, David. *After Ideology.* New York: HarperCollins, 1990.

Walzer, Michael. *Just and Unjust Wars.* 2d ed. New York: Basic Books, 1992.

———. *Thick and Thin: Moral Argument at Home and Abroad.* Notre Dame, Ind.: Univ. of Notre Dame Press, 1994.

Warren, Mary Anne. *Moral Status.* Oxford: Clarendon Press, 1997.
Weaver, Richard M. *The Ethics of Rhetoric.* Chicago: Henry Regnery, 1965.
Weigel, George. *Tranquillitas Ordinis.* New York: Oxford Univ. Press, 1987.
West, Morris. *Children of the Sun.* London: Heinemann, 1957.
Wilson, James Q. *The Moral Sense.* New York: Free Press, 1993.
———. *On Character.* Washington, D.C.: AEI Press, 1991.
Wolfe, Alan. *One Nation after All.* New York: Viking, 1998.
Wood, John A. *Perspectives on War in the Bible.* Macon, Ga.: Mercer Univ.
     Press, 1998.
Zagzebski, Linda Trinkaus. *Virtues of the Mind.* Cambridge: Cambridge Univ.
     Press, 1996.

USEFUL WORLD WIDE WEB SITES

http://www.wnet.org/religion/resources2.html
(an ethics & religion site)

http://www.mcgill.pvt.k12.al.us/jerryd/cathmob.htm
(a Christian theology site)

http://ethics.acusd.edu/index.html
(a site at the University of San Diego that reviews ethics issues)

http://www.usafa.af.mil/core-value/
(a site concerning Air Force core values)

http://www.usafa.af.mil/jscope/
(the site of the Joint Services Conference on Military Ethics)

http://www.au.af.mil/au/aul/lane.htm
(the Air University Library site at Maxwell Air Force Base, Alabama, the loca-
     tion of the Air War College)

http://www.au.af.mil/au/awc/awcgate/awcgate.htm
(home page of the Air War College)

http://www.cceia.org/
(Carnegie Council on Ethics and International Affairs)

Index